The Media
Teacher's Book

Second Edition

The Media
Teacher's Book

Second Edition

Julian McDougall
& Nick Potamitis

HODDER
EDUCATION
AN HACHETTE UK COMPANY

Orders: please contact Bookpoint Ltd, 130 Milton Park, Abingdon, Oxon
OX14 4SB. Telephone: (44) 01235 827720. Fax: (44) 01235 400454. Lines
are open from 9.00–5.00, Monday to Saturday, with a 24-hour message
answering service. You can also order through our website
www.hoddereducation.co.uk.

British Library Cataloguing in Publication Data
A catalogue record for this title is available from the British Library

ISBN: 978 1 444 115 567

First Published 2010
Impression number   10 9 8 7 6 5 4 3 2 1
Year   2016 2015 2014 2013 2012 2011 2010

Copyright © 2010 Julian McDougall, Nick Potamitis

Cover photo © iStockphoto.com/Vasiliy Yakobchuk

Typeset by Phoenix Photosetting, Chatham, Kent

Printed in Great Britain for Hodder Education, part of Hachette UK,
338 Euston Road, London NW1 3BH.

{contents}

Acknowledgments

Julian dedicates this book, as always, to Mike McDougall. Old school Labour and missed every day. And to Alex for everything.

Julian would like to thank the following people:

Lydia and Ned – for being such brilliant kids – and even Stanley, for making the last few days of writing more challenging. And Jan, Val and Barrie for all the help with Lydia, Ned and Stanley.

For listening to all the madness: Dave Trotman and Andy Cramp.

For inspiration, support and ideas over the years: Pete Fraser, Steve Dixon, Richard Sanders, David Gauntlett, Matt Hills, Cary Bazalgette, Jenny Grahame, Richard Berger, Stephen Heppell, Jon Wardle, Mark Readman, David Buckingham, John Atkinson, Julie Goodwin, Rob Carlton, Wayne O'Brien, Jackie Marsh, Martin Barker, Symon Quy, Andy Ash, Mark Reid, Roy Stafford, Nick Peim and Paul Sansom.

Nick would like to thank Andrea Joyce, Barney Oram, Bill Thompson, Dave Harrison, Dave Robertson, Gavin Luhrs, Jenny Grahame, Nikki Blackborow and Pete Fraser for help, advice and ideas for things in the book.

For all their support and encouragement and for putting up with endless videos of Media students 'waving their arms', Nick would like to say a very special 'thank you' to Helen and Evie.

This book has a companion website available at:
http://www.hodderplus.co.uk/mediateacher

To access the learning plans, glossary and weblinks included on the website, please register on the website using the following access details:

Serial number: H2Tjarher593

Once you have registered, you will not need the serial number but can log in using the username and password you will create during registration.

Introduction

Our students are the last generation of people who will have lived before the internet. For the next generation, there will be no concept of 'going online'. Being always connected will be (in the developed world) everyday life. Equally, social media is increasingly competing with – or even replacing – 'command and control' media. This is impacting on public life, politics, democracy and commerce. The idea of 'the media' as a stable object of study, along with 'the audience' and 'representation', is challenged by these changes to the ways we communicate, and what we expect of culture.

The first edition of this book was described in reviews as 'provocative', 'controversial' and helpful to Media teachers in *'thinking through their own positions in a period of profound and rapid technological change and much theoretical uncertainty'* (Masterman, 2006: 37). That edition had a primary objective, which was to offer an update to and also a shift in approach from Masterman's *Teaching the Media* (1985). Masterman's book remains a comprehensive presentation of strategies for the Media teacher and indeed a compelling *raison d'être* for the subject. However it was already clear in 2006 that the Media learner twenty years on was operating within a different set of cultural and technological discourses, and equally the Media teacher has been residing in a very different educational paradigm. Five years on again, in producing a revised edition, the overwhelming feeling is that the change has accelerated, outdating a fair amount of what I wrote in the first edition. This is staggering. The first edition made a few passing references to YouTube, social networking was largely absent and Google was discussed in a case study as 'sort of a media institution'. This second edition is accompanied by a set of online materials dominated by links to web content. In 2010, a book of this nature is an extended discourse but it must lead, as always, to the internet – where the useful 'stuff' lives.

The 'project'

> *I absolutely – in fact, increasingly – believe in the crucial importance of Media Studies; they should be at the heart of any educational system which claims to equip its citizens to deal with the complexities of life in the twenty-first century.* (Lord Puttnam, quoted in QCA, 2005: 4)

What is the role of the Media teacher in contemporary society? Is it merely as deliverer of a prescribed curriculum that is either academic (with claims to 'critical autonomy') or vocational (a more technical preparation for work or at least the acquisition of creative and technical skills for a variety of contexts, not necessarily Media related)? Or is Media teaching a social practice? Undoubtedly the latter makes more sense, as Media learning is a dynamic, creative and highly reflexive endeavour providing the teacher allows it to be so. Media teaching is certainly political, but I would suggest that this no longer translates into lecturing about ideology. It might now be more micro-political, in the sense that students designing web content or game narratives might be engaging in new literacy practices that renegotiate their socio-cultural identities. Ultimately all Media learning is to do with discourse, whether 'practical' or 'theoretical', visual or written. With this sense of the world, the Media teacher, despite the ongoing public derision levelled at her, has a highly important job.

There was a time when media learning could look like an adjunct to English, and the distinction between academic and vocational media activities was clearly marked. The Media teacher in this era would navigate a primarily 'critical' curriculum, focusing on messages, meanings and language (for GCSE and A Level), or she would operate within a highly technicist agenda, in order to 'train' students in specialist skills within a workplace paradigm.

Media Studies is taught within both academic and vocational boundaries, and suffers from many misconceptions as a result. It is derided for its failure to lead to employment in the media (in a way that, say, History would never be), and it is criticised for its apparent 'lightweight' academic nature because of the accessibility of its subject matter. This book seeks to offer guidance for teaching on both types of courses, and to avoid labelling learners in either way. Each chapter is of equal value for teaching on theory or production-based courses. The book makes no political claims; there is no grand narrative of empowerment or emancipation residing here. And there are no value judgements to be made about the purposes of various forms of Media learning. The guidance offered relates to the specifications used by students on GCSE, A and AS and vocational Media courses, and offers strategies for raising achievement and managing learning toward assessment objectives as configured by awarding bodies.

In *Screen Education: From Film Appreciation to Media Studies*, Bolas (2009) offers a forensic history of the struggle to gain legitimate curriculum space for the study of film and, later more generally, 'the media'. Now, Media Studies has passed through the 'relevance boom'. As a National Diploma student in the 1980s (at the time Masterman was writing) I was excited and motivated on a daily basis by access to video cameras in a way that we cannot expect our current students to be. The technology young people use these days in their out of school/college contexts will often be more sophisticated than what we are offering, and they may find our interventions into their everyday digital culture clumsy and awkward rather than inspiring and empowering. Equally we cannot assume a political response to the media when we are teaching a post-Thatcher generation of students (and why should we anyway?) So we need new ways of exploring technology, creativity, politics and culture. We cannot (for better or worse) rely on the models in currency in the 1980s.

So this book tries to offer some suggestions based on these cultural shifts and on our experiences of successful Media teaching. Apart from this introduction, it is very much a teacher's book, as opposed to an overview of the 'zeitgeist', and as such it is intended to directly aid those teaching Media, about to teach Media or intending to do so. According to the QCA's statistics, only 22% of Media teachers have a degree in the subject, and in the absence of a PGCE course in Media alone, each year a plethora of training courses are provided to compensate and to offer resources and approaches. In addition, there is a wonderful range of resources available commercially and for free to support teaching for particular units. These are all of value, and we will be recommending some of these in each chapter, but we hope this book can offer an everyday range of support in a way that such 'days out' from school or college or specific resources cannot, and thus it will complement these existing opportunities and materials. We hope this book, alongside the new *Media Education Research Journal* and the conferences and seminars provided by both the Centre for Excellence in Media Practice and the Media Education Association, will also go some way to bridging the unhealthy insulation between higher education, schools and colleges. Hitherto, media academics in universities have been complacently superior and inward-looking, usually without any justification for so being, as Berger observes in this historical extract:

> Media Theory' as it was now called seemed to be replicating the activities of the academics of Lagada in Gulliver's Travels; instead of trying to extract sunbeams from cucumbers, Media theorists were busy inventing increasingly impenetrable terminology and making vast assumptions about audiences and texts. (Berger in Berger and McDougall, 2010)

This book is not based on classroom research – see Buckingham (2003) for such a perspective on Media education – nor is it purely a theoretical overview (though I suggest it is impossible to be 'untheoretical' in a pedagogic context). Rather, it will offer a broad range of ideas for approaching concepts, texts, technologies and research with students and I hope these will reaffirm your reasons for teaching Media in creative and inspiring ways.

Our biggest challenge is to try to offer strategies for a progressive form of learning and teaching within the constraints of the qualifications framework you are working with. Buckingham (2007) suggests that digital technologies present a challenge or an 'other' to traditional boundaries placed between critical analysis and creative production. Consequently, there are different opportunities for more 'playful' forms of pedagogic practice. In this sense, he asserts, the classroom reduces in significance and thus we need to pay attention to (and value) learning taking place in other locations and at other times.

Our obligations

Quite a daunting prospect, then, to foster these new learning practices at the same time as pleasing the inspectors and maintaining a healthy position in the league tables and the value-added profiles. But it is to these various demands and discourses that we must turn our attention if we are to successfully update our practice and add to the conceptual/ideological approach suggested in Masterman's *Teaching the Media*. To this end, a series of ten framing statements at the outset (or a 'vow of chastity' for the Media teacher, to borrow the *Dogme* term with a pinch of salt):

The Media teacher's 'vow of chastity'

1. The primary value of technology in the Media classroom is to enable creativity – 'ICT' is our enemy.

2. Creativity need not necessarily be challenging or alternative (and these ideas might need a rethink).

3. No theory is 'too hard' for any learners.

4. The distinction between theory and production is a false binary opposition. In fact, much theory is practical and much production is in itself highly theoretical.

5. Media learning should be free of all value judgements and notions of enrichment or cultural worth. All texts are of equal interest.

6. Media learning is not automatically inclusive and great efforts must be made to make it so and the subject matter of Media lessons is not automatically of any greater interest than other subjects.

7. The study of the media and the acquisition of media literacy is of cultural importance but it is not a political project.

8. Media learning is reflective in the sense that its starting point is audience and learners are readers, but all reading is socio-culturally framed.

9. Media Studies is primarily the study and practice of discourse.

10. No Media lesson should be taught in the same way two years running.

In arranging a second edition the author has the luxury of qualification. In a review/interview for *In the Picture*, Stafford took issue with number 7, arguing:

> You disavow that kind of politics so often in the book that it almost suggests some form of denial. Is it that you have fallen into a postmodernist trap – a kind of value free relativism? (Stafford, 2006: 24)

Later, I was able to devote a whole article in the same publication to the 'new politics' of media education, a kind of 'Ragged Trousered Wikinomics', if you will (McDougall, 2008). As part of a much longer and more sustained claim for a return to the spirit of Cultural Studies and a flee from the text, I made this optimistic suggestion:

> Media Studies today can't be about 'unveiling the truth', however strongly we might want it to be. But it can be about making the familiar unfamiliar, about displacing and decentering, about making students uncomfortable. Critically reflective social practice. How does your film come to be, what does it do, along with a real interest in people and how they allocate meanings to cultural material. How do people use anime music video alongside TV drama to (partly) construct identities, which may be complex, hybrid, fluid? These questions are the 'new politics' of Media Studies. Let's embrace the renewal they offer. (McDougall, 2008: 13)

Strategies for inclusive Media learning

There is much attention rightly paid these days on teacher training courses and in professional development to the variety of learning styles at work in the educational encounter. The most sensible approach to inclusive learning is simply to ensure that any group of students will have access to a range of learning contexts which incorporate visual, auditory and kinaesthetic application. Equally, collaborative classroom activity or production work can guarantee differentiation, so long as careful attention is paid to resources and content. And equality of opportunity must be understood in its holistic entirety – the consideration of the learning experience from curriculum choices to learning materials and both cultural and physical access.

With this inclusion agenda in mind, this book will focus (as already stated) on the 'HOW' rather than the 'WHAT' of Media learning. Within the text look for the online icon ⊕, which points you to individual learning plans linked chapter by chapter to a different type of Media lesson in each case.

Nick Potamitis co-authors this second edition and brings with him a plethora of creative and dynamic teaching ideas that are entirely in keeping with this reimagining of the subject. It would be too simplistic to say that Nick's work teaching the new Creative and Media Diploma is the perspective he brings, but what is clear is that the interdisciplinary and active learning required by that qualification has led to the development of new forms of pedagogy. These are transferable to GCSE, A Level and beyond, so Nick brings two things: a balance in the book so that those of you teaching 'vocational' courses will be just as well catered for as your 'academic' counterparts (and we use these problematic terms under erasure), along with a track record in inspiring and energetic teaching that I wanted to harness.

In this new edition we have substantially amended every chapter and included some new themes. We start with a lengthy 'mapping' of paradigm shifts in learning and teaching across the curriculum and then situate the Media teacher at these crossroads. This section includes some of the 'history of the present' (of Media teaching) from the first edition but bears witness to the pace of change with a more sustained theorising of Media learning.

The next two chapters present strategies for dynamic classroom practice in the two domains of practice and theory (media literacy). Although we are apprehensive about this distinction, there are certain pedagogic concerns for each. 'Doing the Big Concepts' and 'Media in Society' update the first edition and the chapters on managing coursework and approaching assessment are substantially revised for the new mediascape. Where the first edition integrated the class strategies and images into the text of the book, this revised version includes a colour plate section of images and links to one hundred online learning plans with an abundance of weblinks to helpful content and resources.

We have made some changes to the structure of the book and to the format of the chapters. In this new edition we begin with a detailed account of how we might study popular culture 'after the media'. Next we look at teaching production and then we turn to media literacy and how this can be developed through engaging, creative teaching. The big concepts and the big debates are rigorously updated to bear witness to new kinds of engagement with new kinds of media. The chapter on assessment is revised to include a wealth of dynamic strategies; the impetus for these was the diploma but one thing we have learned is that 'academic' teaching has been greatly enhanced by adopting such approaches. And a new chapter on supporting coursework brings together strategies for 'managing' independent student activity in the domains of production, research and industry-focused research. We have updated the glossary where required and, on the accompanying website, extended the list of resources to complement the range of web links in the online learning plans.

Clearly, then, the pace of change has necessitated a more rigorous updating than is required for most second editions. Plainly, since the first edition, there has been a move from studying 'new media' separately to – as Gauntlett describes – *'recognition that they have fundamentally changed the ways in which we engage with* all *media'* (2007). This has led to a (sometimes hostile) debate around the idea of 'Media Studies 2.0'. In this discussion, some have called for a change to the entire discipline whilst others have been far more cautious. But there hasn't been much in the way of advice about how to take all this into the classroom on a Monday morning. We hope this second edition will contribute to that.

Julian McDougall, 2010

References

Berger, R. and McDougall, J., 2010. 'Media education research in the twenty-first century: touching the void', *Media Education Research Journal*, 1.1.

Bolas, T., 2009. *Screen Education: From Film Appreciation to Media Studies*. London: Intellect Books.

Buckingham, D., 2003. *Media Education*. London: Polity.

Buckingham, D., 2007. *Beyond Technology: Children's Learning in the Age of Digital Culture*. London: Polity.

Gauntlett, D., 2007. *Media Studies 2.0* http://www.theory.org.uk/mediastudies2.htm

Gauntlett, D., 2009. 'Media Studies 2.0: a response', *Interactions: Studies in Communication and Culture*, 1.1: 147–157.

Masterman, L., 1985. *Teaching the Media*. London: Routledge.

Masterman, L., 2006. Review of *The Media Teacher's Book* in *Media Education Journal*, 40: 37.

McDougall, J., 2008. 'Raggered trousered wikinomics: "Back to the future" for Media Studies', *In the Picture* 60. Keighley: In the Picture Publications.

QCA, 2005. *Media Matters: A Review of Media Studies in Schools and Colleges*. London: QCA.

Stafford, R., 2006. 'Everything you ever wanted to know about media teaching?', *In the Picture* 54. Keighley: In the Picture Publications: 22–24.

Media Studies After the Media?

We want to argue at the outset that you, as a Media teacher, are charged with a paradoxical task – teaching the media after it has ceased to be a meaningful construct. Whilst orthodox power structures still hold, the majority of media exchange is shot through with the visible presence of the audience. People are at least part of the media now, if not as often as Gillmor would have had us believe in *We, the Media* (2004). So the binary opposition that has held firm, at least in the minds of Media teachers, for decades – that there is a 'mass media' that students can look at and that students are part of 'the audience', is really problematic now. The notion of a text, with boundaries around it, that we can 'deconstruct' is also straining to hold against the tidal wave of multimodal, fluid and 'hyperdiegetic' cultural exchange.

Call of Duty: Modern Warfare 3 and *Heavy Rain* were two of the most important media events of recent years. How many readers of this book included them in the curriculum? The former was, like *Grand Theft Auto* 4 before it, significant in terms of scale – millions of people engaging with the same media product at the same time. *Heavy Rain* was more theoretically ground-breaking – the debate over whether videogames are to be analysed as narratives or 'ludic' experiences, or both, brought to prominence by the existence of a game which *'may not only be the best game you've ever played – it could even become one of your favourite films'* (Freeman, 2010).

But these 'texts' only exist when the 'audience' engage with them. And here is the crucial point – that is nothing new. Films only exist when the viewers engage with them, same thing with music, same thing with radio. But we haven't seen it so clearly until broadband 'web 2.0' made it more visible – as audience interpretation and engagement is out there semantically in the outcome of every keystroke. So thinking about teaching Media 'after the media' doesn't take its premise from an idea of a temporal change – that was then, this is now. Instead it borrows from Lyotard's conception of the postmodern – thinking differently about culture, trying to avoid recourse to the reductive idea of 'the media', thinking more seriously about what people do with culture.

A history of the present

There are some emerging narratives of the history of Media Studies, most notably produced by Buckingham (2003), the QCA (2005) and Bolas (2009). Buckingham's account is the result of his many years at the heart of the subject's development, and as such is a very useful reflective account from a wealth of experience, whilst the QCA report is the product of a more contested and contentious research exercise. Bolas provides much more detailed history from the perspective of film education. Trying to make sense of 'where we've been', as part of a broader research project (McDougall, 2004), a range of Media education's 'key players' were interviewed (those involved over a period of time in curriculum design and reform for the subject, and some of the key authors in the emerging narrative canon of work about the subject), as well as a large group of examiners (who are, of course, also teachers of the subject). They were asked questions about the development of Media Studies as a formal, institutionalised subject in schools and colleges. We call this official form *Subject Media*, from Peim's critique of 'Subject English' (1995). And the research was also interested in their ideas about the separation of academic and vocational versions of Media education, and how they could be justified or at least conceptually understood in a shared way.

In summary, the moments of **consensus** from the research were as follows:

- The distinction between academic and vocational courses is that academic courses are more concerned with theory rather than production, analysis rather than skills, assessment through examinations rather than portfolio moderation, prescribed content rather than briefs set within centres and deconstruction through concepts and critical theory rather than construction through technical competence
- The development of A Level Media Studies represented a watershed moment in the professional status of Media teachers and the resources available for the subject, and it also led to a marginalisation of vocational media education
- Film Studies has existed in various forms for longer, and Media teaching has a long tradition, especially in London within other courses in a liberal/humanities tradition and within English
- Media Studies as a subject has a set of key 'stakeholder' groups concerned with shaping its institutional agendas through policy and also through training and developing Media teachers and influencing their practice. These groups' roles are further given import due to the lack of a formal teacher training course in Media Studies, and subsequently the need for in-service training of new Media teachers, many from an English background.

There were moments of **disagreement** over the following issues:

- The role of the BFI in the history of the subject
- The academic value of some kinds of vocational courses
- The importance, and/or purpose of practical work within Media Studies
- The distinction between Media Studies as a formal academic subject and Media Education as a more general term or a term for cross-curricular teaching
- The relationship of Film Studies to Media Studies (interestingly, the respondents were not asked to include Film Studies in their historical narratives, but all did).

Media Studies today

Media teachers come from a variety of backgrounds. This is a strength in so much as it maintains the subject's status as a 'horizontal discourse' (Bernstein, 1990), a set of practices informed by a spread of contexts in the outside world (rather than a more closed and 'handed down' vertical discourse, perhaps). However it can also be a reason for anxiety, if the lack of an established pedagogic 'rule book' results in more variability in the quality of teaching or practitioner 'expertise.' Working at Newman

University College in Birmingham with a group of English students preparing to teach in the 14–19 sector, students were asked to map the insides and outsides of Media Studies specifications from the English teachers' perspective (the insides being the bits that overlap with English). Their particular responses suggested that technical aspects of production, teaching about technologies, technical analysis of visual texts and politics and institutions resided on the outside (this was drawn as a wall, with these bits being on the other side), whilst on the wall itself were critical evaluation, layout conventions, language, written coursework, representation, advertising, print texts, communication of meaning and identity/culture.

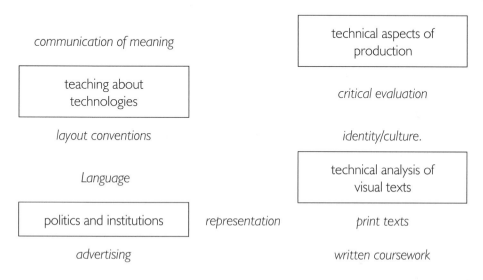

Visual representation of the insides (in italics) and outsides (in boxes) of Media Studies from trainee English teachers' perspectives (Newman College, 2004).

Our view is that ideally we would 'do' the study of culture and move away from academic boundaries which separate poems, paintings, websites and films from one another. This would, for example, create a parity between creative writing and video production, as well as Shakespeare and *The Sopranos*. Peim (2000) suggests that we should consider opportunities to read *Much Ado About Nothing* in terms of gender politics alongside *Eastenders*, for example. This will allow us to scrutinise and challenge the cultural authority of Shakespeare as a 'naturally superior form of fiction'. Literature as a whole might become an unstable category as a result of such practice.

However in the 'state we're in' it is useful to state at the outset that there are many important distinctions between 'doing Media' and teaching English as these subjects are currently configured. Three clear distinctions are these: audience study as a starting point, the importance of theoretical engagement with digital technologies (from students' perspectives) and the constant attention to commercial context. It would still be relatively surprising to encounter an English literature lesson in which the commercial imperatives of an author's publisher and the promotion of the novel as a product were given significant attention in terms of the coded meanings of the text itself. Nor is the arena of negotiated readings of texts afforded much attention.

On the one hand, there is the discipline which we can now call 'traditional' media and cultural studies, where television programmes and films are discussed as 'texts' by isolated scholars. This approach makes no reference to what actual audiences might think – based on the model of English literature, where no-one ever thought it was particularly relevant to hang around in Stratford asking punters what Macbeth meant to them. Whilst English has traditionally got away with this by having a range of interesting people to write about some complex, beautiful and writerly texts, this has always been shaky ground for media studies. Whilst the philosophical justification for why media scholars could do to telly what literary hacks had done with books was solid enough, it just never seemed right to be told about the Catholic-deathwish subtext in an episode of *Eastenders*, when you suspected that not one of the sixteen million viewers at the time has spotted it. It is probably this element of media studies – whether real or imagined – which led, more than any other, to innumerable teenage media students having the piss taken out of them mercilessly by their mums and dads. (Gauntlett, 1997: 9)

Other subject areas provide a basis for Media teaching, but again there are clear shifts in focus. The Sociologist may need to adopt a more fluid sense of the relationship between media and society, whilst the Art teacher may experience some tension when confronted with work that may seem derivative rather than inspired. The vocational teacher with industry experience needs to develop the craft of teaching and find ways to motivate learners within an environment that is 'always-already' artificial. After all, why should students on vocational courses be any more ready for accepting the rule-governed pressure of the workplace than any other learners? Again, we must remember that a Diploma course is highly theoretical and reflective, despite attempts to present it as the other.

Pleasure

Teaching Media has given us enormous privileges despite the derision we have encountered (from the 'just showing DVDs' banter to more prejudicial asides based on intellectual snobbery and ignorance). We have been able to work with students on their terms, and genuinely learn from their interests and their consumption. We would not be so adept at downloading music, for example, if we had earned our living a different way. But we started to enjoy it all the more once we (pretty quickly) rethought our own identities and stopped concerning ourselves with what we should be 'teaching' them, or why they should be interested in, say, the funding of the BBC, and started paying more attention to the ways in which students weave mediated identities and communicate through creativity and consumption. Adopting a more reflexive, perhaps postmodern approach to media theory and research remains abstract if the teacher refuses to shift to a more reflexive approach to the 'educational encounter' itself.

The remainder of this exploratory chapter offers an 'establishing shot' for each of the major concepts, theories and technological areas that will be covered in the chapters that follow, followed by a lengthy reflection on learning itself in the twenty-first century. The mode of address is very much for teachers here and the intention is to provide a contemporary 'spin' on each of the major concepts and theories. It is not our intention to suggest that the kinds of theory mentioned should be accessed by students in a traditional 'scholarly' way. Indeed it may be the case that the teacher's approach is theoretically informed, but learners are not explicitly aware of names or terms.

The 'big concepts'

All kinds of media learning tend to adopt a conceptual framework. Whether the concept is foregrounded (i.e. for learning about the concept itself) or used as a vehicle for creativity and theoretical reflection, most students will, along the way, become familiar with audience, representation, narrative and genre. The most pedestrian work reveals assumptions about how these areas are 'used' by producers and for analysis, whilst the more interesting activity offers a critique of the concepts themselves, or at least a renegotiation of their application.

Audience

Audience should be the starting point for media learning, and audience theory now includes attempts to conceptualise 'the concept formally known as the audience' in the age of the prosumer. This stuff is really up for grabs now. Traditional models describing a linear flow of media information in terms of sender–message–receiver are outdated, as is the over-used 'Uses and Gratifications' model. Seemingly common-sense notions of how audiences are targeted, and how they respond to texts, should be critically reviewed by learners, in dialogue with reflection on how they exist inside and outside of various audience groups. The social-cultural construction of pleasure and the suggestion that audience is increasingly fragmented in the online age are two key themes. Generally audience study has moved to a more critical framework in which the reader's cultural positioning is key (a phenomenological approach) as opposed to a referential approach in which the media representation is treated as fixed and stable. Gauntlett's work (2004) on the internet and also on gender and identity (2002) offer two useful examples of the kind of theory that challenges previous notions of audience and meaning. His response to the effects model is a clear starting point for student work on the active reader. Gee's work (2003a) on computer games and literacy is essential in terms of the question of whether existing models and concepts (such as literacy itself) can survive in the digital era or whether the technological advances require us to create new ways of analysing meaning and identity. McDougall's attempt to 'remix' David Morley's seminal Nationwide study in 2010, with reception of *The Wire* as the starting point, wrestles with the hybrid status of audience theory in the 'post broadcast age'.

Students on vocational courses should not be reduced in their learning to 'common-sense' notions of target audience and audience research. Clearly the commercial context of media production demands great attention to market segmentation and audience profiling, but this activity in itself is theoretical and should be approached through critical reflection. Where do existing ideas about audience groups come from? Were these notions of difference between people already there or are they in some way media-constructed? How are audiences changing and how is production adapting? The 'bedrock' of all this is the agreement that audiences make meaning and that media-constructed identities are negotiated and fluid. The potential interpretations of media texts are subject to a matrix of cultural and symbolic determinants and media learning is to do with bearing witness to this plurality of meaning, whether the vehicle is web design or critical research.

Representation

Whilst this concept is also omnipresent in media learning, it is useful only when called into question. That is, media learning is reductive when students describe how texts represent 'reality' and is interesting when the distinction between reality, media construction and collective identity is challenged. Baudrillard's work (1988) on 'hyper-reality' is useful, for example, in the context of the recent proliferation of reality TV programmes in which we might say that reality is 'fetishised' (perhaps due to the difficulty in pinning it down in our mediated society?). Learning about representation is best facilitated through creativity and play – that is, students engaging with this concept through experimentation, by representing themselves and constructing others. Vocational learners will get more chance to do this as their course will afford them more sustained time for creative activities, so in this sense we might expect them to be the most 'theoretical' learners. The study of (and practice of) representation ranges from analysis of the selection and construction of news to prevailing images of asylum seekers in British cinema. It is concerned with competing notions of reality or realism, with the study of who is under-represented in any culture and with reflection on how our own sense of the world is mediated. A useful starting point for students is a critique early on of the representation of Media Studies itself, as it brings forth for discussion a range of discourses of derision and notions of cultural value which can be returned to throughout a course. And this is not changing – one of the authors of this book was invited onto BBC Radio 4's *Today Programme* in 2009 to be commanded – '*defend your discipline!*'

Narrative

The worst examples of regurgitated 'theory without thinking' tend to involve the application of Todorov and Propp to students' own creative work, or the assumption, for example, that Tarantino 'used' Todorov's model in the development of *Kill Bill 2*. This desire to 'do theory' by clumsily 'applying' a formalist model in this way does little in terms of understanding our roles in constructing narratives, and how narratives carry discourses which appear natural. Certainly in an instrumental sense there is a need to teach students how to use conventions and technical opportunities to construct meaningful narratives, and to explore where our dominant narrative patterns and themes come from in cultural terms. But the most interesting media learning leads us to consider everything as narrative – from videogames to our understanding of science and history, for example (as opposed to the other way around where the structure of narrative is learned, as though a science in itself). Considering narrative as operating to frame our experiences in both micro and macro ways enables media learners to reflect on the interrelatedness of their personal narratives with public media narratives. In this sense narrative is the concept which must be handled with the most care if media learning is to thrive beyond a variant of English.

Genre

A limitation of media learning can be the uncritical acceptance of genre as a 'natural' means of categorising texts which then, it is assumed, acts as a contract between producer and audience. More attention to ideas of audience pleasure can allow us to be more flexible in our analysis of conventions. All specifications for academic or vocational courses offer choices of genres to be studied and clearly there is a shortcut route to this that reinforces existing versions of a genre's history, codes and conventions, key players and the reasons for its popularity. This kind of study will usually progress to the consideration of hybrid texts and texts which extend or in some way parody their genre. Creative production will usually be accompanied by a 'log' or similar written account, which explains to the audience the use of genre conventions. On vocational courses this may well be linked to studies of the marketing context of particular genre products. But the key interplay for interesting media learning is that between reader, text and socio-cultural context and in this arena students can investigate the construction of taste along generic lines in dialogue with other ways of understanding media pleasure. (Mark Reid of the BFI has offered at conferences an interesting, but unpublished, approach to this area, based on Altman, 1982.)

Digital technologies

Reid, Burn and Parker's report on the BECTA video project back in 2002 suggested that media learning is most usefully conceptualised as a 'creative apprenticeship' and that a degree of derivative production is a necessary starting point for more radical or playful creative departure. That still stands and proliferating discourses around the use of digital video editing and gaming in particular tend to involve creativity, engagement of learners who have 'switched off' from the traditional curriculum, and assumptions about vocational education and the importance of skills in the modern economy. More fundamental is the consideration of digital literacy, which if taken seriously by the teacher, can offer the most compelling justification of all for Media education. Undoubtedly, the stigmatised teenager playing *Grand Theft Auto* in her bedroom is constantly learning, and becoming increasingly literate, but it may take great efforts from the parent culture to understand this. Indeed we may have to learn a great deal from our students in this respect – a 'pedagogy of the inexpert' (Kendall, 2008).

Discourse

The suggestions for learning and teaching in this book assume a consensus that Media learning resides in a kind of postmodern paradigm in which identities are shifted and negotiated and the analysis of discourse is paramount. Thus theories like ideology start to look more problematic, especially if they assume an original truth hidden behind false consciousness or media illusion. It is therefore more sensible in our contemporary context to allude to discourse as presented by Foucault (1988), who suggests that discourses *'define, describe and delimit what is possible to say and not possible to say … about a given area'*. Far from being an abstract, philosophical idea as it may seem at first, this is actually of enormous direct use for the media learner since cultural products are disseminators of ideas which are interpreted by audiences through socially constructed discourses which are intertextually coded. So the 'common sense' statements produced through media or about the media are in fact examples of discourses seeking to gain the power that comes from appearing 'natural'. But where this approach differs to the study of ideology is in its refusal to suggest that there is a truth to be found behind the discourse of the ruling group. All discourse in this sense is seen as a 'claim to power' and it is the job of the media learner to deconstruct texts in order to expose the discourses at work (and no more). In production terms, it is an enabling concept as it offers a 'way in' to notions about targeting and mode of address that is applicable and at the same time critical and reflective, and it goes beyond notions of whether your production is challenging the dominant ideology or not (usually too blunt a question).

New ways of learning, new ways of 'being'?

This is a book specifically for Media teachers, aiming to support excellent Media teaching. But all subjects are now operating in a changing landscape, so it is important to set aside curriculum boundaries here to explore some more general issues in relation to learning and teaching in the era of convergence and web 2.0.

> Anyone who can draw as many people into situations related to learning as Nintendo knows something that educators ought to want to learn. (Papert, 1994: 87)

This is a bold claim indeed and one that was made over fifteen years ago! For most subjects taught in schools and colleges, there is still a very clear gap between the curriculum and the wide range of experiences that people have through new digital media that might require us to extend our definition of learning. Examples are videogames, social networking spaces, wikis, blogs and virtual worlds and a new range of websites described by commentators as 'we media'. In these collaborative spaces, people are able to easily create and share material that used to be the property only of media production companies – video, audio, photography and even modifications of videogames. The argument is that learning and the construction of knowledge is going on in all of these digital environments, and that idea poses a considerable challenge for educators. The media itself has been very quick to respond, integrating peer-to-peer elements to mainstream products so the audience can adapt, respond and create. But education's reaction has been staggered and there is a great deal of variety in the ways in which teachers view the relationship between the digital media environment and what goes on in their classrooms. Of course, for Media teachers this is made more complicated by the fact that these activities are objects of study as well. Media education has some tough decisions to make and so far we haven't addressed them. Here are five to get us thinking about where we are at:

Is a videogame a text?

Does a teacher have to play the game to teach about it, as she would need to see a film?

Is Club Penguin a media text – it isn't a game but a virtual world, so how can we teach about it?

Can our subject include student work uploaded to YouTube that was not produced on the course or as a result of our teaching, and if so, how?

How do we regulate online work in progress, research and evaluation, how do we guard against plagiarism and how do we archive this material?

Education 3.0?

Here is a provocation that sets up the history of education as the history of differently configured sets of inequalities:

Education 1.0   Divide in access to schooling

Education 2.0   Divide in distribution into schools

Education 3.0   Divide in 'digital capital'

In this history, education begins by being distributed unequally amongst people based on social class and status. In this era, not everyone is entitled to be educated formally (note that this remains the case in some parts of the world). Since 1944, everyone in the UK has been entitled to free education, but the selective 11+ exam (along with the existence of private schools) enables the state to use the educational process as a form of distributive 'ranking' under the guise of efficiency – people go to schools that will set them up for different degrees of academic or vocational education based on assumptions of what they need for work or domestic duties in their futures. This situation remains for many people of course. But another divide is now endemic, whether intended or not. As the internet provides incrementally more and more opportunities for learning outside the classroom, a digital 'haves' and 'have-nots' distinction is inevitable. But this is amplified by the decision taken by some schools and local education authorities to prevent students from using websites and social networks in school. There is no doubt that students who are denied this access in school and either have no broadband connection at home or lack the cultural capital and media literacy to use the internet educationally are at a huge disadvantage. An affluent student with digital resources at her fingertips in school and at home is even more privileged in this landscape – alongside economic capital and cultural capital, she now has 'digital capital'.

Web 2.0 – just in case

New digital media – what does this mean? What is 'new' is, by definition, always changing. The problem with a chapter like this is that the gap between writing and publication (unlike web publishing) means that there will be new tools in use at the time you read this that take us beyond where we are now – which is Twitter. The reality is that broadband internet communication is actually the 'now' for many people engaged in learning (although not that many as a percentage of the population, as we shall see) so 'now digital media' might be a better term to use. In the history above, 'Education 3.0' is mobilised by unequal access to broadband internet resources. Perhaps confusingly, the shift in the internet from a 'user experience' to a 'creative experience' is described as 'web 2.0'. Sometimes we assume everyone is familiar with what this shift is supposed to have entailed, but just in case, here is some clarification.

This term, 'web 2.0', is fundamentally important for this discussion. Coined by Tim O'Reilly (2004), it describes the shift from internet content produced by website 'owners' or institutions and 'pushed' to users, a largely top-down arrangement of content online to the current plethora of websites and services that allow us to share our own content, edit content and 'remix' content, online spaces that allow us to be more collaborative, creative and participative.

For clarity, here is a short history of 'web 2.0' digital media since 2000 to help us get some purchase on the pace of change and what this means for education. Wikipedia has been with us since 2001. Second Life was launched in 2003, followed a year later by Facebook, now a part of the lives of 300 million people. YouTube, believe it or not, has only been here since 2005 (now owned by Google), closely followed by Twitter (which took a lot longer to become so popular). In 2008, Spotify represented the first in what is predicted to be a long series of industry responses to 'free content' – a music site offering free streamed music, funded by advertising and living in the hope that it will act as a 'giant listening booth' for the audience who will then, having 'test driven' music online, go back to buying music or at least continue to spend money on concert tickets. (Source for dates – *Guardian*, 17.10.09)

Just at the point where formal education is still grappling with the conundrum of how to deliver equality at the same time as safeguarding standards, along comes a range of outside influences that might equally increase or reduce inequality. As each teacher and each school, each lecturer and each college responds differently, and at varying pace, to what is happening outside of the classroom, so the inequality is amplified. Of course, in many ways this is no different to the status quo – more affluent children have always had access to more resources. But the uncertainty over what the resources are and what learners should be doing with them, is what makes this more uncertain.

Teacher responses

The claims for how learning is transgressed (fundamentally changed, enhanced, liberated) by these digital tools and networks are bold, but controversial. And they vary from teacher-led to entirely 'private' learning contexts. It is helpful to imagine this as a continuum. At one end of the continuum we have Tim Rylands, a teacher from Bristol who is now an international consultant sharing his experiences of using the videogame series *Myst* with primary school children to develop further their literacy skills (see http://www.timrylands.com/). This was very successful but in this case the 'use' of new technology is gatekept (very well) by the teacher and the game is a context for more traditional ways of learning – particularly about descriptive language. Rylands discovered something rather obvious – that children would be more motivated by thinking about a videogame's setting, narrative and textual elements that they would likely be about the world represented by classic novels and poems. But the game was played in the classroom and used as a tool for writing – a very traditional form of learning, led by the teacher, but using new digital media as a context in order to increase engagement. The students did not need to play the game at home and the role of the teacher was central.

Sticking with videogames, at the other end of the scale is Patricia Broadfoot's recent suggestion that videogame simulations can be used as an assessment tool to test students' creativity and intellectual responses. In this example the videogame is no longer the object of study or the stimulus for something more orthodox. Instead the game *is* the learning experience, in an educational model which seeks not to replace the intense learning afforded by games with something else but rather replaces traditional educational conventions *with* gaming.

> Games are excellent learning tools in that they are interactive and provide rapid feedback, opportunities for extensive practice, engagement with intellectual complexity, emotional involvement and, increasingly, open-ended outcomes that challenge the creativity of the player. (Broadfoot, 2009 quoted in Newman, THES, 1.10.9: 7)

In the middle of the continuum sits something like the *Moving On, Moving Up* web drama project developed by Chad Vale Primary School in Birmingham. Web drama is a medium that is gaining increasing momentum in education, given its affordance of a 'real audience'. Through the use of a simple blog with embedded video and a polling facility, a more or less 'walled' audience can shape the development of the drama. *Moving On, Moving Up* was the outcome of an after school 'film club' at the primary school for year 5 and 6 students, during which the children created a five-episode narrative through which they were able to dramatise (and thus externalise) a set of anxieties about moving on to secondary school. The innovation, in terms of pedagogy, lay in the voting feature, through which the audience (the rest of the school, staff and students at two partner institutions – a secondary Media Arts College and University College specialising in teacher training – as well as parents and friends) chose the focus for the next episode, constructed as a series of dilemmas presented to the characters and a 'what should they do now?' question on the blog (http://cvtvspielbergclub. blogspot.com/). Interviewed about the process at the end point, the students offered a range of responses but all agreed about three things:

- The web drama had been a suitable vehicle for the discussion of anxieties about 'big school'.
- The creative (and imaginative) process of characterisation and fictional scenario-building had been essential to this.
- Most clearly, there was consensus that the 'real audience pedagogy' could not have been replaced by a more orthodox approach. Had the audience only been able to vote as a response to seeing the episodes in school assemblies or on DVD, something significant would be lost. It was the extended, real, online audience (and the removal of time as a constraint) that made the difference. As one participant has it 'anyone could see it – your Mums, your Dads, your Aunties, your Grandads'.

The reason for placing this example in the centre of the scale is that on the one hand web drama is a transgressive form. It offers 'real audience pedagogy' – a real, live audience who can respond 24/7 – nothing else but broadband internet can do this. It engages and includes students in new ways and sets up the rich learning contexts afforded by risk (dealing with sensitive issues in a public space), performance (displacing anxieties by acting them out through a fictional character) and interaction – a broadband feedback loop, perhaps (the voting patterns of the real audience as an alternative to teacher comments and marks). But at the same time, the context was entirely teacher-driven and the dynamics of the classroom, albeit in extra-curricular framing, were maintained. Everything was produced at the school, the degree to which the participants were involved in technical production of the film episodes and the website was managed by the teachers and the project was designed directly in relation to a formal education issue in order to secure funding. Hence, this is a highly institution-alised form of 'education 3.0'.

It is important to be very clear about some key distinctions. Confusingly all of these are discussed as though they are part of the same educational intervention when in fact they are clearly very different. Using 'e-learning' activities and materials alongside as supplementary to more traditional teaching and learning is now commonplace. But this is not the same as the act of replacing orthodox teaching with 'e-learning' and even that does not necessarily constitute a change in what learning is or how it happens – indeed, the exact dynamics of student and teacher in relation to knowledge and outcomes can be replicated despite the absence of any 'physical' classes. The more interesting area is the kind of learning that technology facilitates whereby the power relations, ownership and construction of learning itself can be challenged, re-formulated and made explicit and transparent through the use of digital space. In this response by Gauntlett (2009) to an article by Brabazon in which his work had been, he felt, misunderstood, this distinction is neatly drawn out:

> The more interesting and relevant bits in Brabazon's discussion are the parts where students themselves might be developing audio responses and resources. This activity seems disappointingly contained, though: the Duke university students apparently used their iPods-with-microphones to record university lectures (very conventional) and their own fieldwork interviews (better, but still conventional). I was hoping to hear that they had started making and sharing their own original pedagogic material. Brabazon's own students are asked to make sonic media artefacts, which must lead to some fascinating work, but again this activity occurs because of, and is poured into, the conventional path of being submitted for assessment. (Gauntlett, 2009: 152–3)

In this discussion, it is the 'making and sharing their own pedagogic material' that would be interesting, that would constitute a shift in dynamics, as opposed to the recording of lessons and interviews on MP3 devices, which is merely the use of a new tool to do the same thing. In our own work training teachers, we find it consistently frustrating when student-teachers (and their mentors in school) tick boxes relating to the use of technol-ogy for learning when all they have done is used a PowerPoint presentation or shown a DVD sequence. Brabazon's examples are a step further than these as they involve students in technology, but they are still a long way short of 'transgressive'.

Responses as discourse

The ways in which education responds to new digital media are constructed in rela-tion to pre-existing discourses – ways of seeing the world that assume consensus. So in order to analyse them adequately it is important to view them in this way – not as organic, free responses but as partly channelled by ideas about learning, society and culture that serve to 'frame' (in Foucault's words to 'delimit') what can be said within a community.

To explore this, here are four extracts from research-based writing on education, tech-nology and 'new media':

I play games whenever I have nothing better to do, which is most of the time. (A Level student and videogame player, Cambridge in McDougall, 2007: 1)

Whichever strategy it adopts, it remains the case that the school is no longer in control of the socialization and enculturation of children – if indeed it ever was. For better of worse, new popular cultural practices have come more and more to challenge the legitimacy of schooling, and hence its claim to sustain established forms of social power. (Buckingham, 2007: 97)

The skill of the practitioner remains key to the effectiveness of learning – an unchangeable factor in a context of rapid change. However, practitioners now need to understand how to draw advantage from an increasingly diverse range of tools and media and select the most suited to their purpose: the appropriate integration or blending of technology-mediated activities with face-to-face learning is an important dimension of twenty-first century practice. (JISC, 2009: 7)

It seems we are witnessing – albeit only for a minority of young people – some genuinely new learning opportunities, centering on possibilities of child-oriented digital creativity on collaborative communication with those who share similarly specialist or niche forms of interest and expertise. It is the successful embedding of these and related opportunities within the formal curriculum, for the benefit of all children, which remains uncertain. (Livingstone, 2009: 90).

If we read the four quotes above several times and try to map them to these three discourses (ways of viewing the world, belief systems or kinds of language) we might categorise the statements like this:

Discourse of Insulation – separating different activities from one another – in this discourse, new digital media will be 'insulated' (kept apart) from formal learning or other more 'serious' activities.

Discourse of Optimism – positive about the challenges ahead for education in the wake of new digital media.

Discourse of Caution – in this discourse we are warned about the challenges ahead and there is posited a lack of clarity about the future and what it may hold for education.

Cognition

Johnson (2005), in his provocative book *Everything Bad is Good For You* – which featured at the very beginning of the first edition as a framing for what followed – challenges us to invert the orthodox view about new media making people less literate, less social and, ultimately less intelligent by arguing the very opposite. In relation to cognitive development, consider this angle:

Think of the cognitive labor – and play – that the average ten-year-old would have experienced out of school a hundred years ago: reading books when they were available, playing with simple toys, improvising neighbourhood games like stickball and kick the can, and most of all doing household chores – or even working as a child laborer. Compare that to the cultural and technological mastery of a ten-year-old today: following dozens of professional sports teams; shifting effortlessly from phone to IM to email in communicating with friends, probing and telescoping through immense virtual worlds; adopting and troubleshooting new media technologies without flinching. Thanks to improved standards of living, these kids also have more time for these diversions than their ancestors did three generations before. Their classrooms may be overcrowded and their teachers underpaid, but in the world outside of school, their brains are being challenged at every turn by new forms of media and technology that cultivate sophisticated problem-solving skills. (Johnson, 2005: 144–5)

OK, but so far so general. Johnson goes on to analyse new media experiences in relation to specific aspects of cognitive development: environmental complexity, a variety of (competing) versions of IQ measurement, problem-solving, pattern recognition, probing, telescoping and experiential learning. And he uses videogames, television narratives and the use of multimodal data online as his examples – the very cultural experiences generally 'taken as read' as responsible for cognitive decline, especially in relation to attention spans and levels of concentration.

Serious games and complex thinking

James Gee (2003a) argues that video gaming develops a form of literacy and that orthodox views of literacy can learn from how gamers develop a 'meta-awareness' of a gameworld that helps them to negotiate their way through a rule economy and cope with the various intellectual demands that the game-text presents. He argues that 'good video games' tend to demonstrate a wide range of learning contexts, far more so than one could observe in any one average school lesson. Gee lists thirty-six principles of 'good learning' and claims that you can find far more being utilised when someone plays a good videogame (he makes a distinction between rich, complex games and less intense ones for this purpose) than in the average school lesson. Gee uses the term 'connectivism' to link constructivist ideas about forming knowledge to the notion of situated learning and concludes that:

> The theories of learning one would infer from looking at schools today comport very poorly with the theory of learning in good videogames. If the principles of learning in good video games are good, then better theories of learning are embedded in the videogames many children play than in the schools they attend. (Gee, 2003: 7)

At a conference on gaming in Vienna, Gee (2008) went further to suggest that the human race faces a problem in that we are conditioned to try to respond through simplicity to complex dangers. In other words, our instinct is to think about solutions to global warming and environmental disasters, the financial meltdown, cultural and religious conflict and public health crises with a simplistic, reductive and generally linear way of thinking. In the wake of complexity, the average human being craves simplicity. However, the one (large) group of people who are wired differently, according to Gee, is videogamers. These people are developing 'system thinking' and can see through the configuration of a game, modify it if they wish and engage in a complex mental process of observing, crafting, experimenting and testing which is, despite the stereotyping and scapegoating that pervades, ultimately a high-order scientific way of seeing the world. Simulation of experience is, then, a rich learning context. When a gamer is 'inside' simulation, she/he develops the kind of empathy for the complex that the human race needs to survive in a more complex world. Switching between one's own point of view and an overall view of the game's system-world is what is needed more and more in the 'real world. So in a context that is almost the polar opposite of school, people theorise play, learn from direct experience and operate strategically to 'modify' the reality they are presented with. Gee encourages us to 'imagine a curriculum based on modding'. In other words, could we imagine a kind of education that is truly constructivist – whereby learners modify the curriculum, adapting it and effectively 'remixing' it for the teacher, who is an agent of this construction – a facilitator in the true sense?

The link economy

A number of recent publications have converged media theory, economics, cultural studies and learning theory. This in itself illustrates the ways in which new digital media have broken down boundaries. Titles such as *Wikinomics* (Tapscott and Williams, 2006), *The Long Tail* (Anderson, 2006), *Here Comes Everybody* (Shirky, 2009) and *What Would Google Do* (Jarvis, 2009) all in various ways add to the arguments from Gee and Johnson – that things are changing for the better but we are always playing catch up to what new media are making happen. The last of these pays most direct attention to education, asking readers to think about the ways in which Google makes the current education system seem illogical. Why do lecturers in universities all spend lots of time producing the same kinds of PowerPoint slides – what is the logical reason why lecturers don't share them on open source networks, thus freeing up more time for tutorials? In effect this is already happening – many 'presentations' are dominated by URLs and material downloaded from the web, most lecture rooms are set up for wireless access and lots of modules feature accompanying VLE spaces where academics upload supporting material from online origins. Jarvis sees the educator of the future (or the present in many cases) as a 'facilitator of links'. To take this further, it is helpful to set this projection against the ideas of Anthony Lilley and Stephen Heppell, both of whom are professors at the University of Bournemouth and speak freely and from a great deal of evidence about the learning possibilities afforded by the internet.

Attention

Lilley (2009) is careful to balance the 'big claims' made in the kinds of books described above with some more cautious (and theoretically underpinned) observations about human social practices. His main idea is that information used to be scarce (so owning the distribution of it was valuable) and now it is overly abundant – put simply, there is too much 'stuff' to ever get through. What is now scarce is our attention. So finding information is easy, but getting your information to be the 'stuff' that is found is difficult. Crucially, Lilley argues that what helps us decide what is valuable from all the abundant material is each other. So we make choices (on the internet) about what is useful and what is not, what is valuable and what is not as we move from 'rationed media' to 'ubiquitous media'. From the proliferation of data (information), we select information which we turn into knowledge and then to wisdom. His polemic is to warn against over-simplifying this and here he agrees with Gee about the centrality of complexity. From complexity and unpredictable outcomes, he suggests, we develop art, adventure and learning. Whereas the 'information fundamentalists' view the ever increasing amount of information as emancipatory in itself, real educators understand the distinction between merely finding material and filtering it. Lilley is a media producer – a 'creative' – but he speaks at conferences about learning because, along with Heppell, his experiences draw parallels between the way that the media has responded to the internet and how teachers might. As Jarvis sees the teacher of the future as an agent in the 'link economy', Lilley views future learning hinging on social filtering of information.

Heppell (2006) bases all of these claims for the future on evidence from the present, which is international in scope. His work tends to reinforce the simple fact that people are much more important than machines in education. When schools are constructed online, the most important criteria for learners in judging the value of any learning experience is *who* is online. He warns against the mentality of 'equivalences' which often restricts creative freedom in planning innovative technology-enabled learning and assessment situations – questions about how the length of a video equates to the word count of an essay, or the number of webpages compared to the time of a presentation.

Heppell imagines a set of transformations, from twentieth-century to twenty-first-century learning and like the thoughts of Johnson and Gee, these are about more than just technological shifts, they are about changes in cognition and in the nature of learning itself. The most important shifts are in the move from 'one to many' education to 'peer to peer' learning and from interacting to participating. These resonate with Vygotsky's ideas about 'good learning' in the sense that the learner is given the power to construct and be active in the formation of knowledge. For Heppell, as his interventions are always based on research evidence, these shifts are certainties rather than debates, as he stresses here in his report on the fifth 'Be Very Afraid' project, which brings together children to share their experiences of learning in new digital spaces:

> We should all worry about the gap that has opened up between the institutions, teachers and learners who have embraced – and are busy astonishing us with – this complex mix of technologies and services, and those institutions that mindlessly ban phones, YouTube, international links, social networking, joy, challenge. The gap is rapidly becoming a chasm. Secondly, we know unequivocally, from a compelling body of evidence and exemplification, that children love to learn together, relish tough challenges, embrace and subvert technology for their learning, engage in it 24/7 and are capable of escaping from so many of the boxes that constrained their predecessors. The concern is that too much of the education system ignores these self evident certainties – witness the laughably blunt metrics of success. The last time the world ignored what we all knew to be true the banking system collapsed with a domino effect of unexpected catastrophes. (Heppell, 2009, at http://www.heppell.net/bva/bva5/default.htm)

Identity

Arguably, online networks and virtual worlds like *World of Warcraft* and *Second Life* allow people to make lots of choices about their identity that are not facilitated in the 'real world'. The extent to which people choose to maintain their own 'core identity' when participating in a virtual space varies from individual to individual. But for the purposes of learning, there are rich opportunities for reflection and imagination created by this potential 'reinvention' of self:

> Second Life provides an environment in which forms of intellectual risk are enabled through the adoption of alternate persona and a different kinaesthetic dynamic of space and time. Second Life, whilst providing new possibilities for a particular form of liberation of the learner, crucially, provides a palpable virtual world in which risk, ambiguity and possibility coalesce to creatively shape intersubjectivity and personal meaning. (McDougall and Trotman, in press)

The argument here is that virtual worlds offer benefits to educators beyond the mere logistics of students being able to stay at home whilst travelling to a virtual shared location, and also beyond the suggestion that 'digital natives' are more at ease in such a 'gameworld' than in the lecture theatre or classroom. (Michael Wesch's YouTube contribution on 'students of today' is compelling in this regard, at least in setting up a deficit model of conventional learning spaces.) Going further, the claim here is that the 'distancing facility' of a virtual world environment not only allows students to do things that are impossible in the real world (experiencing events and/or a location from history, constructing virtual scenarios in seemingly physical spaces) but also that the nature of 'being' in the virtual world creates a more comfortable space for being reflective, for stepping out of one's persona and for taking risks – all of which are established in learning theory as beneficial for education. Egan's work on imaginative education sometimes demonises popular culture, taking instead an 'enrichment' perspective on how learning and culture might co-relate in the development of imaginative education', but perhaps despite this we might be able to connect the kind of immersion and simultaneous 'distancing' available to game players and virtual world inhabitants:

> Imagination is too often seen as something peripheral to the core of education. In this approach imagination is at the center of education. Imagination can be the main workhorse of effective learning if we yoke it to to education's central tasks. To bring knowledge to life in students' minds we must introduce it to students in the context of the human hopes, fears and passions in which it finds its fullest meaning. The best tool for doing this is the imagination. (Egan, 2005: xii)

But there are, of course, debates around virtual worlds and the ontological implications of mixing experience and reality for education. Consider this philosophical response from Zizek:

> Virtual reality simply generalises the procedure of offering a product derived of its substance, of the hard resistant kernel of the Real – just as decaffeinated coffee smells and tastes like real coffee without being real coffee, Virtual Reality is experienced as reality without being so. What happens at the end of this process of virtualization, however, is, that we begin to experience 'real reality' itself as a virtual entity (Zizek, 2002, in Easthope and McGowan, 2005: 231)

Regardless of whether you feel more comfortable with Zizek's defence of 'reality' or Gee's notion of complexity, there are certainly strong indicators that virtual and/or augmented reality is going to become more of a feature of learning in the future so we encourage some 'futuregazing' on your part.

Digital beginnings

Marsh (2010) undertook a research project in a large primary school exploring children's use of online virtual worlds and then analysing the findings in relation to their learning. Marsh observes children learning, in such 'unexpected' contexts as *Club Penguin*, through sociodramatic play and ritualised play and makes interesting suggestions about the proximal relation between online and offline, 'real world' play. But the clear distinction in this relationship is that online play allows for the negotiation of identity and, subsequently, a degree of reflexive learning that is difficult to construct in the real social world. Just as Lilley disclaims the over-simplified distinctions drawn between the real world and virtual media, commenting that most people want to blend the two, so Marsh comments on the blended nature of learning through play in real and virtual spaces. But the richness of the identity play is more visible online:

> Play in itself is mimetic in nature, which in the case of play in virtual worlds, creates layers of modality. … in play, children can move from catotropic mimesis, which involves reproduction of external reality, to metatropic mimesis, a re-creation, re-arrangement of external reality. This movement across a continuum between the two positions could also be discerned in comments made by children in this study. At times, children reproduced narratives observed in their offline worlds and confirmed to the rules of game playing and at other times children played with the rules themselves, reconfiguring the representations of external realities. (Marsh, 2010: 26)

Marsh's observations here resonate with Gee's idea of the richness of 'modding' as an educational practice. Both researchers base their claims on evidence and urge teachers and academics to rethink their responses to digital play and to resist the temptation to reject this range of activity in the 'digital lifeworld'. A much older idea from Illich (1973) can help make this clearer by comparing the free 'convivial' use of tools (organically available) with the institutional management of tools which he describes as 'industrial'. Consider web 2.0 platforms here as tools and the traditional response of education (to control their use through passwords, surveillance and the adoption of formal protocols) as institutional and read Illich in this context:

> Convivial tools are those which give each person who uses them the greatest opportunity to enrich the environment with the fruits of his or her vision. Industrial tools deny this possibility to those who use them and they allow their designers to determine the meaning and expectations of others. (Illich, 1973: 21)

Just as this book is applying Lilley's thinking about the new media landscape to teaching Media, here we do the same with Illich to compare 'Media 2.0' with what came before, a shift that Gauntlett (2009) sees as emancipatory when set against the previous regime of 'elite producers' and big corporations pushing media to us rather than allowing us to construct it for ourselves. To alter this view to focus on learning will be to compare the transmission of knowledge in formal education as industrial and the more constructivist opportunities in digital spaces as convivial. But the role of the teacher merely changes – it does not shrink in significance. What is to be taught is the ability to make sense of the tools, to filter material and to be reflexive, to develop a critical literacy with which to articulate play as learning. It is the 'blend' that is important – as this example shows.

In Learning Plan 01.01, students create a wiki in order to explore two contrasting views of children using digital tools, the 'Toxic Childhood' thesis (Palmer, 2006) set against Jackie Marsh's work, described above. Students participate in a 'hybrid' learning experience – at the same time doing some old fashioned reading to make more sense of some complex arguments, their opinions on which really matter in the real world and also working through these arguments in a new media space, not for novelty or for 'engagement' but just because a wiki is a really helpful *tool* for this kind of work.

 learning plan 01.01 Toxic Childhood Wiki

Motivation

Creativity is an ill-defined concept which is to be left aside here, as it leads to a much broader discussion about individual and collaborative generation. In relation to social digital activity, it is a question of whether to retain an elitist notion of 'great creatives'. In this view, large numbers of people collaborating in digital space will simply not be able to do what Mozart or Van Gogh (the 'great names' used are normally male) could. The more 'evangelical' advocates of digital learning view the 'will to create' as more of an organic, universal human trait and argue that the definition of creativity as elitist has for centuries prevented the rest of us from finding an outlet for this 'will' and that education has been a major culprit in this. The motivation to be creative is thus connected to the motivation to learn and these are not always paralleled with a motivation to achieve. It is suggested that new digital spaces provide a safe, sometimes anonymous context for creativity. Schneiderman (2003) provides a similar framework for 'old and new' learning to Heppell but is more specific about creativity, suggesting that social learning in digital space facilitates a form of education based on collecting information and resources, relating through collaboration, creating knowledge and donating outcomes beyond the classroom. However, we are warned against the assumption that educators are necessarily positive about the 'creativity motive:

> A fundamental concern is that creativity is not universally valued. Many cultures and communities prefer training students to accept existing structures rather than training them to form new ones; they prefer memorization and copying to research and creative writing. These conflicts are likely to remain controversial. (Schneiderman, 2003: 131)

McDougall and Trotman (in press) call this 'real audience pedagogy', discussing three interventions – online web drama, learning in Second Life and 'work in progress' v-logging – in order to explore these as 'transgressive', as is exemplified here in the analysis of the web drama:

> For the young people in this study, the creation of characters, events and scenarios has meant that the dimensions of their work, whilst embracing possibility thinking, has generated a more meaningful engagement in empathic work. The tasks involved in this first

case-study required young participants to adopt a form of empathic agency in their creative work that without which would have rendered their task both meaningless and uncreative in the terms we have previously taken care to describe. Moreover, contrary to the 'moral panics' concerning the de-humanising effects of contemporary media technologies, we see this imaginative-empathic work as entirely in concert with the conceptions of empathy described in the discourses of care theory (Noddings, 2005,) and which enrich the sorts of creative practice undertaken in this case study. Typically the defining features of this work necessitates a 'cognitive understanding of the other's situation and emotional resonance with the other…not only must the one caring emotionally resonate with the other, she must move to do so. She must shift herself into the other's perspective and affective life'. (Noddings, 1984: 16, quoted in Verducci, 2000: 89). (McDougall and Trotman, in press)

Again, relating this discussion of digital learning to existing (and generally accepted) theories about learning and inclusion that inform educational practice and research, a great many have argued that their evidence demonstrates the link between motivation and participation in digital communities of practice. A new body of 'digital ethnography' research aims to support this claim and this section concludes by leading you to construct your own knowledge of that world. We hope you won't feel patronised but in Learning Plan 01.02 **you** are the learner.

🖱 **learning plan 01.02** Digital Youth

We realise that you may be very surprised to encounter this activity as it assumes rather a lot – a whole staff development event! But we need to remember that we should all be learners and researchers, not just instrumental teachers 'from the manual'. If a book like this does nothing more than provide a set of 'off the shelf' lesson plans, then we will just continue the depressing trend towards a de-professionalised teaching workforce. We don't want to do that and, perhaps if there is a huge gap between our aspirations here and your reality in the institution where you teach, that's a problem for us all to worry about?

This preparatory 'mapping' of the landscape will now lead us into the more explicit consideration of Media education in an emerging era which we call 'after the media'. To summarise the 'view from the patch' so far set out, we suggest these foundational observations:

- Research-based thinking in this area has moved on from viewing new digital media as entertainment and new digital learning as separate things
- A range of academics are suggesting that new digital media present us with new ways of learning (rather than just new contexts for learning or new kinds of access to learning) and that these claims raise important psychological issues (how do people learn?) and philosophical issues (what is knowledge?) that we can relate to existing and accepted theories of learning from these two disciplines
- One implication of these claims is that the school, as currently configured, is threatened in the near future. This is not simply due to economic imperatives (why have buildings and teachers when you can provide education online in peoples' homes)

but more importantly because it is suggested that the physical structure and temporal configuration of the school will no longer be able to provide learning for a generation of people who are 'digital natives', not simply because of what they prefer (e.g. screens rather than books) but more fundamentally because of how they think.

Importantly, there is no compulsion for you to agree with these arguments, but hopefully we will all have an informed position on the claims and counter-arguments that we can take forward into more 'subject-specific' ideas for how to 'be' as a Media teacher.

References and further reading

Altman, R., 1982. *Genre, The Musical*. London: Routledge.

Anderson, C., 2006. *The Long Tail*. London: Random House.

Baudrillard, J. (ed. Poster, M.), 1988. *Selected Writings*. Cambridge: Polity.

Berger, R. and McDougall, J., 2010. 'Media education research in the twenty-first century: touching the void', *Media Education Research Journal* 1.1.

Bernstein, B., 1990. *The Structuring of Pedagogic Discourse*. London: Routledge.

Bolas, T., 2009. *Screen Education: From Film Appreciation to Media Studies*. Bristol: Intellect.

Brabazon, T., 2007. *The University of Google*. Aldershot: Ashgate.

Buckingham, D., 2003: *Media Education: Literacy, Learning and Contemporary Culture*. London: Polity.

Buckingham, D., 2007. *Beyond Technology: Children's Learning in the Age of Digital Culture*. London: Polity.

Buckingham, D. (ed.), 2008. *Youth, Identity and Digital Media*. Cambridge, MA: MIT Press.

Csikszentmihalyi, M., 1996. *Creativity, Flow and the Psychology of Discovery and Intervention*. New York: Harper Perennial.

Curtis, W. and Pettigrew, A., 2009. *Learning in Contemporary Culture*. Exeter: Learning Matters.

Egan, K., 2005. *An Imaginative Approach to Teaching*. San Francisco: Jossey-Bass.

Fikiciak, M., 2004. 'Hyperidentities: postmodern identity patterns in massive multi-player online role playing games' in Wolf and Perron (eds), *The Videogame Theory Reader*. London: Routledge.

Foucault, M., 1988. *Technologies of the Self: A Seminar with Michel Foucault*, ed. L. H. Martin, H. Gutman and P. H. Hutton. Amherst, MA: University of Massachusetts Press.

Freeman, W., 2010. 'With games this good, who needs film?', *Observer*, 21.02.10.

Gauntlett, D., 1997. 'Another crisis for Media Studies', *In the Picture* 31. Keighley: In the Picture Publications.

Gauntlett, D., 2002. *Media, Gender and Identity*. London: Routledge.

Gauntlett, D., 2004. *Web Studies: Rewiring Media Studies for the Digital Age*. London: Arnold.

Gauntlett, D., 2007. *Creative Explorations: New Approaches to Identities and Audiences.* London: Routledge.

Gauntlett, D., 2009. 'Media Studies 2.0: a response', in *Interactions: Studies in Communication and Culture* 1.1: 147–157.

Gee, J., 2003a. *What Videogames Have to Teach us about Learning and Literacy.* Basingstoke: Palgrave Macmillan.

Gee, J., 2003b. 'High score education: games, not school, are teaching kids to think' in *Wired* 11.5.

Gee, J., 2008. Keynote presentation to *Future and Reality of Gaming* conference, Vienna, 17 Oct. 2008.

Gillmor, D., 2004. *We, The Media.* Cambridge, MA: O'Reilly.

Goffman, E., 1990. *The Presentation of Self in Everyday Life.* London: Penguin.

Green, H. and Hannon, C. (2007). *Their Space* (PDF) at http://www.demos.co.uk/files/Their%20space%20-%20web.pdf

Heppell, S., 2006. Keynote speech to the Media Education Summit, Bournemouth http://www.cemp.ac.uk/summit/podcasts/StephenHeppellKeynote.mp3

Hopkins, E., 2009. 'The impact of new media technologies' in Sharp, J., Ward, S. and Hankin, L. (eds), *Education Studies: An Issues-Based Approach.* Exeter: Learning Matters.

Horrocks, C. and Jetvic, Z., 1999. *Introducing Foucault.* Cambridge: Icon.

Illich, I., 1973. *Tools for Conviviality.* London: Calder & Boyars.

Jarvis, J., 2009. *What Would Google Do?* London: Collins.

Jenkins, H., 2006. *Convergence Culture: Where Old and New Media Collide.* New York: New York University Press.

JISC, 2009. *Effective Practice in a Digital Age: A Guide to Technology-Enhanced Learning and Teaching.* Bristol: JISC.

Johnson, S., 2005. *Everything Bad is Good for You.* London: Penguin.

Kendall, A., 2008. 'Playing and resisting: re-thinking young people's reading cultures', *Literacy.*

Kendall, A., 2008. 'Giving up reading: re-imagining reading with young adult readers', in *Journal of Research and Practice in Adult Literacy*, 65, spring/summer: 14–22.

Lankshear, C. and Knobel, M., 2006. *New Literacies: Everyday Practices and Classroom Learning.* Maidenhead: Open University Press.

Lilley, A., 2009. Professorial lecture to Centre of Excellence in Media Practice, University of Bournemouth, 11.11.09 at http://www.cemp.ac.uk/summit/podcasts/AnthonyLilleyKeynote.mp3

Livingstone, S., 2009. *Children and the Internet: Great Expectations, Challenging Realities.* London: Polity.

Marsh, J. (ed.), 2005. *Popular Culture, Media and New Technologies in Early Childhood*. London: Routledge.

Marsh, J., 2010. 'Young children´s play in online virtual worlds', *Journal of Early Childhood Research*, 7.3: 1–17.

Masterman, L.,1985: *Teaching the Media*. London: Routledge.

McDougall, J., 2004. Subject Media: A Study in the Sociocultural Framing of Discourse. Unpub. PhD thesis, University of Birmingham.

McDougall, J., 2007. 'What do we learn in Smethwick Village', *Learning, Media, Technology*, 32.2.

McDougall, J. and O'Brien, W., 2009. *Studying Videogames*. Leighton-Buzzard: Auteur.

McDougall, J. and Trotman, D., in press. 'Real audience pedagogy: creative learning in digital space', in Sefton-Green, J. (ed.), *The International Handbook of Creative Learning*. London: Routledge.

Newman, M., 2009. 'The Xbox Factor: Gaming's Role in Future Assessment' in *Times Higher Education Supplement* via www.timeshighereducation.co.uk/story. asp?storycode=408492

Noddings, N., 1984, *Caring: A Feminine Approach to Ethics & Moral Education*. CA: University of California Press.

Noddings, N., 2005, *Educating Citizens for Global Awareness* (ed.). NY: Teachers College Press.

O'Reilly, T., 2004. Opening Welcome: State of the Internet Industry. San Francisco, CA, 5 October.

Palmer, S., 2006. *Toxic Childhood: How the Modern World is Damaging our Children and What We Can Do About It*. London: Orion.

Papert, S., 1994. *The Children's Machine: Rethinking School in the Age of the Computer*. New York: Basic Books.

Peim, N., 1995. *Critical Theory and the English Teacher*. London: Routledge.

Peim, N., 2000. 'The cultural politics of English teaching' in *Issues in English Teaching*. London: Routledge.

Peim, N., 2005. *Critical Theory and the English Teacher*. London: Routledge.

QCA, 2005. *Media Matters: A Review of Media Studies in Schools and Colleges*. London: QCA.

Reid, M., Burn, A. and Parker, D., 2002. *Evaluation Report of the BECTA Digital Video Project*. London: BECTA.

Rusbridger, A., 'Democracy in the Decade of Google' in *The Guardian*, 17.10.09 (also online via http://www.guardian.co.uk/technology/2009/oct/17/communications-decade-democracy-google-rusbridger)

Shirky, C., 2009. *Here Comes Everybody: How Change Happens When People Come Together*. London: Penguin.

Shneiderman, B., 2003. *Leonardo's Laptop: Human Needs and the New Computing Technologies*. Cambridge, MA: MIT Press.

Tapscott, D. and Williams, A., 2006. *Wikinomics: How Mass Collaboration Changes Everything*. London: Atlantic Books.

Verducci, S., 2000. 'A Conceptual History of Empathy and a Question It Raises for Moral Education', *Educational Theory*, vol. 50, pp. 63–80.

Zizek, S., 2002. 'Welcome to the desert of the real' in Easthope, A. and McGowan, K. (eds), *A Critical and Cultural Theory Reader*. Maidenhead: Open University Press.

2 Teaching Media Practice

Research into young people's engagement with media production across a range of curriculum areas and educational contexts supports what we probably all know to be the case in our own classrooms: that the majority of Media students value and have positive experiences of production work in general, and of digital creativity in particular (see QCA, 2005). While many students will leave our courses enthusiastic about having developed their critical and conceptual understanding of the media through textual analysis and deconstruction, it is often the thought of 'making stuff' on 'cool kit' – of producing their own music promo using HD cameras, for example – that initially motivates many Media students to take up the subject in the first place. With cheaper digital technologies becoming more widely available in schools and colleges over the last decade – from camcorders and editing software to graphic tablets and desktop publishing – most centres are now exclusively submitting digitally produced video, print and audio coursework for student assessment. For their part, since the late 1990s awarding bodies have been moving progressively with each new specification to increase the role of such production work to the point where at least one exam board now gives equal weight to practical coursework and summative examinations.

We ought to remember, however, that adoption of digital technologies in Media education is not solely a recent phenomenon. The problematic relationship between classroom set-ups and 'industry standards' has a longer history than current discussion about the necessity of shifting video-work from mini-DV to SD-disks or hard drives. A useful exercise for students and teachers alike is to think about their personal digital histories and to consider their own first encounters with the different digital technologies they use in their media production. Andrew Burn, for example, recalls how his first engagement with digital production work came in 1988 when he began using desktop publishing software on the Acorn Archimedes, working with Year 9 students making 'newspapers with real local reportage in Cambridge, at a time when the local paper, the *Cambridge Evening News*, was still printing with moveable type' (Burn, 2008: 1). For many young people, the first encounter with the kinds of desktop publishing software Burn introduced to his students is more likely to have occurred in an ICT lesson than a Media classroom. While a growing number of students will arrive on Media courses already having clocked countless hours of digital editing experience producing homemade videos for sharing amongst friends online.

learning plan 02.01 Post-Digital Skills Audit

In this example we ask students to reflect on their sense of ownership over the tools of media production and to consider how their creative skills may have been shaped by the formal and informal learning contexts in which they first got to grips with these digital technologies. Being forced to have to edit 'in camera' because of a lack of software, for example, might actually serve to instil an aspiring Media student with a more acute sense of the importance of preparation and planning than someone who has only ever edited in digital post-production. In fact, some of our students still come to digital video having first learnt how to 'crash edit' on VHS, as both the present authors did. Less surprising perhaps may be the fact that rather than sign up for expensive training sessions on After Effects or Photoshop as we as teachers might, most students are a mix of internet autodidact and face-to-face knowledge sharers, teaching themselves to master complex digital technologies by watching how-to videos, reading discussion threads, looking over the shoulders of more experienced friends or siblings, and old-fashioned trial-and-error (see Green and Hannon, 2007).

learning plan 02.02 Creative Buddying

It is important, as Sefton-Green (1999) warns us, not to make assumptions about students' prior access to digital technologies, which may be an issue for production work. Sefton-Green describes a youth project in which it became abundantly clear that the degree of prior access to web design software and computer games related significantly to levels of engagement on the course. We have encountered a huge amount of misguided assumption about 16-year-olds choosing Media courses in terms of their levels of enthusiasm and competence in the domain of risky creative activity. Sometimes we have to remind ourselves, especially in FE, that Media courses attract a large number of disengaged learners who are seeking a second chance, some of whom might have misconceptions about the course being less demanding (see Irvine, 2004 for a fuller picture of this issue in FE, albeit a perspective we don't share ourselves). The introduction of the new 14–19 Diploma has further complicated matters, with the new courses often being pitched as a 'more accessible' alternative for 'less academically motivated' learners, but with many schools and colleges finding it difficult to convince parents and pupils to opt for the new qualifications, and exam boards laying the blame for poor early results on the recruitment of weak students. While a few Media students may see themselves as 'digital pioneers' (Green and Hannon, 2007), and we as teachers may marvel at their facility with some of the new technologies they have grown up with, there are many more young people for whom the use of digital cameras and computers extends not much further than uploading and tagging snapshots onto Facebook or for whom Media Studies is perceived as an 'easy option'.

Tackling the 'digital divides' apparent in our classrooms goes beyond questions of whether students have broadband internet at home, or own a hi-res cameraphone. Instead, as David Buckingham argues, it means thinking about student access, ability and engagement as socially conditioned, addressing the various forms of 'technological, cultural or educational capital that are at stake' when we make assumptions about how young people learn:

> These inequalities in levels of participation are clearly related to wider forms of social inequality; and they largely coincide with other differences, for example, in how families from different social classes use the educational dimensions of the internet or participate in creative or arts-related activities offline. To a large extent, the most active participants in

the creative world of Web 2.0 are the 'usual suspects'. Indeed, if online participation is as socially, culturally and politically important as the enthusiasts suggest, it seems likely that, far from liquidating social inequality, it might actually accentuate it. (Buckingham, 2010)

Two possible ways to attempt to bridge these digital divides would be the use of what we call a Creative Buddying approach, fostering more collaborative practical work as well as to introduce an Invoicing System for encouraging mutual aid and peer-to-peer learning.

 learning plan 02.03 Invoice System

More than just helping students to think afresh about their own learning or to identify peer networks that might be leveraged into helping other students to acquire useful skills, activities such as those we have been suggesting should encourage us as teachers to consider the impact of technological change on the way we make sense of our subject and the objects we study. What effect does a focus on digital over analogue creativity have on the way students find meaning in, and relate to, the media products created with such tools? Does it matter that our students 'do' textual analysis using Quicktime and DVDs and not Steenbeck editing tables, as we may have done at university? Does this affect the ways in which they respond, for example, to the materiality of film and the aesthetics of moving image culture? We would argue that the question of aesthetics should, in fact, be a central part of any discussion of digital creativity and media culture (see Creeber and Martin, 2009). As Sean Cubitt puts it, 'digital aesthetics has to respond to the material qualities of the media it investigates' (2009: 28) and yet we would suggest that as teachers, often we don't ask our students to engage enough with the *digitalness* of digital production.

 learning plan 02.04 Digital Aesthetics 'Taste Test'

It is a commonplace utterance of 'true fans' and analogue aficionados but can your students really *hear* the difference between a digital CD and a vinyl LP? What about between a CD and an MP4? While we might all be able to spot the too-perfect sheen of much cinematic CGI, is it not almost impossible to tell from watching a movie whether it was edited digitally in Avid or spliced together on a flatbed editing table? Add to this the ongoing trend in film for computer technologies to be used to disguise the digital nature of their own post-production (from *O Brother Where Art Thou* to *Grindhouse*) and we have an interesting opportunity with students to explore Walter Benjamin's notion of 'aura' in what is now 'the age of *digital* reproduction'. And though we are most definitely in an age of proliferating digital technologies, we would argue that it is necessary in creative practical work for students to reflect on the aesthetic characteristics of any given medium before they pitch into production. We ought not take it for granted that students will prefer to shoot their music videos on DV rather than Super-8 or that they'd rather take digital photos for CD covers than develop their own images in a darkroom. There might in fact be interesting aesthetic reasons for them not choosing the digital route. For example, it may be more appropriate for a student exploring the work of anti-folk musician and comic book artist Jeffrey Lewis to produce a fanzine or mini-comic using scissors, glue and a photocopier rather than with Adobe InDesign and a laser printer just because we happen to have access to these digital tools in our media rooms. As we suggest in Chapter 1, there are as many interesting philosophical and aesthetic questions to be raised by the affordances of new digital technologies as there are practical and technical issues of which file format or software to use.

Returning to the pedagogy of production, the context for most practical work in Media education (in both 'academic' and 'vocational' courses) is the 'production brief'. This is a small-scale imaginary simulation of the institutional context, creative processes and economic constraints of professional practice in which students 'take on the role of "real" media producers' (Buckingham, Fraser and Sefton-Green, 2000: 134). While the briefs are often fairly similar in both educational contexts – create a promotional video, a teaser-trailer for a film – the pedagogical purpose motivating the tasks has tradition-ally been different. To over-simplify, production work in A-Level is primarily used to demonstrate students' conceptual understanding of critical theories or generic conven-tions. BTEC production prioritises the development of generalised logistical skills and specialist technical abilities, while theoretical issues arise mostly from exploring the practical work in its industry context. However, even if the underlying purpose of a production simulation in A-Level Media Studies is to explore how far students 'get' the concept of the 'male gaze' or the convention of the 'final girl', or in BTEC it might be to examine whether students are able to 'do' a risk assessment or set the white bal-ance on a video-camera, in neither case is the production work seen as an end in itself. A-Level, BTEC and the Diploma require that students consider their creative practice within a framework of critical reflection and self-evaluation regardless of whether or not the rest of the assessment criteria are weighted towards examining conceptual understanding or determining technical competences (see Buckingham, Fraser and Sefton-Green, 2000).

As we have outlined, production takes many forms and has various rationales, but for the purposes of this chapter we are dealing with practical lessons that take place out-side of traditional classroom settings. These might be dedicated edit suites, computer rooms, art studios or various outside locations. Indeed, lessons might be taking place in a workplace setting or in a specialist location hired by the school or college (or a partner institution, if this is a 14–19 Diploma course). Or the lesson might be part of a vocational trip. What they will all have in common will be a move away from teacher-talk and student-listen. Instead, with its focus on hands-on digital creativity, production work engenders a pedagogical shift towards learning-by-making. For educationalist Seymour Papert, when students are making something with their hands (such as sketching out a storyboard), they enter a deeply engaged state of concentration – what Mihály Csík-szentmihályi calls 'flow' – whereas when they are contemplating abstract concepts in their minds (such as the applicability to their own work of a set of assessment criteria), they tend to be much less engrossed (see Papert and Harel, 1991). Anyone who has ever watched a student hunched over a graphics tablet or a computer mouse, engrossed in creating a Flash animation or editing a Final Cut timeline, will recognise that same state of creative absorption as engendered by the possibilities of digital creativity, what Malcolm McCullough calls the 'practiced digital hand' (1998).

learning plan 02.05 Storyboard In Reverse

However, as we have outlined above, digital production work in Media Studies has not tended simply towards fostering creativity for its own sake. For Buckingham, 'media education aims to produce *critical* participation in media, not participation for its own sake' (2003: 84). By making things, so the argument goes, students learn not just technical or creative skills; they are developing their critical and analytical faculties. The question remains, however, to what extent are students participating in *real* media production when they are working in this model of media education? For example, a typical print media production brief might ask students to create a double-page spread from an imaginary music magazine. Students will normally begin by researching the generic conventions of music magazines; carry out research on their target audience; create page mock-ups experimenting with typography and layout; as well as numerous other stages of production from lighting a photo-shoot to subbing their copy for typos. While the process may well *simulate* all the elements required in real-world desktop publishing, what the students will ultimately have produced – however technically polished or conventionally appropriate – is certainly *not* a 'real' music magazine, although the best work may well *look* like an extract *from* a 'real' magazine. This is an important distinction and one that is at the heart of what Media 2.0 is really about. In line with the government's response to Paul Roberts' report on Nurturing Creativity in Young People that highlighted the importance of *purposeful creativity*, we believe that students should be encouraged, wherever possible, to produce *real products for real audiences*, rather than always being tasked only to simulate such creations. As Green and Hannon's research shows, the principle of purposeful creativity

> was in evidence across all forms of digital creative production we encountered. Digital pioneers always had end goals in mind, although these were unlikely to be recognised by any formal assessment system. Their aim may only be finding an audience to critique their work or designing a game rather than playing one. Three children we met at a youth group in Chelsea who learnt how to use a complex piece of computer software had their own distinct motivation. They wanted to be able to record and edit a film of a dance their friends had rehearsed for a festival. Having this objective made their learning more purposeful: 'It's more fun when you've got something to show for it at the end, isn't it?' (2007: 49)

Media 2.0 with its attendant digital technologies and social media platforms is enabling students to become real producers of real products that they can now share online with real audiences, and so the question for us as teachers becomes: should we be reconsidering the significance traditionally placed on encouraging students to develop as 'critical readers' of the media when they now have the potential to become 'creative writers' of their own media content? Doesn't the emphasis placed on *critical* participation, espoused in much media discourse, need unpicking in the light of contemporary transformations in the media ecosystem?

Moreover, digital creativity also has important implications for our own practice as media teachers, beyond the necessity of trying to keep up with the latest software package. 'Understanding new media is almost impossible for those who aren't actively involved in the experience of new media,' write Wardrop-Fruin and Montfort, and 'for deep understanding, actively creating new media projects is essential to grasping their workings and poetics' (2003: xii). The Media teacher can no longer operate within a purely theoretical, textual environment without sufficient attention to digital production, consumption and culture. The simple reason for this is that there *is* no longer any textual meaning, culture or activity to be critiqued outside of the interventions of digital worlds. To be clear, so as to acknowledge that there remains an enormous digital divide, we mean that even non-digital media production and consumption is situated in its status as *other* to digital work. The days when it might seem feasible – even desirable by some – to make distinctions between practical work and theory, between classroom teacher and computer technician, between critical evaluation and creative expression have passed. Such distinctions are no longer tenable in an age of user-generated content, visual methods and cultural convergence. As William Merrin argues:

> Our fears of technology also extend to our personal use of it. Whereas in the broadcast era we broadly understood the technical principles of our media and their use, sharing that knowledge with our students, today lecturers are increasingly left behind in their knowledge of what media exist, their functions and capacities, how they work, how to use them and how others are using them. Unless we can keep up with these changing technologies, and unless they become as central to our lives as they are to our students, we'll lose both the ability and the right to teach them. In an era in which we watched TV we had the right to teach it: in the future unless we're downloading, sharing, videoing, tagging, texting, ripping, burning, messaging, networking, playing, producing and building then we'll lose that right. (Merrin, 2009: 29–39)

Irvine offers a nice illustration that serves to demonstrate the need for the contemporary Media teacher to be less an expert in everything than a master or resources and organisation:

> On the same day, a Media teacher might start with a class doing quite sophisticated work in Quark Express and Photoshop (i.e. things some people do full time) followed by a lesson on silent cinema and then a session of TV soap operas and representation and a final lesson on more production work but this time on radio script techniques. Few subjects demand such a range of expertise. It makes accusations of being a 'Mickey Mouse' subject even less tolerable. (Irvine, 2004: 24)

Whilst it is clear that a Media teacher needs an array of digital production skills – 'downloading, sharing, videoing, tagging, texting, ripping, burning, messaging, networking, playing, producing and building' – these are relatively easy to acquire for teaching at Levels 2 and 3, especially if you have technician support and savvy students to help you with the tricky stuff while you concentrate on organising the learning.

⊙ learning plan 02.06 Visiting Speaker

For all Media courses, students need to demonstrate experience, whether it is technical or not, of the specific kinds of production that 'real' media practitioners are working with at the time they take the course. This means it is your duty to the students to find out, and this in turn is the reason for our suggestion that you make links with people working in the media. If students are working with outdated technology or in vocationally unrealistic ways, then there is little point in the work, and this is equally true for the practical elements of academic courses. Some educational institutions arrange work placements for staff and we would advise any Media teacher to take this opportunity and to develop a scheme of work for students out of the experience. In our view, using outdated equipment or ways of working is as problematic as ignoring recent theoretical developments in your subject area. However, with many places limiting opportunities for teachers to go out for training due to issues over cover, it may actually be more viable to arrange for professional media practitioners to come in to run master classes for staff or students. As well as the practitioner workshop another potential but often under-deployed resource for really helping students with production work is team teaching. Using this approach gives students a live, tangible understanding of the way in which media professionals collaborate. Just as putting students from different creative courses together works to extend their repertoire of skills, so does working with practitioners from other subject areas.

 learning plan 02.09 Team Teaching Media Arts

While teaming up with colleagues in Art, Drama or even Business Studies and Science for help on particular projects will enable students to make connections between different subject areas for help as well as seeing alternative creative approaches in action, some places have gone a step further in fostering whole-college collaboration. In an effort to institute creativity across the curriculum, Dave Robertson, Deputy Arts Director at Kingswood School, Corby, helped establish 'Creative Learning Weeks' for all year groups. Suspending the normal timetable for a week, all students become involved in playful learning projects in a fictionalised context, orchestrated by a team of teachers from across all subject areas:

> The key focus was to place the students in a sustained role (i.e. historian, investigator, entrepreneur etc.) without the sometimes negative connotation of 'role playing' – it isn't a drama exercise. It was essential that there was a learning objective that was explored in possibly unconventional ways. The results have been impressive. Projects to date have included: an exploration of local history contextualised as a ghost story; a murder mystery with the head-teacher as the victim; an exploration of Arthurian legend positioning the students as trainee knights; the research and creation of a crazy golf course; a spy training school with physical, logical and scientific learning.

The 'Creative Learning Weeks' promote and reinforce teaching links across the curriculum, and have made significant crossover impact into the pedagogy of all departments. 'Ultimately,' enthuses Dave Robertson, 'students had fun while learning without the constraints of the curriculum and teachers had fun teaching, something that's becoming increasingly rare.'

 learning plan 02.10 Building the Bayko House

Playful, collective learning experiences such as the Kingswood Spy School – in which students made CCTV footage to analyse; produced photo identikits; and filmed their own mock episodes of *Crimewatch* – and our own *Bayko* house ice-breaker exercise, make a change from traditional, teacher-mediated transmission-style lessons, aspiring instead towards the positive virtues of an *Every Child Matters* curriculum and demonstrating 'open-ended investigation, creativity, experimentation, teamwork and performance' (QCA, 2008: 2).

The notion that learning should be more playful and game-like is not without its detractors. David Buckingham, director of the Centre for the Study of Children, Youth and Media, writes:

> the identification of learning with pleasurable play neglects the possibility that some forms of learning might necessarily involve frustration, boredom and endless repetition – and indeed be actively unpleasurable ... As a keen amateur jazz musician, I know that if I don't put in regular time on practising my scales, my playing will be good for nothing. (Buckingham, 2007: 111)

It is interesting that Buckingham cites music (and elsewhere, sport) as examples of learning acquired through prolonged attention to monotonous repetitive activity, in which any sense of gratification in the process is, by definition, deferred. On the one hand, we can argue that part of what is being learnt by musicians, athletes and by extension artists or chefs, is in fact muscle memory, a kind of learning *embodied* in the interrelationship between cognitive processes and the physicality of the hand, the notion that 'making is thinking' (see Sennett, 2009). Both musicians and athletes *play*. They also work hard to be able to play *well*. The notion that learning through play will *only* involve enjoyment is a misconception, as is the idea that students' engagement in a task is directly related to their immediate pleasure in playing along. Take these two reflective comments made by Diploma students learning to make their own Julian Opie inspired cartoon-style self-portraits in Photoshop, a task that is clearly playful in nature, but one that requires repetitive effort and perseverance to get to grips with the intricacies of the software:

> The outcome for this task was excellent i feel. I'd used it before so i kind of new [sic] what i was doing, but there are always problems and one of them was using the pen tool. It got a bit repetitive and strenuous. I made a good effort at trying to copy Julian Opie's work tho and have succeeded. The task was enjoyable and fun to do. I felt I completed this challenge well. I enjoy doing these so you may see a couple more on these pages :)

> I found the task difficult because I hadn't used Photoshop much before. At first, i struggled with getting the outline of my face using the pen tool and i didn't get it right. After a while I was starting to get the hang of things, and before I knew it I had finished. I like the outcome of my photo and i think after having some more practice with using Photoshop, i might actually end up getting quite good at it!

These two students, one for whom Photoshop is unfamiliar and the other with much more prior knowledge of the software, both demonstrate an engaged commitment to the task in hand despite both experiencing a great deal of frustration at times with their own repeated attempts to try and master the intricacies of digital drawing. Yet both display genuine satisfaction with the outcomes of the activity and their own sense of self-improvement. Both have clearly *enjoyed* the lesson and both have, on a number of different levels – technically, artistically and emotionally – *achieved* a great deal.

Any media production activity can harness enthusiasm and ownership of learning if it is less about a transmission model of technical skills and more about self-expression and collaboration. During a long-term project, it is vital for us not to be tempted by the 'work in progress' model of learning (and get on with a bit of admin, perhaps, whilst they make such progress) and force ourselves to find the energy to inject each lesson with its own flavour and set of objectives. One easy way of doing this is to alter the brief at a strategic point.

 learning plan 02.II Raise the Production Stakes

A great example of a production team having to respond to a change of plan was the promotional campaign for *Spiderman*. After September 11 2009, the original promotional images of the World Trade Centre were no longer viable, so an alternative set of persuasive texts had to be created pretty quickly. The trailer featured Spiderman building a web between the twin towers to catch his enemies, and a poster showed the towers reflected in Spiderman's shades.

At the same time on US television, a scene in which Chandler makes a joke about going through airport security was cut from *Friends,* and in *The Ellen Show* a character's line about a collapsing building was deleted. It is worth reminding students doing production of the inevitable artificiality of the educational version of media work. They need to accept, whether for reasons of future ability to be employed in media industries, or just for information, that creativity rarely takes place in a smooth, planned, timetabled manner. The ability to respond to the unforeseen is a valuable skill.

Practical media learning, when successful, operates on a set of principles that we call 'disciplined creativity'. Teachers from Creative Arts backgrounds will agree that the most inspired creative output arises from the most disciplined, rigorous application, and thus the stereotype of the 'laid back', disorganised Art or Media teacher is deceptive. Pete Fraser has an outstanding track record at Long Road Sixth Form College in Cambridge of supporting highly original, industry-standard production work (again, it is interesting to question whether doing A-Level on his course is academic or vocational) and we encourage readers to access Long Road's Media Studies website for examples of good practice. His published suggestions (2002) for laying foundations for successful creative work are sensible and applicable to all production work on all Media courses. To summarise (and group his many suggestions into a few 'bedrock' principles) he argues that students must start from research into real media texts, audience awareness and planning deadlines. Following this initial research and planning, the generation of simple ideas is more sensible than great ambition. A combination of simplicity and originality is the key to a creative project, alongside rigorous attention to detail. In the case of video, he points to planning the minute details of each shoot meticulously to avoid wasting time on location, testing batteries, lighting and microphones before setting off and planning to improvise when group members are absent. We mention these points, mundane as they might seem, for an important reason. No matter what advice we give you about the creative or technical exchange between you and your students, if you don't accept that your primary objective with production work is a combination of motivation and organisation, the students will not fulfil their potential. Once you and your teaching group have established this rigorous attention to detail, planning, health and safety and time management, then creativity will flourish. Or as Fraser says: 'Treat your project with professionalism and organisation and you will not go far wrong! Enjoy your work. Being creative is brilliant – but you can't beat being organised' (Fraser, 2002: 42).

Stuart McConnell, at Halesowen College, gets results from the same attention to organisation and detail. Students do not embark on production work until they have gained approval, and their progress is monitored frequently against agreed planning objectives. Fraser and McConnell (and countless other successful practical teachers) believe that creativity emerges from discipline, and the management of learning within production units is *more* important than the planning of teacher-led theory lessons.

learning plan 02.07 Production Troubleshooting

While we hope no one would disagree with how vital good planning is to achieving successful results in production work, it is also important to realise that failure, making mistakes or just plain getting stuff wrong should not be held up always as being negative. In fact, you should be encouraging failure as an important step on the way to success, and (odd as it may sound at first) we would argue that you should be pushing your students to go out of their way to get things wrong from the start. As design expert and web entrepreneur Aza Raskin says, 'All designers design to be wrong the first time. The first version, no matter how well conceived, won't be as good as the second, third, and fourth.' It is only by coming up with an idea and trying it out that students are able to discover both the unknown problems inherent in the idea as well as the unknown potentials that will reveal themselves only once they start to explore it in more detail.

In much media production work students will hit on (what seems to them like) a great idea very early on in the research and planning process only to run into problems after a while. They will then insist on keeping to their original idea, often in the face of more and more glaringly obvious production difficulties, until finally giving up on the project in any serious way. One way however, to avoid getting over-attached to your first thought or idea is to abandon the very idea of a 'first idea' altogether. A brainstorming session at IDEO, the innovative design firm behind Apple's first mouse and the Palm V PDA involves each member of the design team initially jotting down or sketching onto Post-It notes *as many* thoughts and ideas as possible for discussion, however weird or way-out. These are then each explored and finessed, with most being abandoned, but often an idea discarded in the early stages may turn out to provide the answer to a problem faced later on in the design process.

learning plan 02.08 Design Thinking

This kind of 'design thinking' espoused by IDEO and other 'creatives' is a long way from the typical classroom approach, in which students come up with one or two ideas in the first lesson and then plough straight on into pitching their ideas or even storyboarding them in the next. Ultimately, if we want our students to produce really creative and exciting material for their coursework then they need to have enough time to make mistakes and to learn from them. As any successful videogame or web designer will tell you, even media production work needs a 'beta period' in which ideas are explored, modified, sometimes abandoned and then eventually realised. It also means providing opportunities for students to play around, to make stuff not for assessment purposes but to practise new techniques, to take risks and to have fun with technology and to keep 'exercising' their own creativity.

References and further reading

Buckingham, D., 2003. *Media Education: Literacy, Learning and Contemporary Culture.* Cambridge: Polity.

Buckingham, D., 2007. *Beyond Technology: Children's Learning in the Age of Digital Culture.* Cambridge: Polity.

Buckingham, D., 2010. 'Do we really need media education 2.0? Teaching media in the age of participatory culture', in Drotner, K. and Schroder, K. (eds.), *Digital Content Creation: Creativity, Competence, Critique.* New York: Peter Lang.

Buckingham, D., Fraser, P. and Sefton-Green, J., 2000. 'Making the grade: evaluating student production in Media Studies', in Sefton-Green, J. and Sinker, R. (eds), *Evaluating Creativity: Making and Learning by Young People.* London: Routledge: 129–153.

Burn, A., 2008. 'New media and the future of media education', *Media Education Journal* 43, summer.

Creeber, G. and Martin, R. (eds.), 2009. *Digital Culture: Understanding New Media.* Maidenhead: Open University Press.

Cubitt, S., 2009. 'Digital aesthetics', in Creeber, G. and Martin, R. (eds.), *Digital Culture: Understanding New Media.* Maidenhead: Open University Press.

Fraser, P., 2002. 'Production work tips', *Media Magazine* 1. London: English and Media Centre.

Green, H. and Hannon, C., 2007. *Their Space.* London: Demos.

Irvine, S., 2004. 'Media in FE: how things stand today', *In the Picture* 50. Keighley: In the Picture Publications.

McCullough, M., 1998. *Abstracting Craft: The Practiced Digital Hand.* Cambridge, MA: MIT Press.

Merrin, W., 2009. 'Media Studies 2.0: upgrading and open-sourcing the discipline', *Interactions: Studies in Communication and Culture*, 1.1: 17–34.

Papert, S. and Harel, I. 1991 'Situating constructionism' via http://www.papert.org/articles/SituatingConstructionism.html (accessed 7.3.10).

QCA, 2005. *Media Matters: A Review of Media Studies in Schools and Colleges.* London. Qualifications and Curriculum Authority.

QCA, 2008. *Every Child Matters at the Heart of the Curriculum*. London. Qualifications and Curriculum Authority.

Sefton-Green, J., 1999. 'Media education, but not as we know it; digital technology and the end of Media Studies', *English and Media Magazine,* 40. London: English and Media Centre.

Sefton- Green, J. and Sinker, R. (eds), 2000. *Evaluating Creativity: Making and Learning by Young People*. London: Routledge.

Sennett, R., 2009: *The Craftsman*. London: Penguin.

Wardrop-Fruin, N. and Montfort, N., 2003. '*The New Media Reader*: a user's manual', in *The New Media Reader*. Cambridge, MA: MIT Press.

3 Teaching Media Literacy

"Media Studies is evidently a blister on the heels of a number of feet. (Barker and Petley, 2001: 222)"

In this chapter we deal with some of the pedagogic principles required to develop *critical* media literacy in students. As much as we dislike this opposition, for the sake of structure this chapter separates this kind of media literacy as analytical from the more creative forms of media literacy associated with practice, which we explored in the previous chapter.

In August 2009, in the wake of A-Level results, one of the authors of this book was 'grilled' on BBC Radio 4's *Today Programme* about the value of Media Studies compared to Maths and Physics. The interview began with the blunt demand to 'defend your discipline' and this theme was consistent – why should people study the media, how can it be as difficult as the understanding of Newton or Shakespeare? We are used to this, of course, and the 'discourse of derision' has been very well analysed, most notably by Barker's rigorous critique of the 'trendy travesty' attacks and the way we annoy by *signifying* (in Barker and Petley, 2001); by Buckingham (2003); and here by Bolas, who focuses on the problem this book is designed to partly address – the institutional barriers preventing Media graduates teaching Media:

> Those students who achieve their degrees on such media, cultural studies and communication courses are not attracted to teach in schools where the scope for media teaching is constrained by the National Curriculum. Currently the number of students able to train to teach media in schools is tiny. (Bolas, 2009: 353)

We might instinctively scoff at these attacks and obstacles, or get angry – after all, our whole professional identity, what we do, is at stake. Or we might rise above it and pay it 'no never mind', as *The Wire's* Marlo might say. But actually it is very important that we can offer more than a defensive and, ultimately, complacent reaction because there is an issue with the current state of play in the subject. It is not to do with whether the subject is sufficiently 'hard' or whether the world needs people who can apply post-structuralist theories to social networking more than it needs engineers. It is to do with the variable quality of teaching. Currently the majority of Media teachers are English graduates. English makes use of a different set of concepts and theoretical premises. There is some overlap but, as we explored in the introduction, divergence is increasing as Media Studies moves away from a text-centric pedagogy. And one thing is clear: it is not adequate for English graduates to simply 'transfer' into Media teaching without acquiring a grasp of the key theories informing their adopted subject that were not a part of their own degree study and teacher training. These theories, we argue, come mainly from Cultural Studies and they are concerned with the ways in which people make sense of the world and their identities and the role that engagement with media might play in this. In the chapter on the 'big concepts' that follows later these will be explored in depth, but here we are concerned with strategies for dynamic theory teaching. That said, a rather obvious foundation for this pedagogy must be secure subject knowledge, so for non-Media graduates there is some homework to do to get started.

Back in 2005, the QCA (now Ofqual) produced a report on Media Studies that included findings from some research with students. Predictably, one of the 'turn-offs' they described about their Media learning was *'lecture-based teaching of theory'* (QCA, 2005: 39). Tellingly, amongst the positives students identified 'deconstruction and analysis'. Proof then, if any were needed, that theory in itself is neither dry, boring or pointless. Indeed, working with texts is seen as active, engaging and essential. But the medium through which it is facilitated is crucial. In other words, if students find theory dull, it is probably a result of the teaching. People tend to feel empowered by the ability to think critically about the world they inhabit once they acquire the tools to do this, but the unhelpful binary opposition that has been established (by educators, mainly) between ideas of thinking and doing has served to reinforce a false notion that theory is the necessary evil that you sometimes need for practice.

But quite a lot has changed since 2005, as we know. Technology used in the classroom and 'in between' formal learning has greatly increased and new specifications have deliberately merged theory and practice at the institutional level; this is crucial since the awarding body agenda tends to lead pedagogy, for better or worse. The Diploma has injected a new variety of practice into the classroom and this has impacted on 'academic' courses as well. A 'making and doing' culture for learning is much more evident across the board, with creativity high on the agenda. And for Media education, the medium is the message in so far as the ambience for learning needs to be in keeping with the vibrancy of the object of study. So how do we bring theory alive from day one of a course? To start with, when students arrive for their 'icebreaker', it helps if we can combine critical reflection and some formative theory (such as semiotics) in a non-threatening and light-hearted way. If students were a car, or a breakfast cereal or a videogame, which of these would they be in each case?

learning plan 03.01 Icebreaker

One problem with these chapter headings, you will have observed, is that they reinforce the very binary between theory and production that we wish to debunk, a demarcation that we have suggested avoiding – as though here we are ONLY thinking about teaching media theory and elsewhere we are ONLY dealing with creativity and production skills. Thus it is important to state that what follows are suggestions for offering energised, creative learning in areas traditionally marked as 'theoretical'. They are presented within a 'safety net' in the sense that the ideas signpost some key quality buzzwords: inclusivity and differentiation, technology for learning, promotion of diversity and active participation. First we need some working definitions for these.

Inclusivity and differentiation

All learners must have, in terms of their human rights to education, equal access to the curriculum and to the learning environment. For the teacher, this means careful consideration of specification, unit, text and topic choices, and these should be made on the basis of student interests and profiles as opposed to teacher preference (for example, resisting the temptation to take the easy option by dusting down the Press Regulation resource box for the fifteenth year running when the students might find more currency in Social Media). Inclusivity extends to the accommodation of a variety of learning preferences (we are anxious not to use the term 'learning styles' as we are uncomfortable with the rather blunt and quasi-scientific assumptions made about right and left brain tendencies, for example), and to the provision of variety in learning outcomes and their assessment. An inclusive classroom will be an arena in which a calm atmosphere pervades and learners feel safe, so there is a classroom management element also. It will also be a space where nothing is 'set in stone' – where teachers are comfortable with what we call 'pedagogy of the inexpert' (Kendall, 2008) – power is handed over, students are encouraged to ask questions about why some things are on the curriculum when others are not and taste is not allowed to masquerade as value.

Differentiation should be a given in learning and teaching and it is alarming that it can be treated by some teachers as an adjunct to classroom practice (it appears as an extra column on schemes of work, for example, separate to 'lesson content'). Equally disturbing is the claim made by some Creative Arts teachers (we include Media in this) that their subject itself guarantees differentiation. A differentiated learning space is one in which students collaborate in their exploration of subject matter, skills and concepts and flexibility is constant: in task and assignment setting, in the rhythm and pace of the work done, in resource allocation, in opportunities to succeed and in feedback. The most common question asked of trainee teachers at the end of observations is, why were they all doing the same thing at the same time? If you want to control a group of people, if that is your primary objective as a teacher, then of course you will want to have everyone doing something that is commonly measurable and you will want to reduce the potential for chaos and confusion. But real life is complex and people learn by being involved in differently punctuated activities and practices, so the more alien the classroom experience from how human beings develop in social life, the harder it is to facilitate learning. And the key question is, why would you really want to control a group of people? What has that got to do with learning?

Technology for learning

If we are dealing with 'transliterate' students these days, who can comfortably learn and communicate across multimodal technologies, then why use a term like 'technology' or a category such as 'IT' at all? When we check our emails at home on a portable device, at the same time as stirring the soup, do we think of this as an 'ICT' activity? Sue Thomas, Professor of New Media at De Montfort University, worries about the failure of teachers to cope with transliterate students and how this effectively renders the academics 'illiterate':

Most would admit it, even taking a certain pride in their part-removal from the world of e-communication. This matters if they find their teaching relationship with students breaking down because of an inability to communicate fully with one another. (Fearn, 2008: 37)

The problem with the whole concept of 'ICT' is its insulation from everything else. The same applies to 'literacy'. When we send a message from a mobile device or pause live TV to make a cup of tea, we benefit from the 'invisibility paradigm' – we needn't be concerned with the workings of the machine, we just push buttons. The same really should apply to how we view technology in learning and teaching – just a range of tools that are easy to use. The idea of booking an 'IT room' for a special session should be outdated, we should be bringing handheld devices into classrooms routinely and using online learning contexts as 'everyday'. Buckingham makes the point very clearly here when describing the inclusion of games and web content in the media curriculum:

> I continue to regard these things as media rather than as technologies. I see them as ways of representing the world, and of communicating – and I seek to understand these phenomena as social and cultural processes, rather than primarily as technical ones. (Buckingham, 2007: viii)

Equally, it is really important to use a value judgement when observing teachers making use of technology in their work with learners. Put simply, technology is of no particular extra value if it does not lead to the enhancement of the learning opportunities provided for students. There is nothing wrong with using technology as a presentation tool (slides and film clips through a data projector is very much the norm), but you cannot stake a claim about learning from this. People are really just looking at stuff, they're not processing it any differently or doing anything with it. Similarly, if students are not equipped with selection and processing skills, then asking them to use the internet will be of no greater value than 'library work'. And if your teaching is actually becoming regressive as a result of using technology (for example, if students are hiding behind monitors where you cannot see them or if your lesson collapses because the network crashes and you have no alternatives or if nobody engages with your lecture because they can look at the slides on Moodle later) then we are very far away from the enhancement of learning!

On the other hand, technology can aid learning in very clear and exciting ways. It can include people who find traditional educational contexts uncomfortable. It can increase access. Beyond this, as well as the very obvious aforementioned democratising impulses of 'Media 2.0' which allow students to be media producers long before they arrive in your classroom, students can use a range of technology to explain to their peers how they constructed their digital photography by annotating the still frame. Blogs and forum tools can be used to extend learning beyond the timetable, and digital editing, image manipulation and videogaming take us into the exploration of new forms of literacy. In theory work, the question will always be about enhancement of creative theoretical practice (for example, building a website and forum to explore ideas about censorship or learning about conditionality in videogame narratives by building a game level) rather than the mere presence of computers in the room or the option to go online to find information. Finally, by far the most important, but challenging, 'use' of technology for the teacher is its potential to 'de-school' learning, taking us away from the constraints of the timetable and the classroom:

> Learners benefit from choosing when, where and how they learn. Technologies that enable learners to manage the pace, time and place of their learning add real value to the experience of learning. (JISC, 2009: 17)

 learning plan 03.02 Digital Student

Promotion of diversity

Often misunderstood as another phrase to describe Equal Opportunities, the promotion of diversity is a requirement for the project of education for citizenship in our multi-cultural society. Put simply, throughout a scheme of work on any area of the curriculum, learners should encounter a diverse range of resources from a variety of positions so that their learning hinges not only on subject matter and skills, but also on an awareness of the diversity of our culture. This is another area where it is tempting for Media teachers to claim that the subject somehow does this automatically, if compared to, say, Maths. But whilst representation will undoubtedly be high on the agenda and this indeed guarantees an awareness of cultural bias, scrutiny is still needed of textual choice in particular. Good practice in this area simply involves attention to texts, theories and case studies from a variety of cultural positions to include ethnicity, gender, sexuality and disability, so that respect for diversity is integrated into the literacy practices of the subject. The Media teacher has to be a critically reflexive practitioner – to ask herself, why are we using these films, these TV shows, these newspapers, games, websites, networks, communities as our objects of study? Why are we making these media products? Will they skew the curriculum towards a particular world view? Might some students question the cultural bias of your course? Or if they don't, should they? This is one key example where the instrumental practices of the awarding body agenda and the National Curriculum have to be set aside so that the lived experiences of the students day by day, apart from their assessment, can be thought about. It is not essential that, for example, National Diploma Media or A-Level Film students engage with the representation of disability in the media, unless this is a topic chosen by the teacher, but perhaps they ought to for other reasons?

Active participation

You will I am sure teach students who do very well but remain reticent publicly. What do you say when explaining to parents that their daughter's coursework is superb but she really ought to contribute more in class discussions when the response is, 'If she is doing so well, then why?' But the 'quality' agenda asserts that a success measure for a lesson is that **every** student will contribute so we need to find ways of making this safe for students who do not comfortably take centre stage. There are a variety of strategies for this, most often through group work which enforces collaboration but offers anonymity in presentation. The crucial 'ask' for our pedagogic practice is that we should do as little talking as possible and students should reflect and express themselves in a variety of ways as often as we can enable.

The starting point for any Media theory teaching should be demystification. Theory as social practice is of great value, and we should encourage young people to be critical, but regurgitation of learned theories without application and any personal narrative is of no particular value other than to gain cultural capital (Bourdieu and Passeron, 1977) through acquiring an 'elaborated code'. So we are going to assume that being theoretical means thinking reflectively about taken-for-granted common sense notions in circulation around us, whether this means that we analyse the common use of sports co-commentators (to add 'expert' punditry) whilst adopting the convention in our own production work, or that we question the extent to which torrent sharing of films online is really threatening the industry. In any case the emphasis is on using theory in a new way for the students' own ends, questioning the theory in terms of its validity in specific contexts, and always aiming to create *new* theory. In this sense we move from a transmission model of knowledge (teacher tells students about news values and they tell the examiner how they work) to an autonomous, reflective model of learning (student develops theoretical approach to inform her own creative interventions).

Most of the time you will want to use group work to foster collaborative learning for theory tasks but you should never just allow groups to develop without a purpose. Over a period of time, any class should experience friendship groups, mixed ability groups based on 'cold data' such as target grades, mixed ability groups based on specific aptitude in a particular kind of learning, randomly chosen groups, groups based on personal interests and 'jigsawing' (described fully as a strategy elsewhere, with a link to a learning plan). Depending on what is at stake and the kind of collaborative learning taking place, you should always have a *strategic* reason for the construction of groups.

Another ground rule for theory is that it should not be taken too seriously. Students should be discouraged from having unconditional reverence for the writers of theories, and it is useful and amusing to remind them that most 'theorists' are teachers no different from yourself. In other words, ideas are important, but status is not.

A good way of establishing this 'face your fear' approach to media theory 'early doors' is to get students to invent their own theories. This serves as a comfort blanket as it sets up the idea that theories are very often just quite obvious ideas that nevertheless help us make sense of things.

(🖱) learning plan 03.03 Invent a Theory

There is a balance to be struck here as we want to celebrate critical thinking at the same time as demystifying and deconstructing the idea of alienating language and big ideas. The Media learner can end up with a profoundly radical perspective on contemporary life. Here are ten justifications for theory work, or active uses of theory for students to suggest as a starting point:

1. Theory informs production – the most important selling point is that you will make better films if you know how they are made by the experts.
2. Theory gives you critical power – we can enjoy media texts all the more if we can develop a creative sense of how they are constructed.

3. Theory is useful for citizenship – we can become more aware of representation and who is being excluded through a theoretical understanding of texts.

4. Theory gives us cultural capital – far from thinking of Media Studies as a trivial pursuit, students' parents will be impressed when they are treated to an analysis of how current affairs are presented according to news agendas, for example.

5. Theory is relevant – Media students get to understand how technology works and to take some of the claims about it with a pinch of salt, so they are 'digitally informed' consumers.

6. Media theory is all about people – audience theory, for example, is just stories about people and how they use media in their lives in creative ways.

7. Theory is reflective – most media theory is about you and your opinions – whether ITV's *The X Factor* is mindless trash or interactive democracy in action – the Media student will have a developed spin on their response.

8. Media theory is 'interdisciplinary' – Media Studies is pioneering in the sense that whether you realise it or not, you are studying History, Politics, Sociology and Art – a *'massala curriculum'* even!

9. Media theory reminds you that things are not real – getting a grip on the space between media reality and whether or not there is another reality to be grasped is a 'life skill'. Better to be aware that you are being manipulated, then you can enjoy it more!

10. Media theory demystifies the world – many people have some idea that behind spin about the global village there are big companies making a lot of money. The Media student knows who they are and how they operate.

learning plan 03.04 Writing Frames for Theory

The simplest ideas are often the most valuable, and whilst Matt Hills' work is far from simple in its arguments and range, the title of his excellent book *How to Do Things with Cultural Theory* (2005) is a classic 'nutshell' of the kind of theory teaching we want to advocate. Hills see theory as active, enabling and ultimately performative – it does something to culture when a student uses it. Students will be working through ideas (including their own) about what matters in the contemporary mediascape, or as Hills puts it:

> Treating cultural theory as performative means considering both what that theory does – how it constructs and affects the world – and also what apprentice, amateur and professional theorists can do with theory. (Hills, 2005: 175)

In this way you can help your students to see themselves as apprentice theorists, learning from professionals, just as a 'vocational' media producer will learn from industry practitioners – theory as a 'trade'.

So what kinds of theory are required? Since the first edition of this book was published, this area has been much more 'up for grabs' than ever before and that makes choosing a specification a much more strategic decision. Scanning specifications for

GCSE, A2 and AS, Creative and Media and National Diploma, the range of prescribed theory still (for better or worse) includes the key concepts (audience, genre, narrative and representation) and then a number of different varieties in the study of media language or literacy (or textual analysis). There tends to still be a distinction maintained between still and moving images and between media (or 'platforms') despite convergence eroding many of these boundaries. Another matter for debate is whether there ought to be a prescribed list of theories for each level/key stage. There isn't, and this is an exception to the rule when set against other subjects, but the reason is that relatively speaking Media teachers get lots of choice over what students will analyse, and so a centralised list would be stretched too far.

That said, if you are not a Media graduate, there will be some work to do regardless of the specification or qualification and to be helpful, here is an 'unofficial' canon of theories in five categories, but please let's be clear – these are just a few examples:

Theorising production

Media language

Aesthetics

Convention and Genre

Formats and House Styles

Modes of Address

Further theories specific to the production context – e.g. auditory verisimilitude; web navigation theory; conditionality for videogames; lighting conventions for film or elements of semiotics for print-based material.

Classic conceptual theories

Crucially, these MUST be treated as ideas to challenge, not to straightforwardly regurgitate.

Genre theory

Altman is recommended.

Narrative theory

The formalists are popular – Propp and Todorov, as well as Bordwell and Thompson for film, and more recently the narratology/ludology debate for gaming – see Frasca for a commentary on this and Diane Carr for applications to games.

Theories of representation

Stuart Hall and the Birmingham School of Contemporary Cultural Studies are usually the starting point, Laura Mulvey, Roland Barthes, Judith Butler – too many to mention. Welsby's recent book – *Understanding Representation* – is a fine 'reader'. But remember to add Gauntlett's 'Media Studies 2.0' idea – the concept formally known as the audience representing themselves. Is the concept in crisis?

Theories about audience

Our strongest recommendation is to look at the work of Neil Ruddock, Matt Hills, Martin Barker and David Buckingham. You can use a standard course textbook with students in the first place, so these suggestions are for you to read.

Ideology

Well, it used to be Marx and Althusser and Winship and McRobbie but these days you need Jenkins ('Convergence Culture') at the very least as well. And contrasting Plato and Mill works well for contextualising the role of 'the media' in society in political science.

Theories about culture

A 'cultural studies' reader is a good toolkit here and then you can move on to the work of Matt Hills, David Gauntlett and Henry Jenkins for a view on how the 'classic' theories of culture might work in the age of web 2.0.

Theories about change

This is hard to pin down because of the delay in between writing a book like this and the publication date, but if the book was printed tomorrow, we would be recommending Clay Shirky, Henry Jenkins and Mark Prensky.

Theories about literacy

James Gee and Cary Bazalgette have made helpful contributions to debates around 'new literacies' and for a theoretical discussion of 'media literacy', David Buckingham, Jackie Marsh and Alex Kendall are key agents.

Politically, all of this is deeply problematic. The last thing we want to do is reduce media education to a list of 'big names' or create a theoretical canon. And this is only a small sample of the field in any case. But it is probably unwise to embark on a professional life as a facilitator of media learning without knowing 'where we've been' and we do feel passionately that having an academic subject taught mainly by people who studied something else is at best strange and at worst damaging.

learning plan 03.05 Fast Track Media Degree

It's really important to emphasise that which of the above is of direct 'use' with students all depends on the topics you want to cover. So the above list is really a 'fast track' to graduate-level understanding rather than a set of teaching resources. Learning Plan 03.05 here offers a range of online content for each area.

Our central suggestion for all theory teaching is that it should be integrated into production and creative work at all times. Complex though it may seem at first, there are enormous benefits for both students and teachers if certain principles can be accommodated.

Reduce the content of the course to the bare minimum by combining units and projects. For example, students might be given the topic 'Media Representations of Britain' and study this for the whole of one or two years. The theoretical prism would be the ways in which the changing demographics of the UK are negotiated on screen. Within this they could produce a trailer for a new British film, study new British cinema (including films like *Fishtank* and *Somers Town* alongside more commercially prominent examples), television drama (take your pick), soap opera, sitcom (again, the range is vast but one key choice might be *Gavin and Stacey*) and reality/talent TV (looking at changing representations of categories from class, gender, sexuality, age, disability and ethnicity and in some cases, located within broader contexts of celebrity culture, globalisation and capitalism) and conduct some research into British directors' use of digital video for low budget production and the impact of downloading on the UK film industry. These areas would, on any kind of course, cross unit boundaries in order to develop a deeper theoretical understanding of these areas. The textual analysis at the heart of this topic is best managed through application in creative tasks. Students would be creating ideas and small chunks of their own soap opera and 'talent show' or sitcom sequences (for theoretical ends) alongside the production of their trailer.

If you work at an institution which offers vocational courses as well as 'academic' ones, then timetable students together to remove these boundaries. Avoid creating territorial distinctions by having different rooms and resources for these learners. Get your A-Level students working collaboratively on aspects of production with the Diploma group, for example. They could analyse the video work of their fellow students using semiotics. And if the A-Level students are studying 'Media Regulation', why not give them a research project on OFCOM which they can present to the vocational group to inform their production research for their next project?

Your aim through these kinds of strategies is to erode all boundaries. The worst examples are the use of words *theory* and *production* to describe lessons. If the unit on 'Media Industries' seems dry compared to 'Web Design', then the teacher needs to work twice as hard to make it dynamic, creative and active. If possible, creative timetabling can mobilise a culture shift, by avoiding housing a theory lesson on Friday afternoon. A 'Media Industries' workshop, perhaps 'rebranded' as 'Media Employment' – with visiting speakers, a short placement, internet research and video conferencing or Skype interactions – can 'transmit' the same content for the same assessment ends, but the journey is a far more exciting one. Impression management of the curriculum itself is what is at stake. Your ultimate goal is to create a course where all lessons are practical and there is a 'buzz' of collaborative energy, indeed where the notion of the 'lesson' in its traditional sense is obscured.

So what does a great media theory lesson look like? Here is an example that might not seem very 'theoretical'.

In this case, students need to be introduced to the idea of gender representation, which is going to be a constant theme of the course. We need a way of capturing their imaginations for this area of study and it is probably unwise to start with Stuart Hall or Laura Mulvey (important though they are). So we start with some music. Instead of a 'theory first' approach, we go for a 'text first' approach. We will be better equipped if we do it this way around to get stuck into notions of ideology and feminist approaches later in the scheme of work as we will have 'user friendly' examples to recall.

learning plan 03.06 Geezers and Birds

Let's take another example of media theory and consider a range of practical methods for making learning inclusive. Most Media courses include a practical element and a heavy emphasis on textual analysis but in their organisation there is often a separation of technical theory (essentially instructions for using equipment) and analysis of existing texts. We might better facilitate learning about the construction of meaning if we remove that distinction (and any subsequent physical boundaries as mentioned previously). In this way we could create a lesson on realism which is both practical and theoretical, both instrumental ('how to') and reflective ('with what assumptions').

Students might (depending on the content of the course) consider this matrix of subject matter through the prism of understanding documentary as a genre or textual form. To focus in on a contemporary format within the broader category is more realistic. In the learning plan that we link to here (03.07), we work with the version of reality documentary successfully formatted by Love Productions (*The Baby Borrowers, Rich, Famous and Homeless, Kidnapped by the Kids* and *Tower Block House of Commons*).

learning plan 03.07 Collaborative Theory/Practice

Looking at the activities in the learning plan on documentary from a 'quality' perspective, we would find a highly active, participative strategy for learning in which tasks are differentiated. The discussion on the purpose of documentary will throw up questions of diversity, and by using time constraints and clear structures for summary and selection, you can signpost key skills in Communication, Working With Others and Problem Solving. And technology is being used in the lesson in a way which genuinely aids learning (providing sufficient guidance is given for effective searching and selecting within the time allowed – this kind of attention to detail is vital). More importantly in terms of media pedagogy, though, we have avoided demarcating this as either a theory or a practical lesson and we have managed to link textual analysis, some of the received conventional 'body of knowledge' and technical production.

But, out of date though this might sound, there is nothing wrong with a good old-fashioned lecture every now and again. Students intending to apply for higher education will need to engage with a sustained argument, illustrated with quotations and examples, and providing a calm but stimulating environment is created, there is no reason why students on any type of Media course should not experience a lecture mode of delivery on occasion. This might even be a joint lecture where several groups are put together – after all, this is what you get for your money when you take them to revision conferences and the like. Indeed, one might argue that if we NEVER teach students in this way, then we disadvantage them and even patronise them by assuming their attention spans or intellectual capabilities are insufficient for such an undertaking.

So if we accept that one lecture is reasonable on any scheme of work, and might even be a stimulating adjunct to our more participative norms, then how should we approach this? Certainly not by transmitting the published ideas of an established writer (for example, Marx on ideology or Mulvey on the male gaze). Rather, we should put together an entertaining argument which draws together ideas about audience, institution and media theory. We should always use visual stimulus, integrated to avoid messing about with remote controls to alter the source – Prezi is our current favourite for this – but we shouldn't simply read from PowerPoint or provide handouts with all the information on and then simply churn through it. The balance is right when this presentation method is used for key headings rather than all the content.

Here is an example. During the study of British television and film, leading to an analysis of how changing notions of 'Britishness' are renegotiated on screen to provide a voice for asylum seekers, working-class white people and 'settled' ethic minority groups, for which *Fishtank, Bend it Like Beckham, In This World, Shameless* and *Gavin and Stacey* will be our key texts, we are to offer a lecture on the conventions of British Social Realism with particular attention to films depicting the North of England (as opposed to 'Swinging London' in the 1960s), often referred to as 'Kitchen Sink Drama'.

 learning plan 03.08 Lecture

The material above lends itself to a lecture style, in the sense that you are presenting a view on British film and television and illustrating it with examples. Good practice is maintained because the 'official' theory comes in after the exploration of less alienating themes (so we are considering the theory through the lens of the clips rather than the other way around). The discussion or testing of Higson's hypothesis will be housed in a seminar context, of course, as would be more 'kinaesthetic' material such as matching British films to the BFI's categories in order to explore the increasing difficulty of actually defining a British film. This would be best done through a sorting exercise in groups where information about films (from, say, *Sight and Sound* or the *Internet Movie Database*) can be matched to the categories as a result of discussion. This material clearly could not be the subject of a lecture.

At the opposite end of the spectrum is a strategy such as role play for debate. The teacher can become completely redundant apart from planning if this works. However there is some essential groundwork to be undertaken for this to be successful. Role play is not a 'given' in terms of skills and confidence so some rehearsal and exemplar material helps. Also you need to be towards the end of a topic because essentially you are in the realm of discourse analysis with such an activity – in order for students to be 'in character' they need a developed understanding of the points of view they will need to 'act out'.

 learning plan 03.09 Role Play for Debate

The approach to censorship in the role play learning plan directly addresses the study of discourse. During the study of such a contested area, students should be introduced (after a letter has been sent home informing parents) to a range of cultural products which have been censored, alongside others that were not but were controversial for that reason. It is important to address the political dimensions of such arguments – for example, films which were seen as shocking when their novel versions were not, films which are of concern not because of the violence itself but because of the moral framework (or lack of) surrounding it and films in which language and/or politics are more important than images in their potential to 'shock'.

For more complex discussion, students need to engage with the distinctions made between the apparently more immersive experience of playing a videogame such as *Call of Duty: Modern Warfare* 3, compared to watching a war film like *The Hurt Locker*, and the far less specific remit of The Byron review and the broader concerns expressed in Sue Palmer's *Toxic Childhood* (see Learning Plan 01.01 'Toxic Childhood Wiki').

Whilst there tends to be an assumption that in Liberal Humanities, the path to enlightenment is to do with understanding competing arguments and then forming opinion, we think in the case of media theory it is paramount to devote most time to the 'understanding' bit but emphasise the socio-political underpinnings of arguments in order to deconstruct them. What we will find, then, is that we are not so much deconstructing texts but deconstructing the interplay of text, audience and society. In particular we are scrutinising the unequal distribution of forms of capital (who is the censor, who do they assume they are protecting, who is a subject and who is an object in these debates?)

However 'technical' a programme of study might appear on the surface (e.g. a unit on the film industry on a vocational course) we must not assume ever that such crucial lines of enquiry about who has a stake in deciding who can see what are not of interest to certain students. Theory tends to take on greater immediacy when it can be related to lived experience. For this reason we favour an approach which starts with texts and/or games (as we have seen with *Geezers and Birds*) and then builds received theory onto this preliminary engagement. Three more learning plans link together to introduce theory in such ways.

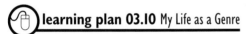 **learning plan 03.10** My Life as a Genre

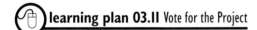 **learning plan 03.11** Vote for the Project

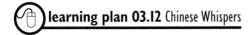 **learning plan 03.12** Chinese Whispers

Let's reassert that it is not in the gift of this book to provide content for lessons, although the PDFs in this second edition will lead you to some 'good stuff' online. Instead the intention is to suggest a 'spirit' and a range of strategies you might try, in order, of course, to develop your own ways of operating. Nor is it possible to cover all kinds of theory for all kinds of courses or to go far beneath the surface – hence it is easier to suggest ideas for lessons fairly early on in a scheme of work rather than later. At the end of this chapter, it is prudent to devote some space to the specialised kinds of theory that are negotiated on vocational courses. One such example is a unit on Web Authoring for an E-Media specification, for which students must work in HTML, explore a variety of tools and features, and go on to produce a 'media rich website'.

This is as seemingly removed from traditional Media theory or concepts as could be, and yet clearly a learner cannot demonstrate imaginative use of technology and its tools without a theoretical foundation. But the vocational learner on this kind of course has the same entitlement to reflective, conceptual study as the A-Level student analysing gender representation in science fiction, for example. Rather than suggesting the vocational student 'learns by doing' we are arguing that all students should work in this way. For this example, the teacher should facilitate analysis of HTML as a language and develop in students the ability to operate metalinguistically – that is, to talk about the language as well as work in it. They will also work towards theoretical consensus on what constitutes a media-rich website, and if they are to demonstrate understanding of vocational practice this inevitably takes them into discussion of professional discourse in terms of hierarchy, team work and different understandings of management, so essentially a range of political discussions will take place. Usually vocational specifications insist on an evaluation, and yet many teachers underplay this as a skill. Evaluative discourses need to be exposed and discussed, they are an institutional language game rather than a natural, common sense 'after the event' inevitability and students will operate much more effectively within this discourse if they understand it as such.

learning plan 03.13 Technical Peer Instruction

For a more developed approach to analysing websites as media texts, see Burn and Parker, who set up this kind of study around the following themes:

> We will begin by looking at the organisational function of the texts and what this organisation allows their users to do; but we will also consider how they present ideas, narratives and representations of their subject, as well as how they address their audience. We want to consider how the visual elements of the design, written language, and the nodes and links of hypertext combine to offer multiple-user pathways. How does these structures represent the content areas central to the sites; how do they construct relations between text and audience? (Burn and Parker, 2003: 29)

This is still relevant for this second edition, but you might want to consider it alongside Jenkins' *Convergence Culture* which takes a less textual approach to web content.

The learning plan idea on site management demonstrates a broader principle which this chapter has explored in some depth. In short, we should be looking to theorise the practical and energise the theoretical so that all Media students are 'learning by doing'. If we do this, then all our teaching is inclusive and we start to erode some of the divisive and unnecessary boundaries placed between different so-called 'types' of learners.

Most of the time we are working in spite of the school, the college, the classroom. What we mean by this is that we have realised that the institutional constraints of how school works are really unhelpful for dynamic, sustained learning. Riele (2009) sets out an agenda for a 'pedagogy of hope', founded on principles of positivity, possibility, community and critical reflection. We hope our ideas for creating active 'theory lessons' for media learners connect with these ideas in three ways – by building up a relationship with students that respects their media cultures and avoids imposing taste; by challenging boundaries and encouraging students to construct knowledge as 'apprentice theorists' and by fostering a comfort zone for 'can do' theory work.

References and further reading

Altman, R., 1982: *Genre: The Musical.* London: Routledge.

Barker, M. and Petley, J. (eds), 2001. *Ill Effects: The Media/Violence Debate.* London: Routledge.

Bourdieu, P. and Passeron, J., 1977. *Reproduction in Education, Society and Culture.* London: Sage.

Buckingham, D., 2003. *Media Education: Literacy, Learning and Contemporary Culture.* London: Polity.

Buckingham, D., 2007. *Beyond Technology: Children's Learning in the Age of Digital Culture.* London: Polity.

Bolas, T., 2009. *Screen Education: From Film Appreciation to Media Studies.* Bristol: Intellect.

Burn, A. and Parker, D., 2003. *Analysing Media Texts.* London: Continuum.

Creeber, G. (ed). 2001. *The Television Genre Book.* London: BFI.

Derrida, J. and Ronnell, A., 1980. 'The law of genre', *Critical Inquiry,* 7.1, On Narrative: 55–81.

Fearn, H., 2008. 'Grappling with the digital divide', *Times Higher Educational Supplement,* 14.8.08.

Hartley, J., 1999. *Uses of Television.* London: Routledge.

Higson, A., 1995. *Dissolving Views.* London: Cassell.

Hills, M., 2005. *How to Do Things with Cultural Theory.* London: Hodder.

Jenkins, H., 2006. *Convergence Culture: Where Old and New Media Collide.* New York: New York University Press.

JISC, 2009. *Effective Practice in a Digital Age. A Guide to Technology-Enhanced Learning and Teaching.* Bristol: JISC.

Kendall, A., 2008. 'Giving up reading: re-imagining reading with young adult readers', *Journal of Research and Practice in Adult Literacy,* 65, spring/summer: 14–22.

QCA, 2005.*Media Matters: A Review of Media Studies in Schools and Colleges.* London: QCA.

Riele, K., 2009. *Making Schools Different: Alternative Approaches to Educating Young People.* London: Sage.

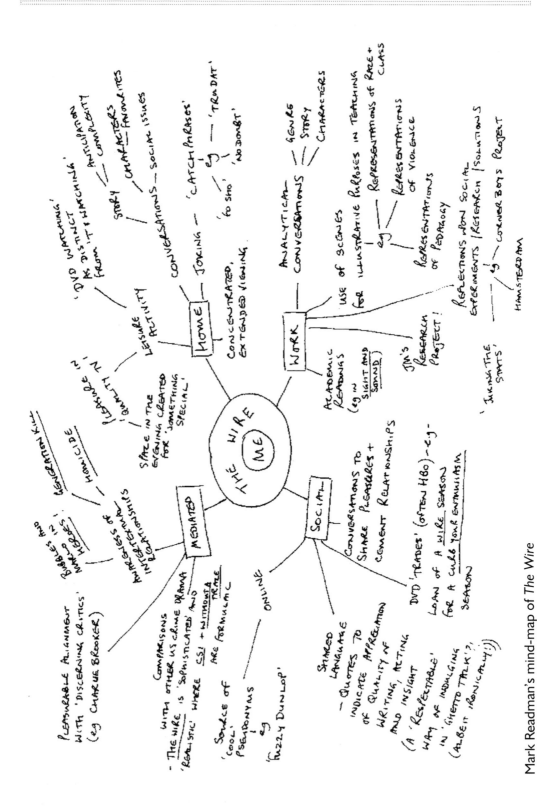

Mark Readman's mind-map of *The Wire*

4 Doing the Big Concepts

This chapter will offer a more detailed approach to working with the key concepts of Representation, Narrative, Genre and Audience with Media students on all courses. This is possible because, for better or worse (and elsewhere we have suggested moving away from this framework), more or less all Media Studies specifications demand the ability to work with this kind of 'conceptual committee'. This approach differs to some in sequence, as we want to argue that genre especially must be challenged as a concept in the classroom, existing as it does as (to some extent) an accident of the other concepts. Equally, discourse as the *practice* of representation is at the heart of this book's strategies, so we suggest that if conceptual learning is productive (and reflecting on this with students throughout is mandatory), then the question of how mediation operates should be the starting point, with questions of narrative and convention following from this foundation.

Audience is a concept which has been shaken to its foundations by notions of 'Media 2.0' and 'we media' so Media students no longer have the luxury of an essentialist position – the singular target audience. Whether you 'buy' the whole prosumer idea or not, the idea of the audience has undoubtedly fallen apart in some places (watching *The Wire* on a box set in your own time and at your own pace) and back together in others (the *X Factor* final and live election debates). It needs thinking about.

> Technological and social change has affected Media Studies at every level of the subject. It is not yet clear whether the existing models of analysing and creating media products are continually adapting to new developments or whether these changes have transformed the whole field of study. (QCA, 2005: 65)

At the time of writing every Media specification with 14–19-year-old school/college students as its 'core business' features a compulsion to be conversant in these concepts. This has largely been accepted and approved of. Indeed at the British Film Studies conference in 2008, David Gauntlett's intelligent (2008) dismantling of this framework (which we will call the Masterman approach (1985); Gauntlett prefers 'Media Studies 1.0') was met with anguish and some hostility. We should think of this conceptual agenda as one approach to be compared to other ways of thinking about Media, and certainly we should not assume either that texts are at the centre of study or that these can best be analysed through such concepts. In addition, creative work, through explanation of process and evaluation of outcome, is usually written about by students in conceptual terms. *Which genre did I choose and why? What conventions did I employ and how? Did I use a linear narrative? Who and what was I representing and how?*

A problem with this tradition might be the proliferation of a set of 'set responses' or 'right answers' about how texts in particular genres make meaning, which goes against the grain of the kind of media learning which acknowledges the negotiated, fluid, situated and 'languaged' nature of audience responses to texts. Our key suggestion is this: building a conceptual approach around the changing nature of audience and representation. Facilitating a reflexive approach to these areas (i.e. focusing on active reading of representation, reappropriation of meaning and identity and questioning assumptions about media representation) will enable students to gain the required knowledge of how these concepts work, but avoid passive and mundane acceptance of academic language. If students are going to engage with genre in their creative activities, then consideration of how their work plays with conventions maintains this spirit. Equally, work which seems to merely imitate is better understood as an application of conventions, as all new activity within a paradigm is ultimately dialectical and constitutes a shift (see Buckingham, 2003: 134). At the same time, if students are looking at texts from an analytical perspective, then the focus should always be on how audiences interpret representations in different ways, and how representations reflect claims to power and truth that may be more or less successful.

Before we crack on with each concept in depth, it is worth taking a look at this resource, simply to keep it in your mind as you read on. What is the difference between the material that follows, insulated by conceptual boundaries, and the discussions you find online here relating to the idea of 'mediated cultures' and 'digital ethnography'?

http://www.netvibes.com/wesch#Digital_Ethnography

There are very different kinds of Media teachers these days and where you connect will depend on whether you feel more comfortable with key concepts or 'convergence culture' or (preferably) a bit of both.

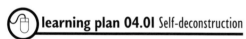 **learning plan 04.01** Self-deconstruction

Representation

"*The notion of 'representation' is one of the founding principles of media education. The media do not offer us a transparent 'window' on the world, but a mediated version of the world. They don't just present reality, they re-present it. (Buckingham, 2003: 57)*"

When Media students analyse ways in which texts and their readers make sense of representations, they are usually thinking about the world of the text in relation to competing notions of what the world is 'really like'. This is evaluative, and it is deeply problematic if it relies on an assumption that we can know the world outside of our own perception, of course. The ideology of a text can be considered, in the sense that it is possible to say, usually, that the text relies on some assumptions and it will work only if its readers share some of these. More importantly, most versions of this conceptual study get to the point (usually fairly late on in proceedings) where students consider the possibility of oppositional or negotiated responses to texts. Who might be excluded? Might there be other ways of reading this? Might it be more complex than we first thought? Our central suggestion is that you start with this discussion.

It might be helpful to consider the representation of Media Studies itself. Two examples are particularly stark evidence that we remain something of a 'trendy travesty' (Barker in Barker and Petley, 2001). First, one of the authors of this book, following the 'defend your discipline!' interview for the *Today* Programme, was criticised in a *Telegraph* column for, well, everything really – as the reproduction in the colour plates demonstrates.

🖱 learning plan 04.02 The Trendy Travesty

Most specifications require students to study representation in two ways. The most obvious and common is for them to use a range of concepts when studying any single text, and in this context *how* the text represents people and things would be one consideration amongst a range of others (and as such it might be given fairly brief attention). The other common approach is for particular genres or time periods to be given attention for their significance in representational terms. For example, students might analyse situation comedy for its comedic representation of common experience, TV drama for its portrayal of gender and social class, videogames for the ways in which military conflict or urban crime is depicted (and *experienced,* in this example), gangster films for their take on the 'American Dream' or magazines for their presentation of gender. In this second context, a more 'macro' approach is taken and students make intertextual and historical connections, with the help of some received theory/research from writers who have become expert in a particular genre or time period.

In both approaches, it is impossible to separate representation from questions of narrative, genre (perhaps) and audience, so again exam questions or coursework requirements tend to be broad in scope. As a result it is possible for students (and teachers) to place more or less emphasis on representation. A student writing about documentary might spend more time on the history of the genre, its development in conventions from Grierson to *Tower Block House of Commons* and its function institutionally, and then place this in a debate around 'quality', access and democracy. Another student might focus much more on the claim to realism made by documentary and, through scrutiny of editing and televisual language in general, question the nature of the reality and its representation in particular cases. A student working on British Cinema might produce promotional materials for their own UK film, and either 'major' on co-funding and commerce (how successful might this film be for an international audience) or on how their text represents British people in the contemporary historical context (the 'history of the present').

To illustrate a range of examples for working with media representation we are going to consider *Shameless* for its representations of class, gender and family in comparison with British soap opera (which we will return to when we focus on genre) and a postmodern reworking by Kid British of *Our House* by Madness. Then we will turn to *Skins* and *Dubplate Drama* representing youth and an audience study of *The Wire* that deals with a contemporary way of looking at encoding and decoding. Alongside this we will describe a study of *Grand Theft Auto 4* in terms of the effect that participation in narrative has on representation.

Shameless, described on the *South Bank Show* by its creator as '*Little House on the Prairie on acid*' and broadcast by Channel 4, is a comedy drama featuring a family living on a fictional estate in Manchester. Frank Gallagher, an unemployable alcoholic, and his many offspring survive through hard work and some criminal activity. Over the duration of the programme and through its developing series, the show has arguably become more parodic of itself and this makes the representational operations more complicated and self-referential. So students need to get to grips with the complex range of representational devices at work in this text. The fact that whether the families depicted and their environments are represented in any one stable way is difficult to say is precisely the reason for choosing this text to work with.

> You know Frank's totally derelict. The fact that you don't want to kill him is a rally serious piece of processing on the audience's part. (Abbott, speaking on *The South Bank Show*, ITV, 2005)

Representation is best understood as a flow of energy arising from a text's status as a site of conflict. Understood in this way, media texts construct narratives through which competing discourses (ways of understanding 'truth') battle for supremacy. A classic realist text sets up one discourse as dominant (usually through the actions of the main character with whom we empathise), whereas more complex texts offer a variety of positions to take (in which case the 'sayable' is less delimited, in Foucault's terms). Students might look at a range of texts with this in mind, not to work out how and what each one represents, but to compare the degree of motivation at work in representation. Representations of law and order, family, religion and sexuality are equally polysemic in *Shameless*. In any one episode, there is no fixed point of moral or social judgement for the audience to take. For this reason, it is really productive to start with a text as complex as this one and then look at more 'black and white' alternatives later – if such exist.

⌨ learning plan 04.03 Group Presentations

Connecting micro analysis to macro critique is always the challenge for Media students thinking about representation. Here is how. In one episode, screened by Channel 4 on 27 April 2010, the title sequence offers its 'all life is here' motif culminating in Frank's '*Make Poverty History, Cheaper Drugs Now*' crescendo. The self-contained narrative in this episode concerns the failed attempt by the McGuires to get divorced on the grounds that they were married by a fake priest in the first place. The micro focus here could productively relate to the use of music (non-diegetic) and how, in its slapstick and heavy-handed, self-parodic agenda-setting way, this distances the programme from more straightforwardly serious realist drama. Almost every scene features non-diegetic music and these are arranged into narrative thread soundtracks – one for each storyline. This convention is shared with Channel 4's *Skins* but is very distinct from soap opera or a more traditional (but still contemporary) approach to depicting the lives of the 'socially disadvantaged' in social realist ways, such as *The Street* or even *The Wire*. The macro extension, then, takes us to an analysis of shades of realism. *Shameless* is realist (but heteroglot) – it has a believable and consistent textual logic, it fulfils its verisimilitude over time without disruption. But it sets up the Chatsworth estate as 'real' in the sense that it is based on the life experience of its first writer at the same time as viewing it through a highly referential (even postmodern) and at times surreal-fantastic lens. Why don't *Shameless* and *Coronation Street* look and sound the same? And how is *Shameless* able, for example, to represent homosexuality in far less worthy and earnest ways than soap opera can manage, precisely because of its playful aesthetic and mode of address?

As the McGuires attempt to legitimate their marriage in order to divorce and the local priest declines, a rich dialogue – '*Throwing your weight around the population of Chatsworth doesn't mean you can throw it about around God*' – and the confrontation that ensues, resonate comedically (and irreverently) with the much revisited theme in gangster films of violent men attempting to reconcile their actions with their Catholic faith – think *Bad Lieutenant*. And so it is that representation so often works only in a chain of signification. For students to deal with how *Shameless* represents the inhabitants of council estates in northern cities, they must go beyond simplistic ideas about the relationship between reality and the text and insert the reality of other texts into the equation.

learning plan 04.04 Micro to Macro

For similar ends, we have used an extract from *South Park* in which white America is lampooned for its racial paranoia, and then shown a clip from *Training Day* in which a white rookie cop is taken to a 'ghetto' by his worldly black partner. In the learning plan on 'The white gaze', this is updated to make use of Eastwood's *Gran Torrino*. Either will work, as will any number of your own examples – Hollywood is hardly lacking films which look at ethnic groups as 'other'. The *mise en scene* (which spells out danger, drug deals, guns and prostitution) is constructed through the eyes of the white character (this is the 'white gaze', to extend Mulvey's theory). This scene is not unusual – we get the view of black neighbourhoods we are used to, from mainstream Hollywood cinema, to the extent that we do not question it on first viewing. But screened in the context of the *South Park* clip, it becomes an example of the ridiculous phobic landscape of white middle-class America. This intertextual strategy serves to show students that texts exist in relation to other texts more significantly than in relation to any fixed sense of reality. The ghetto we see in *Training Day* matches our expectation of such a place in the 'real world' and yet this (mis)recognition is based on other films and television sequences rather than lived experience of such urban locations. Students need to acknowledge these textual operations before proceeding to analyse such concepts as realism.

learning plan 04.05 The White Gaze

There is never any shortage of resources for exploring representations of the British family and the 'social document thesis' is a good tool for analysing these. If we treat media products as social documents that accurately depict the British family, what view do we get from texts that deal with the same social group in different time periods? For example, comparing the video for *Our House* (Madness) – itself a parodic view of the history of the working-class British family – with the postmodern reworking of the same song by Kid British (*Our House is Dadless*) is a very rich exercise. But it isn't just about the internal properties of the texts – the Madness song and video simply representing the family in one way and Kid British sharing some of those dynamics and adding new ones (absent father, multicultural Britain, technology). Fundamentally, the analysis turns on questions of how we attribute meaning to these cultural products – what we do with them, in relation to our own ideas about identity, family and culture. This makes it more interesting, but harder to teach, of course.

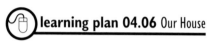 **learning plan 04.06** Our House

What we do with media

One question that media teachers often ask concerns the more difficult work of helping students analyse the meanings that people attribute to media, as opposed to the internal properties of texts (the more 'Englishey' stuff). For example, alongside the excellent resources for studying *Skins* provided by the English and Media Centre's *Doing TV Drama*, we recommend students consider the extra-diegetic elements of the programme, such as a case study on the infamous '*Skins* party'. Consider the 'moral panic' and hostility to *Skins* that arose when a teenager from Northern England posted an open invite to a '*Skins* party' on Myspace, using the subtitle from an episode of the programme – 'Let's trash the average family-sized house disco party'. Two hundred people attended and caused over £20,000 worth of damage deliberately.

Skins has been very successful in engaging its target audience and either representing life as it is or life as the audience might like it to become. Derided by critics for its stereotypical characters and storylines, the programme (broadcast on E4 and made by the same production company responsible for *Shameless*) has been controversial for allegedly representing teenagers as more transgressive and 'out of control' than is realistic. Featuring a gay character, a character who cheats on his girlfriend and another who sleeps with a teacher and storylines involving a Muslim character experimenting with drugs, car theft, eating disorders, suicide and a heroin overdose, the central motif of the series is the recurrence of high-octane, drug-fuelled parties and it is this narrative element that has outraged older viewers (we might call this group the 'parent culture') and delighted teenage viewers in equal measure. Analysing the 'Skins party' in terms of representation, the question to ask (as of all media texts) is whether the programme is merely representing accurately, for better or worse, the world as it is (teenagers are like this and the programme is accurate) or whether it is constructing a version of teenage life which may lead to more drug taking and antisocial behaviour. In which case it becomes a question of how much responsibility you think programme makers have for the potential outcomes of the material they broadcast.

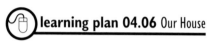 **learning plan 04.07** Skins

Our teaching about representation will be influenced greatly by the curriculum boundaries imposed by specifications. We might be helping students look at a particular set of ideas about media and identity (e.g. British Cinema), or broader categories (changes to media audiences and the idea that we can represent ourselves these days), or more overtly political concerns (how the news represents war, for example). Equally, the determinant might be theoretical reflection on students' own production – how did they set up representational devices in their work? But it won't be about producer intention. Unlike English.

> The idea of literature as a special category worthy of attention in itself, with its own special qualities and specific effects, and its very own modes of engagement is really a very dubious affair. Teachers of English have believed, in a necessary ideological move, that literature really does exist – in itself, somehow – and that it really does have intrinsic qualities that make it worthy of study in itself. They have maintained, one way or another, that literature is generally very good for you, if you're lucky enough – or sensitive enough – to appreciate it. If you're not able to appreciate it this is likely to be due to innate insensitivity or poor social conditioning, or maybe the general decline of culture into technological mindlessness and media intoxication. (Peim, 1993: 176)

Whether or not you are offended by Peim's observation, the fact is that Media Studies needs to start from a different conceit. We are not 'training' students to appreciate media. Equally we are not simply equipping them with critical reading skills – as though somehow they can become different kinds of readers of media to everyone else (a strange view that is commonly held by Media teachers – equally preposterous as the belief in the existence of literature, we would argue). Instead, we are helping students to theorise the relationship between media and the rest of life.

Returning to representation and the connections we might make, from soaps to British film to *Shameless* to Kid British to *Skins* and on to *Dubplate Drama*, the last of these offers us an alternative media domain in which to engage with the concept. Like machinima and game modding, *Dubplate Drama* can make us feel very old in the sense that most of us are unfamiliar with it but come to realise that is much more part of the lifeworld of our students than the 'mass media' material we have been working with.

learning plan 04.08 Dubplate Drama: Idiot's Guide For Teachers

Further angles for representational study include popularity of certain genres in relation to how and what they represent (reasons for enduring success); negative representation and social consequences (for example, objectification of women in music video, the tabloid press or 'lads' mags'), questions of realism, debates around truth (for example the selection and construction of news) and access (the absence of representation, for example of people with disability or the representation/absence of ethnic minorities).

What many of these versions tend to avoid is a scrutiny of some (in our view) outdated assumptions about mediation. There is still a prevalent model at work in media teaching which is not too far away from the 'classic' Shannon and Weaver (1949) sender–message–receiver conception of communication. More interesting media learning arises from placing questions about the *nature* of meaning at the heart of the work. So in the case of *Shameless,* how are viewers culturally situated in their responses? How does intertextual meaning make a difference? To what extent are traditional representations of working-class Northern communities played with in this text (we might look at *Saturday Night and Sunday Morning, Coronation Street, Boys from the Blackstuff, Brassed Off, Looking for Eric and Fish Tank* to consider representational changes over time as well as the *Our House is Dadless* activity). We should avoid attempting to 'stop' the chain of signification for too long, lest we might present media texts in an artificial state of isolation from one another.

Comparing a text like *Shameless* with a seemingly more straightforward soap opera such as *Coronation Street* is most fruitful when the more complex text is dealt with first. We want to avoid a reductive approach which ignores the range of possible readings of characters and situations in the narrative. And you have a choice (one that will be more or less pinned down by the requirements of the specification in question). Do you take students through the received body of work on, say, representation of the family in the British soap opera, and then apply this to particular episodes, storylines and extra-textual dimensions (such as tabloid press treatment of actor/character duality)? Or do you help students create something new, by looking at an area such as disability and considering the presence/absence of such representation in such a popular text? Taking the former approach, there is a body of theory available, including the work of Geraghty (1991) and Buckingham (1987). In addition, we have used extensively Linda Grant's (1996) argument that *Coronation Street* and other soaps (early *Brookside* in particular) act now as social documents of their times, inheriting and transforming the legacy of the 'Kitchen Sink' films of the 1950s and 1960s. Students might test this hypothesis (they should never just accept it) by watching films like *Saturday Night and Sunday Morning* and comparing the degrees of motivation in each case, or in Bakhtin's terms the extent to which each text is monoglot (one discourse comes to dominate) or heteroglot (there are a variety of possible responses available and there is no clear hierarchy of viewpoint at work).

Students can easily get into this kind of work, despite the fact that East European Formalism is considered 'high theory' because these are straightforward analytical questions. In *Saturday Night and Sunday Morning* Arthur Seaton's voice is in our ears throughout. The film is anchored by his philosophy. *Never let the bastards grind you down* (on post-war social class and the nature of his exploitation). *Take a tip from the fishes, they never bite until the bait's good enough. Mind you, they all get caught in the end* (on marriage). Arthur's celebration of hedonism, his rejection of consumer culture (most notably his annoyance at his father's television viewing and his sceptical response to new houses) and most importantly his understanding of his alienation in the factory (Albert Finney was filmed at the exact lathe Alan Sillitoe had worked at before he wrote the novel, for those for whom notions of authenticity are significant) provide a preferred reading, or at least the text is hierarchically organised so that we understand other characters' perspectives (most importantly the women that Arthur sleeps with) only in relation to his view of the world. An episode of *Eastenders* cannot be organised in the same way, as its configuration of space and time is more varied. As a result the viewer (who is often in a social context rather than alone) can form alliances and prejudices in a much more idiosyncratic way.

Students might also throw into equation the suggestion that soap opera has historically been understood as a form of melodrama with a female orientation. Does a film
like *Saturday Night* offer a more *logocentric* sense of meaning founded on a notion of a
present, identifiable take on the world, compared to the more fluid dynamics of the
soap opera? Note that here we are not considering how the text represents people, but
how the text represents. We are reflecting on the concept and its dynamics, as opposed
to applying theory as though it were a science. The best way, as always, to take this
further is for students to design (and preferably film/edit and screen) a soap opera
sequence that will offer a plurality of audience responses.

To return to the more rudimentary questions of soap opera representation, here are
some 'ways in' to this kind of study:

- How is the representation (of a particular group) mediated through the specific
televisual language of this kind of text?

- To what extent does the verisimilitude achieved by the illusion of ongoing real-time
seal a sense of greater proximity to real life than in other texts (for example the situation comedy with its condensed and self-contained 30 minutes)?

- In what ways are soap operas topical and sometimes controversial in their treat-
ments of current affairs/social issues? Related to this, what is the responsibility of a
soap opera producer? Is it to reflect society 'as it is' or 'as it should be'?

- What is the balance of realism and drama in particular soaps? This balance is very
important to the remit of a soap opera – it must cling to a very specific verisimilitude (see the opening credits of *Coronation Street*) which may be outdated, or at least
nostalgic and romantic, at the same time as competing for ratings with other soaps
through the development of exciting, ongoing and climaxing storylines. Students
might trace changes in a particular soap at times of 'crisis' in ratings terms to see
how this operates.

- A case study on the representation of family life will be productive. On 17 October 2002, the *Daily Mail* published 'Scarred by Soaps' (by Steve Doughty, Social
Affairs Correspondent), in response to the National Family and Parenting Institute's research. The article explained that the findings of this research were that
children are encouraged by soaps to believe that family breakdown is the norm
and that soaps fail to promote moral values. On the same day, John Carvel (Social
Affairs Editor) summarised the same research in the *Guardian*, but concentrated
mostly on the research's evidence that parents regularly discuss soap opera storylines with their children. If this is the case, then the texts act as a resource for a
(perhaps) healthy level of discussion about the family unit which may be more
difficult to mobilise in isolation from this media catalyst. Students might (to keep
things active) research this debate through their own work with viewers, and then
experiment with the creation of storylines which might offer a range of more or less
positive (or at least different) representations of the modern family.

- Analysis of the intertextual and/or extratextual meanings circulating around soaps
is essential if students are to understand the specific nature of representation at
work in these programmes. Tabloid newspapers (since Murdoch's intervention)

have routinely confused actor/character and drama/reality at the time of popular storylines. These articles might be analysed in terms of second-hand representation. In addition, soap trailers are becoming increasingly sophisticated (especially in genre study terms, all the British soaps have played with Film Noir and thriller conventions in their promotional work) and there are a range of magazines offering additional meanings for the audience.

- In terms of popularity, students might consider whether the reason for the longevity of the pleasure offered by these texts is to do with representation or not. In other words are there forms vicarious pleasure offered by the (mis)recognition of the everyday in these programmes, or are they 'just' good drama. And ultimately the *social document versus junk TV* debate hinges on theories of popular culture. Is the representation of the domestic sphere the reason for middle-class distaste and closet viewing ('I don't set out to watch it, but it is always on in our house'), and equally for devotion from the 'masses' or is the audience acting in a more discerning, 'pick and mix' way with these texts these days?

Returning to media literacy and creativity as the two-pronged approach suggested throughout this book, we should say that this kind of work should never be divorced from the construction and deconstruction of specific textual moments. Students cannot sensibly approach the kinds of debates and research approaches above without relating notions of realism and representation back to choices made about camera, sound, mise en scene and performance. Technical and symbolic codes are always at work in representational meanings. A simple substitution exercise will highlight important semiotic principles. What happens if one character wears different clothes? What if the design of the set was changed so that one family's house got a designer makeover? These interesting, entertaining and very 'low level' questions lead to rich discussion about stereotyping and myth. It is not a million miles from here to Roland Barthes.

learning plan 04.09 Anonymous Statement Banking

The focus on disability is an example of media education at its most important. At a BFI Media Teacher's Conference, Andrea Stanton reported to delegates on the 'Invisible Children' conference that year, with the following statement:

> There was general agreement that to continue to portray disabled people as invisible or one-dimensional re-inforces the discrimination and isolation disabled people experience in all aspects of life. This can include becoming targets for bullying and physical attack. It was felt that children are particularly affected by the images to which they have access. Unfortunately most children and young people rarely meet disabled children in their schools and form their views of them mainly through the media. The inclusion of disabled people in producing and creating images and portrayal of disabled people as 'real people' is crucial.

A production task in which students are charged with collaborating with disabled people (if they are not themselves disabled) can bring to life these issues and lead to some worthwhile and transforming experiences. The focus should be on the production of narratives in which characters are disabled but this is *not* what the story is about. It is not only the relative absence of minorities from media representations which students need to consider, but also the focus, when they are represented, of their 'status' in narratives. Put another way (and using a different example), imagine a world in which Bruce Willis' character in *Die Hard* was gay, and the audience got to know this because his male partner was in danger, but this was of no consequence to the story otherwise. That would *really* be equality.

Working with videogames in the classroom forces us to address once again the question of whether the traditional conceptual approach still holds water in the wake of digital technology, or whether we need to adapt our modes of thinking about such concepts as representation to the 'hyper-reality' of our contemporary condition.

Toland (2004) sought to 'apply' existing ideas about representation in the text; by suggesting that games position and situate us to accept, in many cases, old-fashioned and simplistic representations of gender and ethnicity. For example, in *Grand Theft Auto*, Chinese characters tend to be gangsters. Brey et al (1998) developed a different, more 'semiotic' way of reading games to consider oppositions and relationships between elements and characters that add up to a coherent system of meaning. Students adopting this method will ask who has the most agency (ability to influence), who is absent from the game (e.g. the disabled), who is active and passive in certain situations, which characters have voice and what roles are allocated to which characters. Toland shows us that games have two levels when understood through this semiotic theory – on the one hand it's 'just a game' but on the other it reinforces a range of meanings from outside of the play experience:

> At one level the game is recreational and escapist, at another, its depiction of winners and losers sends out a broader social signal – 'win' and 'lose' carry connotations or 'right' and 'wrong'. (Toland, 2004: 18)

 learning plan 04.10 Play and Represent

One way that games might be connected (and intermedial) to books and films is the prominence of threat and the construction of 'the other'. Some games feed on the established themes of science fiction, in many cases being 'spin offs' of films. Others create their own gameworlds in which civilisation is threatened by an enemy. Lots of game design software available to Media students that you may have worked with takes this construction of heroes and villains as a starting point. Burn and Durran (2007) talk about 'game literacy' and suggest using the theories of Propp and Todorov to link games to folk tales, books, plays, films, TV drama and a whole range of other forms. Being sufficiently literate to play, then, rests on the understanding of character types.

This is true and useful as long as we are clear that there are more games that don't fit this model than those that do. As long as we are limiting our analysis to more 'literary' games with fictional characters, then applying Propp will help us to work at this intermedial level well. But if we are studying *FIFA 10* or *SingStar* it won't get us anywhere.

This is why it is so important to set out the terms of your analysis when dealing with games – what types of games are we dealing with, exactly?

But we are not for a moment suggesting that playing a football game does not involve an understanding of representation – just that the way it is mediated is fundamentally different. The *mise en scene* is important so that the player feels like they are really operating a team in a tournament. When selecting teams, stadia, tactics, these options rely on a verisimilitude constructed through resemblance to 'real life' experience (or mediated exposure, actually).

On screen avatars may be pre-designed and chosen or created by the player. There will be ideological features in this – the reinforcing of visual codes about physical shape, possible branding and ethnic representations will be there to analyse. For games like *SingStar* there is gender representation to consider. Clearly this kind of game has played an important role in bringing more females to the games market. But there are issues here about the polarised nature of games marketing. The games industry is less progressive than the people it tries to reach who enact 'gender trouble' when making unexpected decisions about how to 'be' in the gameworld.

> Over the last decade, as it has attempted to expand its market and sell more games to more people, the videogames industry has become increasingly interested in women gamers. This may have less to do with righting the apparent wrongs of previous eras and more to do with economic opportunity but, nonetheless a number of strategies have emerged….(But) critics point to the potentially ghettoising nature of 'games for girls'. In a retail environment, the (usually small) 'games for girls' section might be seen to serve as a indication that everything else is 'not for girls'. (Newman and Oram, 2006: 72)

However, our research has provided empirical evidence of a more 'performative' gaming experience than either industry strategies or academic assumptions would expect.

Just Gaming

Grand Theft Auto 4 was, for a while, the biggest media event of all time. If that is a surprise it just goes to show how Media Studies has at best marginalised and at worst ignored videogames, preferring to construct the curriculum around less 'slippery' mass media products, or at least ones that the majority of professional adults understand. Looking at *GTA4* through the lens of representation is very straightforward and students will easily find lots of things to say about gender, morality, violence, crime and urban decay. They will certainly identify a 'male gaze' and a capitalist discourse. But it gets more complicated if we actually spend time, as the Just Gaming research project did, talking to gamers about their situated practice. This ethnographic dimension is completely absent from most Media Studies learning, but for the study of how games come to 'mean', it is essential. This research intervention involved a group of 16–17-year-old male players of *GTA4* blogging their play experiences and being interviewed afterwards:

> Bloggers evidently took pleasure in taking centre stage in these baroque performances and some further enjoyed the opportunity to re-tell their stories; sorting, selecting, editing and

glossing their experiences for maximum reader impact. For these participants it seems that gaming offers an opportunity for performance and achievement but at the same time some reflection, with 'knowingness' as important to the performance as the events in the game. (Kendall and McDougall, 2009)

What you get from this kind of research, that you don't from just looking at game sequences or promotional material for games – or from Alan Titchmarsh (if you don't know what we mean, count yourself lucky you missed that one) – is a sense of how the 'text' comes into being in a multitude of different ways each time a player makes it happen. Equally, we find that the gaming experience is a performance. This resonates greatly with Judith Butler's idea of 'Gender Trouble' – we perform our genders in relation to all kinds of everyday experiences and in the ways we attribute meaning to culture – including media. This is why really interesting Media Studies teaching needs to be more about what people *do* with media and how representation works in this convergence of reception and exchange and (much) less about what media 'does' in isolation from the people who engage with it.

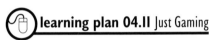 **learning plan 04.II** Just Gaming

Narrative

As we have already considered, interactive and social media are threatening the kinds of approaches to narrative that Masterman was describing in 1985. We are currently renegotiating our ways of analysing text–reader relations in the context of media experiences where the line between activity and passivity is exposed as fragile (it always was thus, but now we can see it):

> There are layers to narratives, to be sure, and they inevitably revolve around a mixture of the present and the future, between what's happening now and the tantalising question of where it's all headed. But narratives are built out of events, not tasks. They happen to you. In the gameworld, you're forced to define and execute the tasks; if your definitions get blurry or are poorly organised, you'll have trouble playing. You can still enjoy a book without explicitly concentrating on where the narrative will you take you two chapters out, but in gameworlds you need that long term planning as much as you need present tense focus. (Johnson, 2005 : 55)

The best way to introduce narrative as a concept is to ask each student to talk for one minute about what they did the night before. Inevitably you can deconstruct their linear sequencing, selection of material and, far more importantly, omission of minor detail. For comic effect, you might say 'What, so you never went to the toilet' to illustrate this point, providing your rapport is robust enough!

We want to suggest an approach to narrative theory that does not use Propp or Todorov, and in this sense this might be unique! Not because there is anything wrong with an approach which uses these old models to demonstrate the fixed, narrow and predictable nature of storytelling in the West, but because we think it presents a model of narrative flow as fixed and 'applicable' and we don't agree that we read texts in this way necessarily. Teachers and students, we think, tend to be comfortable with such theory because you can apply it and be right or wrong about it, but having marked exam scripts and production commentaries in their thousands we have started to wonder about the more interesting discussions of narrative that we might get to if so much time were not spent painstakingly describing disequilibrium in *Flight of the Concords* or working out who the donor is in *Avatar*.

Narrative is rarely (if ever) studied in its own right on Media courses at Levels 2 and 3, so narrative theory as such is less important than a working approach to texts and production work which can be used to articulate an understanding of space, time and active reading at work in the following of a story. Essentially in fiction texts we are talking about plot and story and in non-fiction order, selection and convention. In a film, a character getting on to a train, reading a paper and then departing from the carriage can be 'told' in 20 seconds without an outraged audience complaining at the preposterously rapid nature of the journey (especially in these times in this country!). Equally, we take for granted the relative 'importance' of the first news item and the 'natural' location of sports news at the end. In many ways, narrative can be understood in terms of cognition or as language acquisition. If we make sense of our lives through re-presenting them in narrative form, then are media narratives socially and psychologically beneficial? Next to me on my desk I have a handwritten list of the order of content and learning plans for this chapter. Further down the screen from where the cursor is now as I type I have inserted reminders to myself to write about these things. In the process, this is forgotten and I later on stumble back to this ordering and try to cut and paste the text into some kind of logical flow. Narrative informs all these processes (and their attendant anxieties in this case).

Once again, rather than starting with older narrative theories and ending up with postmodern approaches as a kind of quasi-extension activity, we suggest going straight for the more complex, less straightforward work with students. The 'element' of postmodernity which is of interest here is the ambiguities around space and time. Films by Michael Winterbottom and Wong Kar Wai or the Coens; games with online elements like *GTA4* or the game/film *Heavy Rain*; DJ Shadow's *Endtroducing*; *The Mighty Boosh* – it's a long list, goes on for ever if you let it. As Nick Lacey describes it:

> Postmodernism places the reader in a self-conscious position as the (re)creator of the texts she or he is experiencing. Similarly, the central concern of postmodern media texts is less to do with the traditional objective of 'knowing' (epistemology) and more to do with being (ontology). The reader is not simply using information to create the text, he or she is interacting with the text in 'reference spotting' almost as if it were a quiz. (Lacey, 2000: 99)

We think all media reading has always been so, and postmodernism is not so much an approach to textual production as a way of understanding reading in new ways. In other words, knowing has only ever been a subsidiary of being. In classroom practice, then, how can we translate this set of philosophical considerations into accessible media learning?

We can get straight into this by talking with students about how plot and story work. In simple terms, we can say that the reader constructs the signified story from the plot as signifier. Through the study of editing (which would be our preferred starting point for dealing with narrative on any course) students soon realise that what is not there is of more meaning than what is (as we found with representation, of course). Received theory in this area leads up to consideration of 'Classical Narrative', but as with Propp and Todorov, we are not sure of the function of such an approach we prefer to complicate, rather than simplify students' perceptions of how meaning gets made in media texts. The reductive nature of classic models (for instance, the Classical Narrative is normally equated with Hollywood's dominance of cinema since the advent of sound) can be that their 'application' presents a rather narrow view of how the reader operates. This then jars with other moments in media learning where we ask students to consider the reader as the key negotiator of meaning. Certainly, students need very early on to create sequences, most easily in video, and talk about what they left out and why, and (returning to Eisenstein and, if you like, D.W. Griffith) how the combinations of their images (the sum) makes more meaning than the parts in isolation. If we are looking at film then linking the micro features of a particular narrative (for example, shot/reverse shot, cross-cutting, examples of continuity, ellipsis, dialectical montage and referential moments which rely on inter or extra-textual understanding) with the macro narrative approach, is the obvious next step. The central concept is diegesis (the world of the text). What happens outside of diegesis is where the active reading can be located.

In Susan Levan's analysis of *Fargo*, she describes the directors' approach in this way:

> 'The term postmodern is often used to describe the work of the Coen Brothers … their telling of stories which comment on the nature of stories and of storytelling' (2000:18).

Levan's analysis points out a significant error made by critics who distance the Coens from other directors, as though other films are not 'stories about stories' when really the 'postmodern embrace' is just a new way of thinking about texts, rather than new kinds of texts. We should be working with our students to think about all media meaning as 'postmodern', if what we mean by this is an approach to texts which is most interested in the conditions of their possibility, of their textual nature, as opposed to what they 'mean'. As stated earlier, there is little in Media specifications to demand a consideration of narrative as a concept (this is different for genre, for instance) and for this reason, you will most likely be helping your students to apply narrative models. We think this is a problem, because all the key concepts are best understood through being challenged and made complex. That said, the key questions for students to consider about the construction of any text might be:

- Is it linear?
- What meaning is made outside the diegesis?
- What micro examples best illustrate the overall narrative approach?
- How does the narrative serve conflict between discourses?

To deal with the micro elements, we suggest two approaches. Firstly, the elements of media literacy should not be divorced from narrative at any time. So if students are working with technical codes in their own work and in their analyses, they can consider how these add up to a narrative style or approach overall (although equally they must articulate the complexity of texts which shift between approaches). Alongside this 'meat and drink', an example of 'handed down' theory we do advocate is Roland Barthes' narrative codes. A summary of these, in the form of questions for students, looks like this:

1. How does the text use images and meanings which tap into already-held oppositions and responses to symbols?
2. What enigmas are set up and what simple, understandable actions are evident (and what is the balance of action and enigma)?
3. What cultural meanings are created by mise en scene, performance and setting?
4. What inter/extra textual references help make meaning?

This is not a faithful paraphrasing of Barthes' original theory. Instead it reformulates his ideas in simple (we hope) questions that lead to longer, more negotiated answers than some other narrative models offer.

The work we do with students on narrative as a formal mechanism has strengths and weaknesses. It helps us (and students) feel secure that there are some 'right answers' about how stories are told, but it risks simplifying the very interesting and ever-fluid interpretive work that audiences do with stories. For Gauntlett (2008), semiotics works as a kind of pseudo-science which asserts the idea that the signified is a 'thing' we can know in isolation from situated reception and attribution. There is a dilemma at the heart of this: if we want to teach students about binary oppositions and their function in media meaning – we don't have the time for the ultra-sophisticated Derridean approaches we might want to take. For this reason, can we avoid reinforcing and perhaps over-playing the very polarising tendency in discourse we are really seeking to challenge? Well, we can if we adopt a questioning approach, especially to the students' own narrative creativity. Turning back to Barthes, we would encourage students to consider those questions about their production activities during production, rather than before they start (in which case you end up with a rather artificial attempt to 'evidence' conceptual understanding through making a film) or after they have finished (in which case you can end up with some less than heartfelt claims – *my video has lots of images and is postmodern*').

The degree of closure offered by a text is another measurement students will make, and clearly this is best done through comparative work. Going back to our example from the representation section, *Shameless* is partly closed each time as each episode has a central self-contained narrative alongside others which will continue over the duration of a series. This flow is perhaps disrupted (in terms of the rhythm of a TV serial) by the option to immediately watch the next episode on E4 instead of waiting a week for the next scheduled broadcast on Channel 4 and, of course, to stream episodes or download them completely in isolation from any schedule or linear order. The important point here is that we move very quickly into asking questions about narrative, as opposed to applying models to provide stable answers. The nucleus of these considerations, we think, is one question which is always useful: what assumptions are made by the narrative, and who is more and less included by such an approach? Pretty soon these discussions take us back to the consideration of media discourse. In other words, when students are thinking about cause and effect, space and time, plot and story, cultural codes, intertextual references, diegesis and conflict between characters, they are never far away from deconstructing their own understanding of the world through discourse. The strength of the 'postmodern' approach, for us, is that it emphasises and indeed celebrates the difficulty of this reflective work.

Chris Mottershead, in a conference workshop on Teaching Narrative, offered this rationale:

> Narratives do not just have a beginning and an end in the sense of starting and finishing. Rather they offer a movement from a situation to another situation. The initial situation presents some kind of problem or disturbance to the world of the fiction. The events which follow are about the solution of the problem which is when the narrative ends with a change from the initial situation overcoming whatever was wrong and offering some new future. It is in their choice of both problem and solution that narrative fictions offer accounts of 'how life is', of 'what makes a happy ending', of how 'a hero' should behave and provide explanations which seem to make sense. (Mottershead, 2001: 5)

Mottershead here brings to our attention a big point about narrative which takes us away (helpfully) from the 'nothing changes' adherence to Propp and Todorov. It is a commonly held view that whilst subject matter and ideology change to reflect socio-cultural preoccupation, the structure of narrative remains intact (in other words it is just the type of disequilibrium and the nature of the villains that change). However, consider a text like *Dr Who*, which relies on an 'old-fashioned' set of concerns (not to mention images and effects) to make sense at all. The notion that we have two separate elements to a story – its content and its structure – and that we can say that popular texts tend to update the former but it is only postmodern texts that play around with the latter is unsatisfactory.

Matt Hills (2010) takes this idea further. Hills is an academic who takes fandom very seriously and in his latest book on *Doctor Who* he assesses the importance of fandom as authorship and the relationship between fan-authorship, textual gamekeeping (a spin on Jenkins' 'textual poaching') and the brilliantly irreverent academic concept of 'fanwank' (one of those terms which describes its field in such a way that a definition can be understood without further elaboration):

> The creative input of fan 'gamekeepers' on Doctor Who has counter-intuitively deconstructed fanwank and resisted smoothing out prior textual discontinuities, against what might have been expected. But it has nonetheless sought to incite fans' speculation, disavowing production authority – even whilst enacting it – in favour of a romanticised view of Doctor Who and 'unfettered' audience imagination. Fan-producers have also incorporated other 'fan discourses' into the official text, such as celebratory affect. The fact that fans love the Doctor has been imported into the text. (Hills, 2010: 64)

Elsewhere (Bennett, Kendall and McDougall, 2011), we have contrasted the (necessarily, perhaps) straightforward approach taken by the OCR TV Drama exam, which in June 2009 required students to deconstruct the representation of gender in *Doctor*

Who, with the way that Hills bears witness to the elusive nature of representation in the drama, as above. The learning plan linked here will help students get their heads around Hills' ideas.

learning plan 04.12 Explain Matt Hills

Returning to less complex models, with their attendant pros and cons, such a template is offered by Medhurst (1994), who pinpoints seven narrative patterns that are in perennial use as story currency in Western culture. Let us not forget, by the way, that we will have many students who can tell us about narrative forms from other cultures. According to Medhurst, pleasure is repetition and in this sense we could get pretty easily to a version of Nietzsche's 'eternal recurrence' through a study of media narrative. That is, if we accept Medhurst's premise (or Nietzsche's for that matter!). The seven narrative types, prevalent from Greek mythology through the obligatory Shakespeare and into soaps and sitcoms, range from *Romeo and Juliet* (dramatic irony) to *The Spider and the Fly* (the web of deceit) and *Cinderella* (rags to riches). This is a really useful model if treated as a hypothesis for students to test out through research and analysis. If treated as a model which is absolute, then this is an example of critically bankrupt media learning.

It is important to spend some time on non-fiction narrative. Popular areas for study are news in broadcast, paper and online (selection and construction of news are activities of narrative construction no less than novel writing, we can propose to students), games (see other sections of this and other chapters for discussions of how narrative works in game design and playing, but the question of whether games are fiction or not is also open to student reflection), pop video, documentary and reality TV. We have also done some work with students on football coverage, considering the narrative construction of a live match with particular attention to ellipsis and the plot/story dynamic. What narrative energy is created by presenter and pundits, commentator, editor, interviewer and the characters (players, managers and more often than not, referees)? Most importantly, what inter- and extra-textual knowledge and referential understanding is required to be included by the text?

Again, to get into issues about narration, starting with more complex texts makes it more interesting when we return to seemingly more straightforward ones. On the one hand, a programme like *Secret Millionaire* in which the narration (outside the diegesis) is anchored to the pleasure of the 'dramatic irony' of knowing the secret before the agents in the text find out, might seem complicated in terms of how the meaning is worked out when compared to a film like *Taxi Driver* which features main character narration. But we would argue that whilst the discourse might be more predictable (the millionaire is rich but has to pretend to be 'normal' to do the good work), *Taxi Driver* situates us uncomfortably. The film's approach puts us in Travis' mind and we only get to see others through his eyes. It is very hard, therefore, to distance ourselves from, ultimately, a psychotic killer. So Scorsese uses a highly conventional storytelling approach for an unusual and challenging representational effect. *Secret Millionaire* (or *Rogue Traders*) is more structurally complex (in terms of time and space and the 'undercover' dynamics) but much more simple in narrative terms if we are interested in the rich/poor, problem/solution binary, compared to *Taxi Driver*'s more complex representation of good and evil. This alerts us to the danger of assuming that complex structure means more complex interpretation. Another example is *Seven*, a really useful film for discussing structure and representation, despite it being outside of the contemporary focus we tend to prefer. It is our view that part of the narrative effect of this film is to make the only satisfactory outcome (for the viewer) the completion of the final murder and the subsequent tragedy for the hero of the film. This is the effect of the 'will to linearity' that we get from exposure to the conventional narrative format. In order for the film's slick, clever narrative to ultimately serve us with the pleasure it offers, our morality must be tested, subconsciously at least.

Narratives reside in daily lived experiences; we re-present our own lives as narratives. When we present the events of the day, we make sense of our day (and the notion of a day is itself a narrative construction) through what we leave out more than what we include. How we represent things will never be neutral, but more importantly, how the audience for our telling of 'how the day went' interprets the detail will be (for them) how the events were.

Genre

In this section we will begin with attention to the concept of genre, and ways of helping students test and challenge its value. This will be followed by case study examples looking at spectacular cinema, British soap opera, situation comedy, Bollywood and reality/talent TV. These examples are all moving images, but we hope the approach to genre will be adaptable to any other text-type, in any media.

learning plan 04.13 Collaborative Reading

As the learning plan for collaborative reading indicates, the most productive study of genre does not start with definitions of the contract between producer and audience (see Hartley, 1999), nor with a set of examples of classic genres and their more 'fluid' counterparts. Instead, we should begin by challenging the status ascribed to the concept. How did the notion of category evolve or shift into genre? Whose interests do generic ideas serve? The most useful writer for this is undoubtedly Altman (1999), who sets up a series of assumptions made around genre for critique. These include the notion that genres are defined by producers and easily recognisable by audiences, that texts 'belong' clearly to a particular genre in each case, that genres develop in predictable ways, that texts in a genre share key characteristics, that genres are ideological, that they are not specifically located in history and crucially that genre critics are distanced from the practice of genre, or its workings. This last point is vital as the arrogance of theory is never more visible than when it claims detachment from its objects (or as Foucault has it, power is that which is not manifested as such). Students need to consider the concept of genre from the vantage point of their own relationship with theory and practice, not from the illusory premise of merely 'looking on'.

Genres have traditionally been treated as an 'other' to art texts (Stafford, 2002). The range of perspectives at work when dealing with texts in this way might be student as producer, as consumer/fan, as critic and as analyst. The interplay between these is an interesting area for discussion. Students can get into genre from a critical perspective by drawing up an arbitrary list of categorising features of radio programmes. This might include radio programmes presented by people with long hair, programmes which are listened to more in the car than in the home and radio programmes which last longer than 40 minutes (they can come up with more interesting examples). The function of this is to start to ask questions about the 'order of things' in categorical terms. Might ways in which we label and divide objects, texts and people be constructed so as to serve particular interests rather than in logical, natural patterns? The answer is, of course, a matter of opinion. The important thing, if media learning is to be 'empowering', is not to forget to ask the critical question, which for Altman is whether we read genre as noun or adjective. Mark Reid's approach to teaching genre (2001) takes this further (or at least grounds it in the work of 'doing genre' more clearly). He offers tomato puree as an example, suggesting we ask students a philosophical question: what would happen to this item if it were shelved in another part of the shop? Would the 'thing itself' be any different?

> How something is categorised is determined by who does it, for whom, where, and when. The same is true for films. (Reid, 2001: 1)

And indeed for all media texts (or products). So the more interesting, and ultimately useful approach for us to take with students when considering genre is not 'How does genre work?' but 'Why does genre happen?' In terms of literacy, language teachers have advocated an approach which equips students with the ability to operate within the idioms of dominant linguistic genres (now discussed as 'functional literacy') and the most progressive work is that which does so at the same time as analysing how these dominant modes of communication have become so (and indeed in whose interests). Yet some Media teaching, despite the subject's claims to being a radical cousin of English, is more conservative in its simplistic and unquestioning transmission of received histories about dominant genre practices. Buckingham (2003) points out an irony when observing that the more familiar the students already are with a genre (such as soap opera) the more likely they are to demonstrate critical reflection whilst working with the conventions, whereas introducing students to new generic forms is less likely to yield criticality as more time is spent on familiarising themselves (or being taught about) the genre practices in question. An approach which acknowledges this, whilst putting in play Reid's use of Altman's interventions, would be one in which students create texts based on familiar genres, whilst considering not only the reasons for the success of the genre but the conditions for the genre's possibility – that is, the interests served by its labelling.

To 'anchor' this to an assessment point, the most successful students in responding to questions about genre in exams are those who get into this area of uncertainty. Those who write very fluently about how genres function without addressing the practices of genre in this way are restricted to lower levels in the marking. On the other hand, some specifications do not make such demands, and diploma courses more often require an industry-driven understanding of genre, especially in terms of marketing products to the generic spectator. However, we would argue that working with genre for commercial ends is still likely to be more skilfully done if the theory behind the practice is familiar (to take the industry/vocational angle further, this is surely no different to the scientific theory which underlies good engineering practice).

learning plan 04.14 Genre Busting

According to Neale (1980), genre theory is to do with a circulation of expectation between industries, media texts and audiences. This leads to (or is an effect of, perhaps) 'regulated variety'. Hartley (1999) describes a contract between producer and audience which 'disciplines' choices and reduces desires. All genre theorists agree on the 'slippery' or 'fluid' nature of labelling texts in this way. There is consensus amongst this community that the exception to the rule is the 'pure' genre text. In other words most texts span more than one genre, or can be claimed by several or seem to present a degree of reworking, or play with conventions in some way. So a grasp of genre theory actually leads students away from the notion that genre is an easy, blunt tool with which to produce texts along conventional lines. For Neale, genre is a state of combinations, more or less randomly distributed, and genre texts are those which form particular patterns of combinations, or at least are seen that way by audiences or critics.

The good news for the Media teacher is that there are a plethora of books, websites and teaching resources available to help you work on particular genres with students. By far the most useful is the English and Media Centre's *Genre Through Practical Work*. Produced for English Key Stage 3 or GCSE Media students, this is a simple plan for an activity (to construct, storyboard and film a two-minute video sequence of a rendezvous in a particular genre) which draws on existing knowledge of popular TV genres with minimal teacher input. What we really like about the exercise is that it asks students to be creative first, without any concern to introduce the concept of genre before they start filming, and at the debrief stage students are asked to reflect on the degree to which their work is typical of the text-type they were trying to produce. Through a simple, low-maintenance exercise the practical, creative tone for the study of a concept is set. This is so much more educational than students producing a genre piece after a lengthy study of the concept and its dominant textual manifestations.

In the Picture's study pack on Science Fiction begins with an interesting consideration of genre in a Cultural Studies context:

> Genre, referring to paintings or to forms of literature, has a history going back to the Ancient Greek philosopher Aristotle, but it wasn't until the nineteenth century and the development of new technologies, such as the cinema and mass production printing as well as basic education, that popular culture began to be talked about as belonging to genres. When the whole population and not just the educated elite could experience and appreciate narratives the need for classification changed. This switch from high culture genres to popular culture genres is interesting in that genre went from being a term associated with intellectual discussion to a term of abuse which was then used to dismiss much popular fiction and most cinema as 'mere genre entertainment'. (Stafford, 2002: 1)

This brings us nicely to the five examples we will use as case studies, all of which are firmly situated in these debates over textual status.

Spectacular cinema

We are using this term instead of 'action films' to describe films that offer pleasure related to the visually spectacular alongside or instead of more narrative-driven pleasures. At the time of writing, the most notable example is *Avatar*, a media event marketed almost entirely in relation to its status as a threshold text – marking new territory in the landscape of cinema. Work on this type of film gets off to a good start if students decide on a range of criteria for judging individual texts. For example, they might differentiate between action and effects as a criterion as opposed to plot, or they might locate films as more or less sophisticated in terms of deeper meanings. This is good practice because straight away you are into discussions about how different people evaluate texts for different purposes. One group might see spectacular cinema as 'popcorn movies' which do not require intellectual engagement. Indeed students often say they watch films which 'don't make you think', for pleasure and escapism. Fans of this kind of film might, on the other hand, make complex and discerning decisions about texts. This perspective is informed by Mark Kermode's sensible arguments about horror films, that the people who best understand the generic dynamics and relations between screen violence and reality are the people who watch the most horror films (and thus they are the least 'vulnerable' of all of us and thus in the least need of protection through censorship). Students should also be aware that, with the publication of BFI classics and other academic work on individual films, spectacular cinema is enjoying a little canonisation, and certainly a renegotiation of its status in critical terms.

Jose Arroyo has a very interesting view on spectacular cinema, analysing the visual spectacles and ultra-sophisticated arrangements of time and space at work in the genre as works of art. Arroyo argues that the Frankfurt School tradition of critique (popular I think with some Media teachers still) misses the point that revealing the ways in which texts reaffirm capitalist culture, as sinister pleasure with hidden power discourses embedded in the sugar, only deals with one element of the text's operations.

Arroyo suggests that a film like *Mission Impossible* is so thrilling in aesthetic terms that the ideology is if anything, secondary and relatively uninteresting for the audience (and after all the middle classes are allowed to ignore ideology when wandering around the Uffizi):

> *Mission Impossible* is so thrilling that even hermeneutics are left behind for a while. On the ride, the viewer is too busy rushing through its aesthetics to think of anything but its erotics. *Mission Impossible* is a delight because, in pleasing the eye and kicking the viscera, it continually asks the audience to wonder. How did they do that? And that the film does this, and how it does this, is at least as important as why. (Arroyo, 2001)

Working from the 'how can we judge' exercise to Arroyo's ideas, we start with (again) a complex questioning of how the genre gets the press it does. The obvious link from this is some small-scale audience research to get some discursive data about consumption and pleasure. By the time you introduce conventions and 'micro' analytical work, students are familiar with the range of competing views of the meanings of the genre. As a result you can avoid generalisations about ideology and the audience, and consider how viewers might enjoy the pleasures afforded by the action and spectacle without 'buying in' to the view of the world represented as dominant in some of the most popular films.

Some teachers prefer a historical genre approach, placing contemporary 'spectacle' films in a tradition in order to explore reasons for the longevity of this text type. I have tended to spend more time on analysis of the specific technical and symbolic elements that typify (perhaps, but this is my interpretation) famous examples. The combination of sound and image is particularly rich for analysis. Dialogue spoken during moments of intense action can be definitive in audience recall and pleasure alongside music (which should not be described by students as 'dramatic' – their job is to explain in detail why the combination of rhythm, pitch and tone, when placed alongside images in an anchoring relation, is dramatic).

Students should focus in on editing and consider montage effects and the role of editing in creating spectacle. In this context, you might show students the early Lumiere Brothers films and ask them to make some connections in the light of Arroyo's theory. The notion here is that audiences at the dawn of cinema were interested only in spectacle, with narrative as a secondary feature of cinema. What has changed up to today?

For spectacular cinema, clearly there is lots of work to do around representation and gender, and the question of masculinities. This can be the most challenging, as students can be pretty homophobic, and the more interesting work, from Dyer in particular, comments on the homoerotic nature of action cinema:

> Come to think of it, for the male viewer action movies have a lot in common with being fellated. Whatever the reason, men cherish the illusion that their masculinity is not compromised by being fellated. Yet it's the other person, male or female, who's doing the work, really being active. So it is with action movies. In imagination, men can be Arnie or Keanu; in the seat, it's Arnie or Keanu pleasuring them. Now that's what I call speed. (Dyer, 1994: 10)

We will leave you to decide whether to get into this with your students! But certainly there must be some reflection on the construction of gender identity through response to spectacular cinema, and depending on group, course and the scope of ambition, this might be limited to some interesting audience research on female responses to spectacular cinema, or it might develop into a Lacanian analysis of male physique and the imaginary. To avoid these questions at all is to the detriment of the analysis, as this statement from Tasker suggests:

> The proliferation of images of the built male body represents for critics the kind of deconstructive performativity associated with postmodernism, whilst for others they articulate, in their 'promotion of power and the fear or weakness', traditional images which are also 'deeply reactionary' (Foster, 1988, p61). Within the action cinema, the advent of the body builder as star poses quite complex questions for the development of narrative,

largely to do with the need to incorporate moments of physical display. (Tasker, 1993: 73–4)

learning plan 04.15 Consequences

British Soap Opera

Like the action/spectacle film, soap opera is a lingering example of 'Media 1.0'. Whilst the tyranny of the schedule (more important for this genre than any other if we think about the role played by enigma and tease in the narrative – the soap opera audience must wait, often) has to be maintained for this genre to function, the success of *Kate Modern* and *Dubplate Drama* has shown that the 'on demand' domain of the internet can be used for a more conventional approach to phased storytelling as well.

Whether this topic is housed on your course in genre study, textual analysis, broad-casting, audience or media debates, and whether it is more or less integrated with, or only studied through, production work, we strongly suggest that the learning is structured around a consideration of popular culture debates. This is because in our view production practices and questions of convention, realism and melodrama cannot be understood in isolation from the competing discourses around the popularity of the genre. So rather than starting with analysis of episodes and key scenes in terms of conventions, we suggest setting out from a simple discourse analysis of the plethora of pro and anti responses in a range of contexts: the press, academic texts and pro-motional material. If you are organised enough, you can always record TV and radio material dealing with soap opera. We used a BBC Radio 5 phone-in (broadcast in the aftermath of research into soaps' treatment of family life) and gave students a simple chart on which to plot the callers' statements in various categories (soaps as documents of society, soaps as sensationalist junk and more negotiated positions in between). The discussion we had as a result was about the location of each discourse and the role of soap opera as a scapegoat or catalyst for a range of other identity issues. We discussed gender, the closet male viewer and the myth of the 'addict' in this con-text. Again, as with all of the topics discussed in this book, when we got to the 'nuts and bolts' of genre convention, illusion of real time, continuity, tease devices and cliff-hangers, action and enigma, two-shots and over-the-shoulder shots, establishing shots and tableaux, social issue coverage, meeting places, outdated depiction of community, interweaving storylines, partial closure, balance of realism and melodrama, music as motif, intertextual time and location, anchorage, semiotics of set design, costume and mise en scene, and the complex range of representational devices at work, we were already well informed on the wider debates around the status of these texts.

Another regular, rich resource is the magazine or website *about* soaps which can be deconstructed in terms of the ways in which they manage the relationship between text world and production world, or verisimilitude and documentary. Again, a dis-course analysis in terms of the assumptions relied on by the producers takes you into a more interesting discussion about the genre than simply listing production details. On the other hand, it is important to introduce students to some of the specific context of soap production, by asking them to research budgets, the writing by committee process and marketing strategies. In the section on representation, we dealt with Linda Grant's social document thesis, and as soap is a genre associated closely with representation of 'ordinary life', this is the reason why a more complex analysis of the relationship of text to students' lifeworlds is crucial for a mature understanding of this genre and its contested existence. This can only be satisfactorily achieved through production work, so we would argue that any study of soap opera must include the creation of at least a scene from an episode. Whether this creation challenges conventions or imitates the current orthodoxy is up to you, but we agree with Buckingham that many teachers make invalid assumptions about imitation:

> A brief glance at even the most outwardly 'imitative' student productions would suggest that there is nearly always an element of negotiation, parody or critique. Furthermore, in using existing media forms or genres, students do not automatically take on the values those genres are seen to contain. On the contrary, they are actively and self-consciously reworking their prior knowledge of the media, often by means of parody or pastiche – a process which might be better understood as a form of intertextuality or dialogic communication, rather than mere slavish imitation. (Buckingham, 2003: 134–5)

 learning plan 04.16 1/3/5 minute essays

Situation comedy

As we keep reiterating, strategic use of 'theory' works for any Media student. Regardless of level or the nature of the course/unit of study, if the theory is right, the student will benefit from considering media in this way. Here is an example:

> The sitcom character, because he (and the gender is significant) cannot learn from his experiences – or if he can learn, cannot put his lesson into practice and lacks the will to escape or improve, is therefore shamed and unmanly, and in Sartre's terms, lives in 'bad faith' (the opposite of the existential hero). (Hirschorn, 2003: 17)

In a way this reminds us of a comment made by an eminent TV executive who did a Media Studies degree and was surprised when it kicked off with a lecture on Hegel. It is a matter of 'use value'. Sometimes we over-compensate for the 'everyday' nature of the subject with absurdly intellectual approaches or redundant theoretical models that have little currency in contemporary media practices. You may think we do this at times with our insistence on working with Foucault, Derrida and Baudrillard. But if a 'thinker' has written something which has direct relevance to media texts, audience responses and pleasure (as we think Hirschorn rightly spots in Sartre), then it helps students make the leap from viewing to analysis more easily. Understood in this way, theory is a kind of distracting device.

There are three angles to take on this topic, all with representation as the key concept. One approach is to compare British and American sit-coms (where different configurations of social class are likely to be evident), another is to look at the genre in Britain historically (and trace social changes, prejudices, myth and taboo in this way) and a third option is to analyse the reasons for the popularity of the genre and debates around its status (similar to soaps in this respect). We suggest that rather than starting with more 'traditional' examples like *My Family, Gavin and Stacey* and *Outnumbered* and then moving on later to the complex alternatives, you start with *Extras* and *Glee* and work back. How do these texts rely on an understanding of the genres they parody (the documentary as well as the sitcom are up for grabs) to form their 'otherness' for comedic effect?

Narrative is of great importance to any study of sitcom. Circular, partially self-contained, stories are centred fundamentally on the comfort provided by the absence of change. Some unease prevails when sitcoms move to the end of their lives, and to get to this point writers introduce life changes that will make closure inevitable. A classic comparison is/was *Men Behaving Badly* and *Friends*, looking at episodes with the same narrative theme: unexpected pregnancy and male reaction. In addition to a comparison of gender representation (laughing *with* women *at* men), students analysed the narrative in relation to the typical sitcom structure. What we could see was that these episodes were taking the audience to an unfamiliar territory (the inevitability of growing up, moving on and taking responsibility) and this allowed us to consider the ways in which characters in sitcoms are really 'frozen in time' in terms of the life cycle. Representations of gender, occupations, ethnicity, social class, location and consumption (*Gavin and Stacey* pays great attention to popular culture tastes, for example) all function only in relation to this temporal stillness – things don't change. Interesting work for students to do (again, most effectively through producing their own example) includes considering the moments at which sitcoms meet other generic forms (for example *The Mighty Boosh)* and ways in which the form and structure can adapt to societal change. You may wish to get more or less into an historical account of this, along the 'social document' road, depending on the outcomes you need.

James Baker's *Teaching TV Sitcom* (2001) is a useful resource. Baker's suggestions focus on conventions – typical locations, themes and characters, target audience, typical storylines and, less straightforwardly, why these are funny. He suggests a scheme of work which considers 'buddy' sitcoms, female sitcoms and case studies on sitcoms which were exported to the US (*Men Behaving Badly*, which failed, and *Absolutely Fabulous*, which was a success). You can update this with a look at the 'cultural translation' required for *The Office* to work in the States. Baker explores the ways in which characters are trapped, ultimately by themselves:

> The majority of sitcom characters are frustrated by the situations they find themselves in and which they cannot escape. The situation can be physical or emotional, and although they often strive to change their situation, they are inevitably doomed to return to a similar starting point. (Baker, 2001)

Asking students to consider how their own lives might be represented in sitcom form gets us into this easily. In order to provide this adaptation, an individual needs to exaggerate certain characteristics that might be considered typical of a certain social group or disposition, and then amplify the 'typicality' of their situation through stereotyping and myth. So this might involve stereotypes of teenagers, of college life and then more specific combinations of gender and regionality codes.

It is vital that your attention doesn't wander away from the fact that readings of sit-coms are polysemic. The fact that comedy is notoriously difficult to analyse is important here. It actually isn't any harder to make sense of, it is just that we have mistakenly made assumptions about other media forms and the ways audiences respond that we can't make with comedy simply because when people don't laugh you can't ignore it!

Bollywood

Bollywood is often mistakenly described as a genre, when actually it is a film industry producing popular Indian cinema out of former Bombay (now Mumbai) which rivals Hollywood for worldwide appeal. It produces an average of 800 films a year which are distributed globally. In Britain today, several cities and towns have a Bollywood cinema showing Indian films. Increasingly Hollywood studios are developing their own versions of Bollywood film and there is a proliferation of co-funding. Cinema-going (and home-viewing) in India and of Indian cinema in the UK is said to be more of a whole-family experience than is the norm in the West and an old-fashioned (in British terms) intermission is a common feature in Bollywood cinemas. Bollywood audiences in the UK can subscribe to Star Gold through digital and cable providers, or via the internet, to view Bollywood films, whilst on the internet, Eros International recently teamed up with YouTube to launch a Bollywood channel on a free subscription basis.

In terms of box office success, Gant (2007) recently reported the following trends for Bollywood films in the UK. Most films open at around forty screens, and are increasingly shown at multiplexes rather than only at Bollywood cinemas, independent or art-house venues. Of these, Cineworld holds over half of the market, and its top venues are Ilford and Wood Green in London and Bradford and Wolverhampton. The most successful Bollywood films in the UK are those that offer something different to Hollywood, such as sentimental comedies as opposed to spectacular cinema. But in audience terms, there is still a sense of 'ghettoisation', as Gant explains:

> Thanks to a huge disparity in ticket prices between UK and India, the export market offers producers richer margins. But in the UK films have so far failed to cross over much beyond the Asian-ethnic audience. (Gant, 2007: 9)

There are a number of variables here that we need to set out in order to avoid making assumptions. Like downloading and modding, this is an area where we have always been lucky enough to have students to provide the content, as they know much more about the topic than we do. Another privilege we have enjoyed has been the highly reflective nature of these presentations. Bollywood consumption is, according to these students, highly postmodern in the sense that the films are taken incredibly seriously and yet not at all seriously at the same time. Our job then has been to place their knowledge in a theoretical framework and to provide a range of ways into a more critical approach. If you do not have Bollywood enthusiasts, then more teacher input will be necessary.

As already stated, Bollywood is not a genre. But how it relates to (Western) genre theory is really interesting and it will cast a critical light on other genre study. Finally, Bollywood is a massive industry (students are often surprised by the data) but it is not

Indian cinema. So a working definition needs to be established, and the most accurate one is simply that Bollywood films originate from Bombay. They are often described as 'Indian popular cinema', which of course reinforces the derisory use of 'popular' as a distinct from 'serious'. The 'ollywood' relates more to industry practices and global successes than it does to textual elements, as the content and style of Bollywood films is usually very different to Western cinema, as is the audience response. Tyrell offers a sound introduction:

> Bollywood – the affectionate name for Bombay's Hindi cinema – is the biggest film industry in the world. In India Hindi-dubbed Hollywood releases can't touch it (even the occasional Hollywood hit takes but a tenth of Bollywood's average box office) but it is also an international export with audiences in Africa, the Middle East, Russia, South East Asia, China, Europe and the United States. These viewers are not always Indian – Bollywood offers an alternative popular cinema for nations with a religious or political aversion to Hollywood (as in the Middle East) as well as crossing over from an Indian audience to a mainstream one (as in East Africa) on its merits as entertainment. (Tyrell, 1988: 20)

So students at the very least need to avoid making mistakes by understanding that Bombay's film industry is what is being studied, that this industry is more successful than Hollywood financially (to compare the cultural imperialist effects of both is a very interesting, but different question), and crucially that whilst the success of Bollywood products is often described as oppositional to Hollywood conventions (bound up with theories about Classical Narrative Cinema touched on previously), the films in question clearly share elements with popular American cinema. So notions of 'alternative' media come into question with this topic area. Once again, Bollywood is not a genre, but we might come to understand genre theory (and whether we believe in it or not) through scrutiny of the ways in which popular Indian cinema plays with genre conventions.

If we are defining Bollywood as an industry, how does it fit into genre study? Analysing the pleasures provided by films like *Chak de India* or even *My Name is Khan* reveals that genre theory in its traditional Western form doesn't really work. On the one hand, a film like *Sholay* is a reworking of the Western genre but it isn't satisfactory just to assess it as 'parody' because of the collision of cultural codes at work. Equally, most Bollywood films contain so many different genre elements (music, action, thriller, romance, comedy) that they take the concept of hybridity so far it no longer has credibility. This range of elements had led to these films being called 'Massala movies' (the range of ingredients) but the question students need to consider is whether Bollywood 'shows up' genre as an inadequate device that only works in a simplifying manner, or whether it is just that it does work for Western films but not for popular Indian cinema, in which case it is not flawed but it is deeply culturally specific. Either way, studying Bollywood from this perspective will lead to a much more informed, considered and less 'naturally' situated use of the concept of genre. More interesting work around Bollywood concerns the theory of diaspora in relation to cultural imperialism and globalisation discourses. The diasporic aspect is Indian culture being dispersed, through immigration, around the world and the way that this leads to people using the media as part of a network of hybrid identity (Ruddock, 2007).

⌐ learning plan 04.17 Diaspora

Taking one specific Bollywood film can be useful for students, as long as you help them avoid assumptions. You can illustrate this danger by asking them to identify a 'typical' Hollywood film and then ten others that are nothing like it.

Ideally, any scheme of work on Bollywood should include the viewing of a film in a Bollywood cinema. We have always taught in cities where these are easily accessible, and it is opportunistic but true regardless to mention that the day before writing this Julian's daughter attended her school's annual Bollywood disco. We appreciate for some of you this may be a mission, but worth it for the rich discussions about spectatorship it can yield. The behaviour of audiences in Bombay is certainly very different to that of English multiplex visitors, and it is common for audiences to dance during films. Finding out to what extent this form of spectatorship is preserved in Birmingham or Leicester is an interesting research activity (although those of us who teach the initiated need to make clear that we are learning *from* them, else there is great danger of patronising assumptions – the exotic other and all that).

Reality/talent TV

Since the first edition of this book, *Big Brother* has been replaced by *The X Factor* in the hearts of the nation. Another example that serves to 'problematise' the concept of genre more than apply it, documentary and its relative 'reality TV' (and its cousin, talent TV) are not fixed in genre theory. Again, this makes this all the more useful to study in this context. A range of approaches to this might be to place reality TV in the context of debates over quality and choice in the digital era. There are actually more documentaries available on the schedules than ever before, but many critics would not accept that this makes our current television more informative (in the Reithian sense). Why is this? What are the debates in the deregulated era? Were there really 'good old days' of public service broadcasting, or was this 'golden age' merely an era of middle-class prescription and acceptance by the masses?

> In the digital era, the world's most accessible medium has become even more so, and it's had a democratising influence on programme content, the viewing experience and on our ability to access information. So rather than there ever having been a golden age of television, it's my contention that it is the television of today that offers a gilt-edged opportunity to viewers and broadcasters alike. (Dawn Arey, Sky TV, Huw Weldon Lecture, 2005)

Developing this view, Peter Bazalgette of Endemol (the creators of the *Big Brother* format) argued that the proliferation of ordinary people on television is democratic public service broadcasting in action and furthermore that it offers liberation from state control and a patronising, middle-class approach:

> *Big Brother* arrived just at the point when, with multi-channels, content began to be driven more by popular taste than the dictates of a cultural elite. TV was no longer different or special, as it had been with only one or two networks. From the start *Big Brother* was different too. With its nudity, sex and bald [sic] language it was an extreme provocation to

television regulators and governments. Across the world it became the catalyst for fierce censorship debates, clashes between Church and state and constitutional crises. No single television idea had ever had such an effect before. (Bazalgette, 2005: 270)

Simon Cowell has inherited the crown as king of the format from Bazalgette in recent years, to the extent where, at the time of writing, there is serious discussion around a political TV format in which the audience get to vote in response to political debate, live – effectively an interactive current affairs/politics show in fusion with a talent contest.

Whilst Bazalgette and Cowell adopt the position of contemporary bastions of democracy and engagement (a view endorsed academically, intentionally or not, by Michael Wesch, who talks about young people's 'unseen' engagement with democracy in social media), others argue they are the mass producers of cheap, intellectually bankrupt entertainment serving to distract us from more enriching matters.

learning plan 04.18 What Do I Get?

Students must decide for themselves of course, but an approach based on contesting assumptions made by documentary about reality, representation and authenticity will inform them better. Consider this suggestion:

> Winston argues (1995) that much traditional documentary has as its subject 'victims'. For all its postmodernist style, this is essentially true of Big Brother. This series appeared to produce, as did the multitude of TV docusoaps, those alter egos, victims and celebrities. (Withall, 2000: 40)

Close textual analysis of a range of 'traditional' documentaries alongside new reality TV shows should revolve around how each text, through 'old' and 'new' conventions, constructs for itself and its audience a 'claim to truth'. How does voice-over, selection of material, use of experts, hidden camera footage and most importantly of all, the editing together of all these and the subsequent rhythm of the text (who speaks when, after whom and before what) construct a particular version of reality, and whose interests does this serve. And why is it that audiences seem curiously more trusting of this kind of media text than a range of others? Working with audiences is useful for this last question, of course. In keeping with the approach this book has advocated throughout, and at the risk of repetition, let us state that a sophisticated understanding of how documentary constructs these 'truth claims' in complex ways can only be acquired if you make a documentary, or design a reality TV show yourself.

For talent TV, the questions are slightly different as they raise issues about the cult of celebrity and how this format might relate ultimately to capitalist discourses of opportunity and escape. Our interest in reality TV in relation to democracy is all about the issue of access. Clearly more ordinary people are on TV than ever before and this trend looks set to continue. So we are moving away from the idea that 'being on telly' is for an elite group of talented individuals and moving towards the idea that the television is an arena for 'the masses' and that fame is obtainable with or without a clear reason for being famous! Whether this is a good or a bad thing depends on your view of what

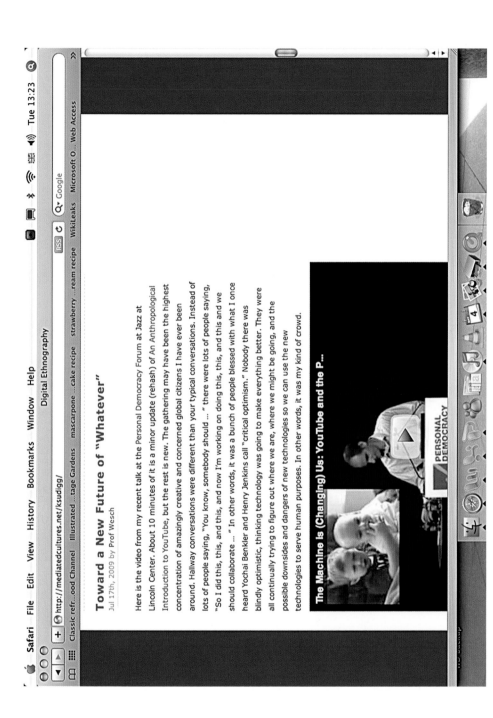

Figure I A page from http://mediatedcultures.net by Professor Michael Wesch

Figure 2 The leaders of the UK's three largest political parties debating on television before a live audience during the 2010 General Election © Ken McKay/ITV/Rex Features

Figure 3   A still from Channel 4's controversial teen drama *Skins* © Channel 4/
Ronald Grant Archive

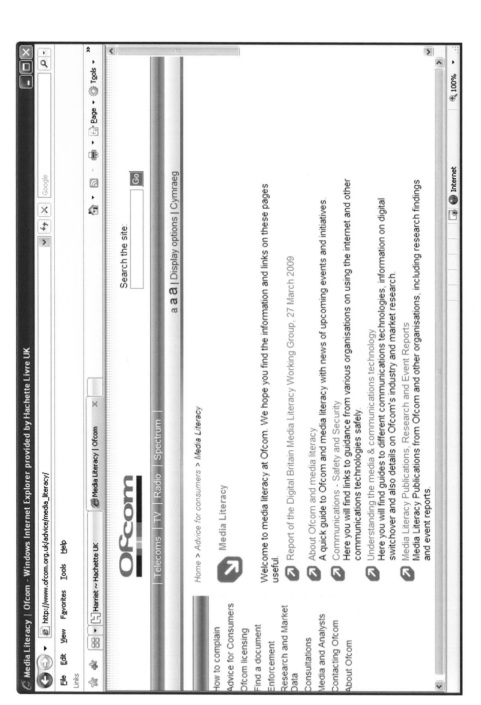

Figure 4 The online Media Literacy page of OFCOM

Figure 5 Creativity is a very broad and elusive category

Figure 6 A video-gamer coming face-to-face with a real-life gaming character

Figure 7   *In This World* © BBC/Film Council/The Kobal Collection

Figure 8 Jim Groom's *Edupunk* knuckle tattoos © Jerry Slezak

television is for, what the implications of our celebrity culture might be for social life, and what is meant by 'talent'. *The X Factor* and *Britain's Got Talent* can be seen as part of a 'lottery culture' in which the 'American Dream' idea of a level playing field whereby anyone's dream can come true is the subject of more and more entertainment.

Those who wish to uphold the idea of television as enrichment – to educate, inform and entertain in equal measure, as Lord Reith of the BBC declared almost a hundred years ago as a template for public service broadcasting's obligations – see reality TV as a 'dumbed down' year zero for our culture, distracting us from more serious matters and using the public as a freakshow. So these shows are criticised as dehumanising and immoral as well as just being of low quality, whatever that might mean. Therefore they are 'counter-democratic' in so much as they serve to disempower citizens from the political arena. Instead of challenging the political status quo, we are voting for *Britain's Got Talent*. The plot thickened when, for the first time, live TV election debates were a feature of the 2010 General Election, with huge audiences and build ups/follow ups that mirrored the conventions of major sports events. This is interesting to us for a range of reasons but, in the context of this chapter, because of the way that it makes the study of genre and audience more complicated – what genre would we place a live election debate in? Discuss.

 learning plan 04.19 Genre-Making

Audience

The concept of audience is really up for grabs. Whole academic conferences are devoted to the question of what to do with 'the concept formerly known as'. The most sensible view, we think, is that the audience is fragmenting in many ways but that it still comes back together quite a lot. Take a much-analysed and critically acclaimed TV series like *The Wire*. On the one hand, here is a text that, in the UK, was mainly viewed outside of any broadcasting schedule – DVD box-sets and torrent downloads mainly – but nevertheless was hugely popular and constantly discussed, often labelled the 'best TV show ever' by the likes of Charlie Brooker and other 'discerning critics'. Elsewhere (McDougall, 2010), we have reported on a detailed audience research project that attempted to 'remix' David Morley's seminal Nationwide study for the 'post broadcast mediasphere' by working with a range of different audience groups with different research methods (http://www.participations.org/Volume%207/Issue%201/mcdougall.htm). The findings seem to suggest that we are in a state of hybridity in audience research. On the one hand, we need to find new ethnographic methods for looking at how people make sense of media in new ways when the methods of consumption are so fragmented. But at the same time there is still a yearning for a collective viewing experience and a readiness to sign up to a kind of 'preferred reading' which may be – as in the case of *The Wire* – secondarily encoded in a viral mode.

Whilst Morley's formative cultural mapping revealed a set of different readings from different social groups, the data in question here offers different versions of a preferred reading. The five groups, almost without any exception, adopt immediately the dominant discourse – that 'the game' depicted in the show is really being played in social reality – and that the producers of The Wire are offering a window to this world, and that the show has things to teach us. From Charlie Brooker to our Youth Workers, this motif is recurrent. (McDougall, 2010)

 learning plan 04.20 Wiring the Audience

The point is that we can't just say – oh, this is too complicated for our students. Instead, we need to find ways to get them working ethnographically, spending time thinking about how people attribute meaning to media. The only way to do this is to integrate empirical audience research into the curriculum. Combined with production work, we are aware that this makes the majority of Media teaching awkward. But that's a good thing for learning.

Awkward is Good

Banksy's 2010 film, *Exit Through Gift Shop,* is a rich resource for us, since it allows students, through an engaging and accessible 'text', to see the limitations and the challenges of each key concept. As such it offers synoptic and extending material. According to Cynthia Fuchs (2010), posting on the Pop Matters website, the film offers *'an investigation of art and politics, galleries and value, repetition and meaning'.* Again, in keeping with our notion of Media Studies 'After the Media', we want to encourage students not to see the Banksy film as different to 'normal media' in its postmodern acts of deconstruction. Instead, they (through you) should be thinking about how *Exit* merely makes explicit what media theory has failed to notice – that ideas about boundaries (between genres, producers and audiences, between narrative, space and time and between media and 'the real') are always constraining and limited, that media theory ought to be about the space where attempts to 'pin down' meaning fail – our 'jouissance'.

 learning plan 04.21 Essay Through The Gift Shop

Whether the key concepts of Media Studies dealt with in this chapter are here to stay or up for grabs will be determined by you and your students over time. Certainly there is an entrenched legacy and an industry in producing resources to support this way of studying. Our view, which we hope we have consistently applied in the examples above, is that the concepts are only as useful as the testing of them, and as such they should be treated as hypotheses for students to work with. Can we label media texts on genre lines? Do media texts share common approaches to narrative, or does the audience make sense of things in more complex ways? And what do we mean by audience in these days of 'Media 2.0' in any case? Can we ever say for sure that a text represents the world in a particular way or is the meaning of any representation more polysemic and hard to pin down? In these ways, and especially through practical work and audience research, we can help students experiment with these models, and we can learn from their results.

References and further reading

Altman, R., 1982. *Genre: The Musical.* London: Routledge.

Arroyo, J., 2001. 'Mission sublime' in Arroyo, J. (ed) *Action / Spectacle*. London: BFI.

Baker, J., 2001. *Teaching TV Sitcom*. London: BFI.

Barker, M. and Petley, J. (eds), 2001. *Ill Effects: The Media / Violence Debate*. London: Routledge.

Bazalgette, P., 2005. *Billion Dollar Game: How Three Men Risked It All and Changed the Face of Television*. London: Time Warner.

Brey, P., 1998. 'The Ethics of Representation and Action in Virtual Reality', *Ethics and Information Technology*, 1:1.

Buckingham, D., 1987. *Public Secrets: EastEnders and its Audience*. London: BFI.

Buckingham, D., 2003. *Media Education*. London: Polity.

Burn, A. and Durran, J., 2007. *Media Literacy in Schools*. London: Paul Chapman.

Creeber, G. (ed), 2002. *The Television Genre Book*. London: BFI.

Dyer, R., 1994. 'Action!', *Sight and Sound*, October.

Fuchs, C., 2010. Review of *Exit Through the Gift Shop* by Banksy – at http://www.pop-matters.com/pm/review/124099-exit-through-the-gift-shop/

Gauntlett, D., 2008. *Media Studies 2.0* – at www.theory.org.uk

Gauntlett, D., 2009. 'Media Studies 2.0: a response', *Interactions: Studies in Communication and Culture* 1.1: 147–157.

Geraghty, C., 1991. 'Representation and popular culture', in Curran, J. and Gurevitch, M. (eds), *Mass Media and Society*. London: Edward Arnold.

Geraghty, C., 1991. *Women and Soap Opera: A Study of Prime-Time Soaps*. Cambridge: Polity Press.

Grant, L., 1996. 'Plays for today', *Guardian*, 21.12.96.

Hartley, J., 1999. *The Uses of Television*. London: Routledge.

Hills, M., 2010. *Triumph of a Time Lord: Regenerating Doctor Who in the Twenty First Century*. London: I.B. Tauris.

Hirschorn, A. 2003. 'Sitcoms and absurdism', *In the Picture* 46. Keighley: In the Picture Publications.

Jenkins, H., 2006. *Convergence Culture: Where Old and New Media Collide*. New York: New York University Press.

Johnson, S., 2005. *Everything Bad is Good for You*. London: Penguin.

Kabir, N., 2001. Bollywood: *The Indian Cinema Story*. London: C4 Books.

Kendall, A. and McDougall, J., 2009. 'Just gaming: on being differently literate', *Eludamos: Journal of Computer Game Culture*, 3.2: 245–260.

Lacey, N., 2000. *Narrative and Genre*. London: Macmillan.

Lacey, N., 2010. *Image and Representation*, 2nd edn. London: Macmillan.

Levan, S., 2000. *York Film Notes: Fargo*. London: York Press.

Lyotard, J., 1984. *The Postmodern Condition*. Manchester: Manchester University Press.

Lyotard, J., 1992. *The Postmodern Explained to Children*. London: Turnaround.

Masterman, L., 1985. *Teaching the Media*. London: Routledge.

McDougall, J., 2010. 'Wiring the Audiencies' in *Participations* Vol 7 Issue 2, at http://www.participations.org/Volume%207/Issue%201/mcdougall.htm

McDougall, J. and O'Brien, W., 2008. *Studying Videogames*. Leighton-Buzzard: Auteur.

Medhurst, A., 1994. 'The Magnificent Seven rides again', *Observer*.

Merrin, W., 2008. 'Media Studies 2.0' at http://twopointzeroforum.blogspot.com/

Mottershead, C., 2001. How to Teach Narrative. BFI Media Studies Conference Workshop, London.

Neale, S., 1980. *Genre*. London: British Film Institute.

Neale, S. and Turner, G., 2002. 'What is genre?' in Creeber, G. (ed.), *The Television Genre Book*. London: BFI.

Newman, J., 2004. *Videogames*. London: Routledge.

Newman, J. and Oram, B., 2006. *Teaching Videogames*. London: BFI

Peim, N., 1993. *Critical Theory and the English Teacher*. London: Routledge

Peim, N., 2000. 'The cultural politics of English teaching' in *Issues in English Teaching*. London: Routledge.

Phillips, N. 'Genre' in Nelmes, J. (ed.) (1995), *An Introduction to Film Studies*. London: Routledge.

QCA, 2005. *Media Matters: A Review of Media Studies in Schools and Colleges*. London: QCA.

Raynor, P., Wall, P. and Kruger, S., 2001. *Media Studies: The Essential Introduction*. London: Routledge.

Ruddock, A., 2007. *Investigating Audiences*. London: Sage.

Shannon, C.E., and Weaver, W., 1949. *A Mathematical Model of Communication*. IL: University of Illinois Press.

Strinati, D., 1995. *An Introduction to Theories of Popular Culture*. London: Routledge.

Stafford, R., 2002. 'Formats and genres across media', *In the Picture* 44. Keighley: In the Picture Publications.

Tasker, Y. (ed), 2005. *Action and Adventure Cinema*. London: Routledge.

Toland, P., 2004. 'What are you playing at? Representations of gender, race and nationality in videogames', *Media Magazine* 7. London: English and Media Centre.

Tyrell, H., 1988. 'Bollywood in Britain', *Sight and Sound*, August.

Withall, K., 2000. 'Exploring documentary truth?', *In the Picture* 40. Keighley: In the Picture Publications.

Media in Society: Doing the Big Debates

This chapter will address the areas of Media Studies that explicitly demand an opinion (or as it tends to be described in awarding body criteria, 'personal engagement'). The language changes from specification to specification – issues, debates, critical perspectives – but these all describe the more sociological, political, economic and cultural areas of 'Subject Media'. Whilst all Media learning is multi-disciplinary in the sense that texts cannot be analysed or produced in isolation from questions about audience, and a variety of ways of understanding the socio-cultural status of the mass media, these are the bits of Media courses that tend to be assessed through coursework essays or exams and through student response to a question on a particular topic where there are no right answers and the 'stock' of personal engagement is high.

We want to avoid any sense that this chapter is distinct from the chapters that deal with technology and more transgressive ideas about pedagogy. Theory and practice are not discrete in our philosophy so it is very important to utilise the affordances of Web 2.0 when teaching about media issues and debates – not just to revert to more traditional classroom dynamics. That said, in the essential 'Web 2.0 for Schools' (2009), Davies and Merchant suggest that a more liberating use of Web 2.0 across the curriculum (and in our case we mean across the whole Media curriculum) may only be possible with a broader reform of school structures. But we want you to be at the frontier of experimentation 'doing Media theory' in new spaces. With regard to Media in Society, why not make the process of shifting the learning contexts to digital spaces part of the discussions and reflections – what responses and responsibilities are pertinent for media educators in collaboration with their students?

> Response refers to the ways in which educators may be able to harness the power of these emerging technologies to develop new kinds of learning communities – online spaces that reach far beyond the walls of the classroom, connecting learners in different social settings, and crossing the boundaries of age and culture in new kinds of participation. Responsibility refers to the ways in which teachers will need to be aware of how new media also serve the needs of what Buckingham calls 'capitalism's relentless search for new markets' (2002: 203), as well as other undesirable forces in society that might ultimately put students at risk. (Davies and Merchant, 2009: 103)

At the same time, we don't want you to lose sight of learning – this is not an area of Media education that is transmitted – 'Big theory' being passed on to students. Instead, this area of the subject is shot through with the obligation to negotiate, collaborate and reflect on how we all construct our identities in complicated ways and partly (crucially, only partly) in relation to media. Jarvis (2010) writes about how we learn to be people in society and we think this is a helpful framing idea for this chapter:

Experience itself has no meaning…but our meanings stem from our relationships with other people in our lifeworld, from our own interpretations of our experiences, from questions about the cosmos or any combination of these. There are metaphysical and socio-cultural perspectives on this. (Jarvis, 2010: 70).

The 'role' of media in society, then, is not to provide a service or to give information or 'just' to foster entertainment or even to facilitate participation and exchange. Media has no role, its relationship with our lifeworlds is complex and unpredictable and *different*. But it is undoubtedly part of our experience and – as Jarvis alludes – thinking through how we give meaning to such experience (not what meaning a media text itself produces) should be the starting point for critical media literacy.

We hope that by now, if you have approached this book in a linear fashion or at least dipped into a few earlier chapters, we can take it as read that the best way for students to learn about gender magazines is to make one using digital photography, desktop publishing and photo-editing software. British cinema and identity is best understood if you create a British film and setting up a twitter feed to reflect on local politics in your area gives you a pretty good understanding of how new technologies might impact on news and politics now and in the future. But at the moment, we are still dealing with Media Studies specifications that often require students to show themselves to examiners through the medium of the exam paper or written coursework in this area, so that is what we will address in this chapter.

A few rationales for this kind of learning are:

With appropriate pedagogies and classroom work, the concept of audience has the potential to develop understandings of the cultural power of media institutions in ways that won't reduce down to 'brainwashing' or 'ideology' the variety of relations we enter into with texts. (Branston, 1991: 9)

and

All technological extensions of ourselves must be numb and subliminal, else we could not endure the leverage exerted upon ourselves by such extension. Although the medium is the message, the controls go beyond programming. The restraints are directed to the 'content', which is always another medium. The content of the press is literary statement, as the content of the book is speech and the content of the movie is the novel. To those who have never studied media, this fact is quite as baffling as literacy is to natives who say 'Why do you write? Can't you remember?!!' (McLuhan, 1994: 305)

and

On average we spend over fifteen years of our waking lives just watching television. Films, videos and the time spent reading newspapers and magazines, listening to music and surfing the net, means that we spend one third of our lives immersed in the media. Our abilities to speak, think, form relationships with others, even our dreams and our own sense of identity are now shaped by the media. So studying the media is studying ourselves as social creatures. (Sardar and Van Loon, 2000)

Since the first edition of this book, as we keep saying, lots has changed. So let's add this fourth statement to bring us up to speed:

> We are entering a period of prolonged transition and transformation in the way media operates. Convergence describes the process by which we sort through those options. There will be no magical black box that puts everything in order again. Media producers will find their way through their current problems only by renegotiating their relationships with their consumers. Audiences, empowered by these new technologies, occupying a space at the intersection between old and new media, are demanding the right to participate within the culture. Producers who fail to make their peace with this new participatory culture will face declining goodwill and diminished revenues. The resulting struggles and compromises will define the public culture of the future. (Jenkins, 2006: 24)

These four statements illustrate the same idea in different ways. Branston encourages us to equip our students with awareness of the complexities of audience behaviour. McLuhan provides the most explicit sociological approach, suggesting that media, as 'extensions of man' change culture profoundly. Sardar and Van Loon offer a popular justification of Media learning, as inevitable and necessary as it forms our reality (in this way Media Studies is the new Theology, I suppose). Jenkins is arguing that we understand our relationship with media – including our own creations – in new ways now. This one is up for grabs, and this chapter aims to support the kind of teaching that gives students space to explore the landscape and form their own, intellectually informed, opinions.

Our distinguishing these approaches from more straightforward topic areas hinges on the need for an understanding of different opinions. So while a student can answer a question about a film genre by presenting a description of the genre's conventions, its history, specific textual examples and an account of its popularity, the same student responding to a question about film censorship would need to balance out the conflicting discourses in this area, and think much more about the nature of film spectatorship and claims about social effects.

As always, we are all about the pedagogy so we urge you to consider as many new and innovative ways of engaging students in these theoretical debates about media in society as possible. For example, you might be able to use a virtual world environment such as Second Life to explore questions of (virtual) identity. If you can, then you can use this experiential ontological work as a basis for returning to seemingly more 'grounded' discussions of how our idea of 'reality' gets represented in media. Sometimes the set topic should come second, after something more fundamental and – frankly – interesting. But if we do take that route, we must always be mindful of what Sanders refers to as the 'conditions of possibility' for new modes of learning (rather than assuming students are all 'digital natives'):

> When bringing together experiences from the past 2 years, our most important findings relate precisely to the fact that we experienced levels of discomfort and concern amongst these students who were far from 'native' when inducted to 'avatar-learning'. We also experienced more behaviour management requirements in Second Life than ever in the

seminar room. If the conditions of possibility for Media undergraduates to learn reflectively when the object of study is the ontological exploration of the virtual, then perhaps we should tread even more carefully with students for whom the virtual world encounter is more of a shift in relation to their learning outcomes? (Sanders and McDougall, 2010: 7)

Back to the work in hand, here are some examples of the kinds of questions that call for such a socio-cultural understanding:

- Do media images contribute to gender difference or just reflect it?
- Why does Britain need a film industry?
- Should the media be more or less regulated and why is the idea of regulating media in a democracy so complex?
- Does Public Service Media have a future?
- Why has Hollywood dominated cinema?
- What is the relationship between the media and politics?
- How useful are various theories of media audiences?
- How credible is the 'effects model' of audience behaviour (often studied through the example of film censorship)?
- Are we living in a postmodern world?
- Are the boundaries between different types of cultural product (e.g. art, film, literature, music) broken down by the internet?
- Has the internet turned us all into 'prosumers'?
- Debates over the effects of advertising in contemporary society.
- Analysis of debates around particular types of media text and their cultural status.
- Is the media now more global than local and more or less democratic than before?

We want, at the risk of repetition, to reiterate our strongly held belief that we should rid ourselves of any notions that certain kinds of students can handle 'theory' and others are less prepared for this kind of work. This is absurd. Firstly, it assumes an understanding of theory (derived from a discourse of 'academia') that falsely separates it in a binary opposition from practice, and the craziness of this is hammered home to me every time a 'vocational' student explains to me how digital coding works. Secondly, it sets up an insulting deficit model of 'vocational' learning which completely ignores the time factor. As Media learning is currently arranged, a Diploma student will spend roughly fifteen hours a week studying films and television. An A-Level student might (at some points in the course only) get three if they are lucky. How can the former fail to become more scholarly than the latter? So please take it in good faith that the approaches and topics suggested in this chapter are for **all** Media students, for when they need to engage with theories that inform debates. Whilst it will be harder to find explicit references to such debates in assessment criteria for vocational courses, in the higher grade/level descriptors we tend to judge students on their ability to deal with the contexts in which audience response is played out, and these higher-order reflections will often take students into the kinds of questions listed above. Equally, whilst

GCSE students (and some AS) may seem to be more focused on *how* the media work rather than *why* they work in this way, or put another way they will be preoccupied by the micro (texts) as opposed to the macro (the media), a differentiated approach to Media learning will provide opportunities for those who are in a position to tackle some of these broader questions.

Another disclaimer – we want to encourage you to teach Media Studies 'after the media' not only in steering students more towards the study of people than the study of 'media texts' but also in working across boundaries. Both the Creative and Media diploma and a great number of degree courses foster interdisciplinary learning – looking at arts, media and culture together, producing creative work across modes and platforms and extending notions of 'textuality' across hitherto constraining categories. This is partly due to the affordances of the internet and partly because we are arguably looking at postmodern culture as the 'norm' – see Learning Plan 04.21.

This is reciprocal. We can learn from Ash (2010), an art practitioner and teacher trainer who is fairly rare in his appropriation of strategies from Media education – specifically moving image. We say unique because, in our experience, Art teachers are often suspicious of what they see as pervasive imitation in Media Studies. For Ash, in discussing a collaboration with the BFI whereby Art students visit a 'Mediatheque' gallery, the advantage of working across media is partly to do with pedagogy and partly just a matter of responding to the proliferation of moving image art in exhibitions by inserting media literacy into the Art curriculum:

> We would like to suggest that Media Studies focuses on learning the language of media through the study of context and reflection on the texts and images. It is 'about developing young people's critical and creative abilities. . . The notion of media literacy…implies that reading the media and writing the media shall be inextricably connected' (Buckingham 2003: 82). Art educators like wise are also concerned with contextualising the image and reflecting on the creative process and outcome. Buckingham (1995) (2003) suggests that Media Studies educators have a concern with 'Romantic' notions of 'creativity' and how to assess that. He quotes Bob Ferguson writing in 'Screen Education' 1981 who condemned the 'puerile' results of imitation and parody. Buckingham argued that the way forward was not to reproduce the 'dominant ideologies' but to challenge them, a deeply held belief that has been the backbone to media education since the publication of Marshall McLuhan's 'Understanding Media' 1964 and John Berger's 'Ways of Seeing' 1972. In contrast, 'creativity' is first in the list of Key Concepts in the A&D curriculum and is defined as 'producing imaginative images, artefacts and other outcomes that are both original and of value' (QCA 2007:18). Can moving image be taught effectively in Art & design classrooms without the support of a Media Studies department to help teach media literacy? Unless pupils are media literate how can they begin to climb the heights of creative originality? (Ash, 2010, in press)

Ash is arguing against the tradition in Art pedagogy of treating media literacy with suspicion. But what lessons have the Media education community learned from Art teachers? Our view is that we need to look more closely at how Art education works out what it means by 'creativity' – we have inserted this criterion into our work without due attention to its complexity, as is explored in the work of Readman (2009) and Trotman (2010) here, disseminating research into 'creative' learning in digital spaces with an explicit connection to the established work of Paul Willis:

> New digital spaces enable the creation of previously unexplored landscapes for the exercise of functional freedom, ambiguity and informed risk. In our analysis, we not only retrace earlier studies of creativity but also align our interests with a number of related developments in the field of ABER research. In particular, Willis' (1990) work on symbolic creativity in the lives of young people provides a study that is situated beyond the bastions of formal education, illuminating a powerful dynamic of creative work in young people unfettered by institutional restraint and approved pedagogy. (Trotman, 2010: in press)

With regard to the scope of this chapter, we are suggesting before we move into the realm (and to some extent the tyranny) of the 'topic' that you encourage students to look beyond 'media in society' toward the arts and the realm of culture more broadly – not only by producing 'cross-media' production work but also by extending the range of what they look at (and listen to) when 'doing theory'. The BFI's Mediatheque project might be a helpful way in to such an endeavour.

Having said all that, these types of study do tend to be 'meat and drink' more consistently for A2 students and in our experience students are at most risk of under-performing in this area of their course because the leap from textual analysis and creative production to this type of cultural investigation is so profound. Students need to deal with media realities, discussing the relationship between the world, lived experience and media representation not only in a descriptive sense (how does the media present the world?) but through a philosophical lens (what is the nature of reality understood as separate from media imagery in these times?). Alongside this they need a sophisticated grasp of current thinking about audiences (if they get this wrong, a simplistic account of audience is more damaging to their cause than getting some facts wrong in an account of institution, for example). And they need to handle debates well, which is a learned skill – the fine line between personal engagement and unsubstantiated opinion tests out third-year undergraduates, so we need to work hard on this with our 'Level 3' charges.

When we talk about this kind of Media learning, there is a tension which divides the subject community to some extent. Whilst some see exam papers that test students' ability to write essays about the media in society as the last bastion of an essential theoretical approach (which will be bound up with notions of critical autonomy and media literacy on a broader scale than mere textual analysis), others worry that this model of 'doing media' is outdated. Regardless of the opinion you have, this kind of work is likely to stay 'big business' for Media students for a while, and there is a lot at stake for them. No matter how practical you make your course, regardless of how much technology you enable students to use, and how radical and transgressive your pedagogy, students will have to write essays, either for coursework or exams, and demonstrate understanding in that medium. So the remainder of this chapter will offer six detailed examples of 'doing debates', accompanied again by a set of class strategies. These 'study sites' (and their range of elements) are:

Magazines and Gender: how do publishers create a sense of belonging based on gender codes and to what extent do students think these presentations of 'us and them' have negative social implications? And another view – the postmodern reader plays with gender identity and as such achieves 'metacognition' of the constructed nature of gender. Here we will consider this example as part of a broader discussion of media and collective identity.

Media Effects: in two parts – firstly, a discussion of moral panics and less extreme manifestations of concern about children's media consumption and secondly an analysis of the 'protection' thesis at the heart of justifications of film censorship and calls for tighter regulation of games and social media. In both cases, a wider range of theories about popular culture are considered. The recent Byron report and its recommendations, followed by the subsequent review of progress in 2010, are of mandatory interest here. In addition, the concept of media literacy as a protectionist measure against 'effects' is a recent example of the ongoing public discourse around the power of the media in its various forms and the importance of critical skills through which young people in particular will be able to 'resist' influence.

British Film and National Identity: does Britain need a film industry, distinct from its status as an annexe of Hollywood? And if so, is this for commercial/economic reasons or is it to do with culture – the need for us to tell stories about our changing understanding of Britishness? Again, the idea that we form ideas about our national culture partly through engagement with media is an element in a broader discourse around the media and (collective) identity.

News, War and Politics: taking the reporting of September 11, the wars in Iraq and Afghanistan and the 2010 election as case studies, an analysis of the selection and construction of news, the relationship between corporate-political news agendas, party campaigning, spin, social media and the introduction of live TV debates into the UK political arena. What is particularly interesting here is the complexity of a situation where on the one hand the media audience is 'falling apart' – accessing 'pull' media in a wide range of contexts 'on demand'. But at the same time politics enters the space normally filled by talent TV and live sport – 'event TV' which has to be viewed when it happens. To what extent this influences the nature of contemporary politics – alongside the blogosphere and how this might re-engage younger citizens – is the debate at stake here.

Fandom: new for the second edition, we believe that the 'prosumer' convergence culture has foregrounded fandom and that Media students must not ignore fan behaviour in their studies of audience. The work of three people is recommended for attention – Matt Hills, Henry Jenkins and Jon Wardle – and in this section we will suggest some ways of making connections between the kinds of topics Media students have to choose between (which exclude fandom as a discrete area) and this work on active engagement.

Reality and Talent TV: investigating competing discourses at work in reality TV programmes and doing work with audiences to explore the status of reality and Talent TV and to develop student responses to the key debates – around realism, exploitation, truth and 'quality'.

We also look at the BBC's pioneering response to digital consumption. Here students need to be adept and handling the various factual pieces of the equation – the success of the UK in franchising and exporting format TV, set against arguments about public service broadcasting and the sovereign but ever more threatened licence fee, Anthony

Rose's development of the iPlayer and a range of theoretical forecasts for the future as revenue streams – in the wake of the decline of TV advertising – become more scarce. Alongside the facts, they need to understand the critical perspectives about the proliferation of reality and talent TV – from Michael Wesch's digital ethnography of young people's 'below the line' engagements with democracy, to Jenkins's *Convergence Culture*, John Hartley's concept of the post-broadcast 'mediasphere' and the relationship between reality TV and debates about postmodern culture.

Inevitably there is overlap here with previous chapters, as many of the texts and conceptual approaches discussed in other parts of this book share some common ground with these topics. We describe some institutional areas for study related to the BBC in the chapter on coursework, and blogging has featured all over the place. The section on representation threw up British cinema as an example, and reality TV texts were prominent in our discussion of media literacy. These are not particularly original areas to focus on. They are the 'meat and drink' of most media debates/contexts coursework. And of course there are a plethora of resources available to support these areas, and most student textbooks offer chapters on these areas. So we are hardly making a radical intervention here. But what has changed since the first edition is, somewhat obviously, the internet and as we support Gauntlett's view (2007a) that the internet is now at the centre of media exchange, we have to update the way we look at the relationship between the media and society, given that the web is part of both and, if we believe Jenkins in particular, the 'virtual revolution' has transformed society itself, which would make the distinction between media (in its online form) and people at least blurred.

On the other hand, we are more interested in *how* students learn in these areas, and this is about more than content and provision of materials – it is about a way of seeing and a way of doing language, a language game you need to play in order to articulate (which is different from understanding) some 'deeper' questions about your identity in a mediated world.

Magazines and gender

This topic appears explicitly on some Media specifications, can be addressed as an aspect of a broader study of magazines or print publishing for others, or as an example within work on gender representation or as a selected 'case study' in an exploration of media and identity for any Media course. The approach suggested here begins with a consideration of women's magazines, drawing on some 'classic' examples and a readily available body of work on these texts, then introduces 'lads' mags' for comparison, and then – crucially – moves students away from the nature/nurture, positive or negative binary-structured approach to this debate, towards a more postmodern conception of audience behaviour.

🖰 **learning plan 05.02** Discourse Mapping

Discussing the notion that publishers and editorial teams create a sense of 'belonging' on the part of their readers is a good starting point, but in order to avoid a reductive reinforcing of stereotypes, we need to keep our thinking sharp enough to remember that readers do not really believe in this community. For that reason, I think it is a common bad practice to ask students to use A3 paper and cut and paste to produce classroom displays about '*Loaded* man' or '*Cosmo* woman'. Better if we start with a view that '*Cosmo* woman' is an editorial construction and then start to deconstruct her. Some semiotic work can get students started here, focusing on cover design, to address the simple question of how the reader is 'drawn in' through the language of signs and symbols. Students can then be given two very different theoretical perspectives to apply to their semiotic findings. Winship (1987) offers a feminist application of 'male gaze' theory to women's magazine covers, arguing that '*the gaze between cover model and women readers marks the complicity between women seeing themselves in the image which the masculine culture has defined.*' We have put this idea alongside Althusser's (1971) notion of 'interpellation' (the social/ideological practice of misrecognising yourself). If students put the two together, a feminist-Marxist reading of magazine covers is straightforward – Winship's complicity is being prepared, for gratification, to recognise the ideal version of oneself, despite the anxiety this will cause. For feminists, the male culture reinforces its power by defining women in this way and encouraging this anxiety. The alternative is to challenge it, but students will know from their experience that this is difficult. For Marxists, this is a form of 'false consciousness.' Put simply, the post-feminist backlash has served to 'redistract women' – rather than continuing to lobby for equal pay and positive representation in media, they are reading *Hello* and commenting on the waistlines of their sisters.

To get to this point of debate, though, as well as cover design deconstruction, students need a more developed understanding of the constructed audience. The easiest way to obtain this is by contacting publishers for advertising packs. These will define, for potential advertisers, the reader – where she shops, what she likes, how she understands herself.

 learning plan 05.03 Knowledge or Belief?

 learning plan 05.04 Hot Seating

Male magazines, or 'lads' mags', provide us with one of the most challenging, hotly debated areas for analysis. We have developed a case study on *Nuts* and *Zoo* (McDougall, 2004) and a more sustained focus on *Men's Health* (McDougall, 2008) to explore questions of audience and 'effects'. With the latter, we have asked students to consider the question of whether, for feminists, 'two wrongs make a right'? In other words, does the proliferation of male concern with body image and health reflect a maturing society within a wider discourse about the 'new man' or can we trace here a worrying objectification of men that actually reinforces that of women (a different kind of level playing field)? Again, we get to this discussion through the 'legwork' of textual analysis, content analysis and study of journalistic approaches, as well as evaluating the advertising content (again, using the publisher's briefing notes as a starting point). A comparison of *Nuts* with *Men's Health* gives students the chance to consider different variants along a continuum. Whereas *Nuts* is explicit in its sexism and reduction of the male gender to its stereotype (undoubtedly in a playful way, as we shall discuss), *Men's Health* lays claim to a more sensitive, aspiring version of the male, yet the majority of its 'quick fix' approaches to everything from 'impressing the boss' to 'getting a six-pack' and 'making her beg for more' are based on a traditional hunter-gatherer discourse about male behaviour. There is little in the way of (female?) complexity in its pages so whereas the mode of address is very different to *Nuts*, is the discourse so far removed?

At this point, then, having come to a developed understanding of how a range of magazines for both genders operate in textual and commercial terms, we can introduce a triangular approach to considering representation. Three questions should be asked of each text – how does it represent its 'own' gender to the reader, how does it represent its 'own gender' to the other gender and how does it represent the other gender to its reader? This pays attention to the importance of female readings of *Nuts* and male readings of *Sugar*, as this duality of representation serves to reinforce ideas of the other. Bring in discussions of sexuality and the 'secondary reader' (e.g. the gay male reader of *Cosmo*, or the female reader of *Men's Health*) and things get more interesting, and remind us again of the complexity of representation. It is a fact that the cover models on *Men's Health* are always in black and white because the editors assume that the readership will be able to cope with a male cover model only on these terms (the black and white male torso becomes less sexual and more medical/muscular). And why do students think that, with a few exceptions, women's magazines feature female cover models and so do men's? Finally, a consideration of rival perspectives.

Laura Barton asserts that:

> These days, the insinuation that all gents are satisfied by 29 cans of Stella and a slightly stained copy of *Razzle* is as quaintly outmoded as the suggestion that the lady loves Milk Tray. Nevertheless, *Zoo* and its brethren seem to act like some elaborate cultural muck-spreader, coating everything in an impermeable layer of tits and ass and porn and fighting. And the intimation is that any bird who can't handle that can feck off and take her scented candles with her. (Barton, 2004)

Barton, Althusser and Winship all offer a variation on the theme that gender magazines do some damage, and that there is a correlation between the representation of gender in their pages, the readers' acceptance of them and problems in society. There is no better example for students to engage with than the scandal leading to Danny Dyer being dropped by *Zoo* magazine after a 'production error' led to a shocking piece of violent misogyny which, presumably, is considered 'fair game' among *Zoo* contributors being printed.

learning plan 05.05 Devastated Danny Dyer

But another, and contrasting, view that students absolutely **must** appreciate and take a stance on, is the growing idea that we 'pick and mix' our media and we similarly select in more or less regular ways how we form our identities in relation to media. Gauntlett, through sustained audience research, describes readers' active negotiations in response to both women's and men's magazines:

I have argued against the view that men's lifestyle magazines represent a reassertion of old-fashioned masculine values, or a 'back-lash' against feminism. Whilst certain pieces in the magazines might support such an argument, this is not their primary purpose or selling point. Instead, their existence and popularity shows men rather insecurely trying to find their place in the modern world, seeking help regarding how to behave in their relationships and advice on how to earn the attention, love and respect of women and the friendship of other men. In post-traditional cultures, where identities are not 'given' but need to be constructed and negotiated, and where an individual has to establish their personal ethics and mode of living, the magazines offer some reassurance to men who are wondering "Is this right?" and "Am I doing this OK?", enabling a more confident management of the narrative of the self". (Gauntlett, 2002: 180).

Kendall researched young people's reading habits and, predictably, magazines featured heavily. Kendall was concerned with readers' notions of themselves as particular kinds of readers; after all, young people today are demonised for their lack of literacy in conventional terms. She found that male readers adopted a less critical stance than their female counterparts:

The magazines functioned, as for female readers, to offer prompts and possibilities for representing self through negotiation of symbolic codes. However, the male readers were characteristically less critical and more acquiescent to the identities inscribed through the modalities of their 'hobby' magazines. (Kendall, 2002)

Why this would be so, is open to debate. Perhaps males take a less negotiated position in response to these texts, or perhaps the longer history of the woman's magazine is a factor. Either way, both Gauntlett and Kendall remind us that the only viable approach to these debates ultimately is audience research.

Gauntlett's last sentence is perfect for an old-fashioned academic essay, we think, reformed as *According to Gauntlett (2002), gender magazines 'enable a more confident management of the narrative of the self'. Discuss.* To answer this well, students would need to introduce the texts in their commercial contexts (circulation, publishers, etc.) and the big issues – nature/culture, representation and broader debates about effects. They would move on to discuss the function of magazines, in terms of editorial policy and selling of audiences to advertisers. They would next approach, through textual examples, a range of theoretical positions, referring in particular to Winship and Gauntlett as alternatives. Next they would apply these positions to one example, and then, most importantly of all, describe their own audience research in this area. It is from this primary work that their conclusions should be drawn.

Audience, effects, protection and regulation

There are a number of designated topic areas under this umbrella. Considerations of film censorship, children and television, audience research, media and violence, the effects model compared to others and analysis of the effects of advertising all demand (if they are to be done well) an awareness of and sensible response to contemporary theories of media audiences (which means considerably more than Uses and Gratifications, or the Hierarchy of Needs!). Since the first edition of this book, videogame effects have high currency alongside, of course, the 'moral panic' over the proliferation of online social and virtual media. As far as children's use of these spaces goes, the Brown Government commissioned Tanya Byron to produce a set of recommendations for online and digital child protection and for the regulation of gaming. These are essential reading and the learning plan we link to here is all about making connections (where they are to be made) between policy interventions.

learning plan 05.06 Byron, Media Literacy, Every Child Matters

In the section on narrative we made some negative remarks about students' dutiful yet bland application of Propp and Todorov to contemporary films, and we want to make a similar case against the Bo Bo Doll here. We don't believe there is much mileage for Media students in using dated behaviourist models from psychology to support an argument about media effects in the twenty-first century. As students will be aware of the media effects hypothesis from lived experience, better to start with a variety of research on media audience and the more complex challenges to this orthodoxy. To this end, the sections on the effects debate in Dutton (1997), Barker and Petley (1997), Gauntlett (1995) and Buckingham (1995) are essential 'historical' reading for students (or at least selected extracts from each), alongside Byron, OFCOM's media literacy bulletins and the most recent BBFC statements about how they rate films and games. From this range of reading (guided, through the kinds of learning strategies offered throughout this book), students will encounter the history and nature of ideas about how audiences are 'effected', alongside some alternative perspectives, and the key policy criteria in use by institutions and regulators. Any one of the three paradigms in this triangle is meaningless in isolation from the other two.

We also strongly suggest you make links with other topics, so if students were looking at horror films they could usefully make a synoptic bridge to Dyer's work (1994) on action film pleasures, or they could return to Kermode's views on film censorship:

> It is very hard to maintain freedom of speech in a culture which has become terminally infantilised. We've allowed the censors to view us all as children, and we've handed over the reins of responsibility for our viewing habits because we are not willing to accept that responsibility for ourselves. (Kermode, 2001, in introduction to Channel 4 screening of Bad Lieutenant).

The film Kermode refers to has recently been re-made and shifted to post-Katrina New Orleans, so there is an opportunity to bring this idea to life through engagement with the specific case Kermode makes, as long as you are comfortable with the 'shocking' (allegedly) content.

> The lack of firm evidence for negative long-term effects from video games on the attitudes, beliefs and behaviours, means that we need to consider the question of harm and risk of harm within the broader biological, psychological and social context of the child or young person playing the game. This approach can help to highlight specific potential areas of risk for some vulnerable children and young people. (Byron, 2008: 149)

Students will need to think about the difference between the 2008 Byron report, quoted above, and the *Child's Play* case as documented by Martin Barker. Whereas the subsequent report on 'video nasties' was highly specific in its range and assumptions about the problem at stake, the Byron enquiry was much less clear in its remit. There is clearly a kind of 'moral panic' at work in the discourses around 'toxic childhood' and online safety and we wouldn't want to undermine the idea that there are serious risks in the digital world. But, unlike the Bulger case, Byron was not dealing with anything specific – more a general set of anxieties. Avery (2010) refers to this broad anxiety about children and digital creativity and – more specifically – the attempts by intellectual property owners to hold back the tide of access through legislation as 'The Great Media Compromise':

> You can of course understand the reluctance of professional content creators to make a decision that could see them out of pocket, especially at a time of uncertainty in the economic model of the media industries. In the meantime however, before this great media compromise is reached, a potentially wonderful outlet for young people to become more actively creative citizens, commenting on the world around them, is made illegal. (Avery, 2010: conference abstract).

Avery is not only concerned with legal gatekeeping; a term he applies to the media literacy moral panic that is especially helpful for our focus on regulation is *ephebiphobia* – the extreme fear of youth. Might the root of the latest attempt to regulate young people's activity be this long-held anxiety about young people in general – as The Smiths had it, *'sir leads the troops, jealous of youth'*?

learning plan 05.07 Mediawipe

The important role for the teacher in managing this learning is to prevent students placing walls around different areas of Media study. It is common for the same student to deal with subtle nuances of audience pleasure when writing about a particular area of contemporary music, but then take a reductive, deficit-model approach when considering arguments for film censorship. Another caveat is this – if you decide to use a case study like Barker and Petley's analysis (1997) of the moral panic arising from the Jamie Bulger case, make sure students are aware of the difference between general audience work and highly specific research.

In any case, *Child's Play* was viewed on video, so it cannot be applied in work on children and television or film censorship, for example. To tackle audience work with confidence, you need to support students in their understanding of demographics, dominant readings and other possibilities, cultivation, moral panic, myth, reception theory and reader-response, research methods and theories of popular culture. We are setting up a sophisticated grasp of audience theory as a pre-requisite for dealing with debates around censorship and effects for the obvious reason that there is a great danger otherwise of basing one's opinion (or demonstration of personal engagement) on a simplistic conception of how people read media texts.

To prepare students to write well about censorship, we suggest you foreground the notion of protection within a broader discussion of 'concern' over popular culture:

> There is a continuous and necessarily uneven and unequal struggle, by the dominant culture, constantly to disorganise and reorganise popular culture; to enclose and confine its definitions and forms within a more inclusive range of dominant forms. There are points of resistance; there are also moments of supersession. This is the dialectic of cultural struggle. (Hall, 1981: 228)

We utilise this sociological perspective from Stuart Hall because it reminds us that we cannot sensibly isolate the notion of the state censoring media content from power struggles over the function and limits of popular culture (and indeed all of Media Studies is negotiated within this contested terrain). Equally, students will often demonstrate, in free discussion, myths about 'the other' which are useful if they are reflected upon (i.e. we all do it, but knowing why we do it is helpful). Students will often admit to watching films and DVDs they are excluded from by classification, but will sometimes articulate the classic line that there are other people who wouldn't be 'suitable' for such illegal consumption. So again, discourse mapping is a sound methodology for dealing with the idea of protection. Going through some case study examples, such as *Crash* (not banned in novel form), *A Clockwork Orange* (banned by its director), *Battleship Potemkin* (banned for some social groups, but not others), students can map the assumptions made against discourse categories. Alongside this work, it is interesting for students to consider the dilemma the 'cutter' faces and to analyse famous examples of problems with context (for example, *Straw Dogs* where there is a view that the censor made the images more disturbing than before).

To focus on the politics of censorious claims, films like *The Magdelene Sisters, Dogma* and *The Passion of the Christ* (and a comparison with Philip Pullman's recent novel is interesting here) serve to highlight the ideological nature of such specific debates over faith, and this exercise is then useful for illustrating that actually all censorship is based on power-claims; there is no single text that is universally offensive. For example, as Kermode has argued recently, the BBFC (which, it should be noted, is funded by the film industry rather than the government) appears more heavy handed when dealing with English language films compared to subtitled arthouse movies with controversial content. The assumption about audience is obvious. As always, we suggest that the most productive, active strategy for student work in this area is audience research, not to try to 'prove' whether their peers or family are influenced negatively by film images, but to collect qualitative data through interviews and focus group discussions about films and censorship, so they can analyse the discourses articulated and where they come from historically and culturally. Where at all logistically possible, ethnographic work is the goal.

learning plan 05.08 Easy Ethnography

Students' own responses to shocking films will, naturally, be of great importance. Davey (2005) offers a really interesting student view:

> Films are a form of expression, and many forms of expression are prompted by sorrow and loss which, in many cases, are prompted by violence. Therefore, without violence, a vast number of films would never have been made. If violence has played a part in the

making of a film, then it's understandable that in the content of the film, violence may play a part. We cannot distinguish between violence and film, because that would mean distinguishing between violence and life. (Davey, 2005: 30)

 learning plan 05.09 Critical Discourse Analysis

A note about resources. Film magazines regularly devote whole issues to banned films, and there are regular documentary series' aired that look into the history of censorship as well as the arising debates. In addition, Film Education and the BFI produce study packs on this topic, a number of publications from Auteur and the English and Media Centre are helpful and DVDs of controversial films will usually contain documentary material or a director's commentary on these issues. The crucial role of the teacher, though, is to choose the resources to support the approach you already wish to take. On the one hand, content-driven Media learning can frustrate, and on the other, you will need to make decisions (and perhaps obtain parental agreement) that are sensitive to the cohort you are working with. Here are two responses to the film *Crash* – the one about sexual gratification linked to motor accidents, not the more recent film about racial tension in Los Angeles – to illustrate this point:

> A film, by an important director, of a book by a great novelist, which has generated much media heat (and of course, very little light) should be dealt with in the Media Studies classroom because if we're not doing it then sure as hell nobody else is. (Nick Lacey, quoted in Stafford, 1997: 7).

> Inevitably, trying to understand what people 'do' with media products will involve discussing the issue of violence in moving image products. This does mean analysing the views of both those who maintain a direct 'cause and effect' relationship between 'violence' on screen and violence in society and those critics who reject such a crude model or way of describing the debate. There are enough examples from recent years to enable a thoughtful, intellectual debate. I just don't think a film about obtaining sado-masochistic sexual pleasure from car crashes is one of them. It is just too extreme for use with 16–18 year olds. (Graeme Kemp, quoted in Stafford, 1997: 7)

Roy Stafford, the first author quoted above, led a fascinating workshop at a Media Education Asssociation conference called 'Don't Panic'. Stafford showed clips from 'shocking cinema' and made the same argument he articulates here in relation to *Crash* – that one of the reasons for us doing Media Studies at all is to cover sensitive issues about taboo and taste. It was perhaps surprising that the delegates were divided over whether or not they would 'use' the range of extracts Stafford showed. To some extent this is a matter of confidence and context – if you are a nervous NQT with a new career ahead are you really going to want to steam in with a narrative which involves an amputee soldier dying in hospital being fellated by a nurse whom he gang raped with other soldiers earlier in the war (a 'coincidence' she is aware of)? So it is your judgement call, as the two contrasting views above illustrate very well. You may or may not make use of the learning plan on Chris Morris's latest controversy, definitely the most intense example of a film to test the boundaries of this debate that we could find.

learning plan 05.10 Top Trumps

The MEA event also featured a keynote from David Buckingham about his work producing an extensive literature review on 'effects' to inform the Byron report and the learning plan we link to here asks students to analyse the results of his labour.

 learning plan 05.11 Byron and Buckingham

Our own view is closer to Stafford and to that end we do our fair share of working behind closed doors and explaining ourselves to colleagues in adjoining classrooms, but we have always played safe in this area and written to parents explaining the educational context of showing graphic scenes in class, and giving them an opt-out option. This has never arisen, but it means you need a back-up plan, perhaps even a different topic to run in tandem if necessary. There are also demographic and cultural contexts that make things different for us; some of us work in faith/multi-faith institutions – this ought not to make any difference in a free society, but sometimes it does, as many of you will know.

This brief discussion about our own practice and the judgement calls we have to make is helpful in returning us to the central questions at the heart of this critical perspective: do we need more or less regulation of media, is the regulation we have adequate (and for what) and why is regulation of media in a democracy so controversial and difficult – especially when the internet transgresses national and cultural boundaries? Critically it is always-already about judgement (who judges and according to what criteria) and othering: who are these 'other people' (not us) who will be harmed in some way by access to media? The learning plan we link to here asks students to explore the way the BBFC have to make these tough decisions.

 learning plan 05.12 BBFC Judgement Calls

Moving away from film, another 'classic' and not quite outdated (yet) area for our attention is research into children and television. Students might again start with some historical studies in this area, most obviously Buckingham (2000), Livingstone (1999) and Hodge and Tripp (1986). Then they might look at more recent work – the English and Media Centre's activities on *Skins* in 'Doing TV Drama' (see Learning Plan 04.07) and Dafna Lemish's *Children and Television: An International Perspective* (2006). This reading needs to be organised through a range of individual and collaborative tasks (see the various learning plans that support these approaches) but only in a few instances should it be isolated reading and note taking. The key critical questions to address are:

- *How are children defined and by whom?*
- *What research methods have been used to produce these findings?*
- *What model of audience behaviour is evident?*
- *What difference (if any) is the changing nature of television viewing making to this?*

learning plan 05.13 Living(Stone) Through a Decade

Having asked these questions of some academic work, students should research media coverage of this debate and start to position articles and TV documentaries in relation to theoretical perspectives. Next they can place regulators' practices (namely OFCOM) in this context. Again, as for film censorship, we are establishing a triangular approach where academic theory, public debate and state intervention are understood only in relation to one another.

Primary research with parents and children is incredibly enlightening for students, as long as ethical issues are high on your agenda early on. Outcomes are only useful if students are aware that parents cannot be treated as objective subjects if they are asked questions about how much television their children watch, as this is an emotive area with an underlying subtext about parental neglect. Equally, children are great subjects for open-ended discursive work, especially in response to images. Students should be discouraged from trying to answer questions (e.g. are children influenced by TV advertising – the answer is probably yes), and encouraged to find out about the range of different responses out there. Some interesting examples of work we have supported students with in this area have been *In what different ways is* The Night Guardian *considered to be educational?* (Note – **not** is it educational or not?); *How do children understand the function of advertising; How do children and parents discuss the suitability of television?; What are children's responses to soap opera representations of family life?*

In each case, we had two objectives in discussing these projects with students. Firstly, we had in every case to move them away from a 'headline' approach to research (they wanted to prove something negative). And secondly, our job was to present them with existing research, help them find a way of doing sensible, small-scale primary research with the people in question (and learn by making mistakes) and then relate the latter to the former. In this way, they were able to respond to a 'gap in the market': very little theory about children and television, until relatively recently, had included children in the debate!

> We need to begin by exploring what children make of the films and television programmes that they themselves identify as upsetting or indeed as 'violent' – which, it should be emphasised, are not necessarily those that adults would identify for them. In a debate that is dominated by adults purporting to speak on children's behalf, children's voices have been almost entirely unheard. (Buckingham, 2000)

learning plan 05.14 Writing Up Research

We are choosing not to devote space here to the 'discrete' study of the effects debate or of media audience as an isolated topic, despite the appearance of such areas as 'stand alone' options on various Media Studies specifications. Such an activity makes no sense without the kinds of case studies described here, and furthermore I have argued that, conversely, no media work on these case studies can begin without some serious attention to contemporary debates over audience behaviour. As always, the best way to get students into these debates is to get them talking to audiences. So for us it goes without saying that any work on censorship or effects is really an audience research project.

Internet regulation

Whilst at the time of writing it is clear that television is surviving the internet revolution, it is only doing so by supporting shifts in viewing contexts – shifts in time (recorded or downloaded content) and in space (viewed on a phone). Perhaps the reason for this is partly related to trust. In 2010, OFCOM reported that only one in three of us trusts internet content, compared to 52% who trust television. This is, of course, rather a broad set of brush strokes – people would probably make a distinction between, say, the BBC website and a blog, just as we might have a different kind of 'trust' in World Cup coverage and *Derren Brown Investigates*. For sure it is, like everything we cover in this chapter, complicated.

 learning plan 05.15 Making Sense of Change

Internet regulation, though, must not be avoided in any student work on media regulation and effects. And it cannot be annexed to the end of a piece of writing – this is what Gauntlett refers to as 'Media Studies 1.0' – where we treat the internet as an exception when really it is very much the rule.

There are a wide range of angles students can take to explore issues around the internet and regulation. We will just choose five questions for you to unpack: How does the global nature of internet media exchange make state regulation of content, commerce and access more problematic? What regulatory machinery is needed to protect children and young people online? How does the internet threaten intellectual property? How do attempts to regulate ownership and power work in relation to online media? and What kinds of identity-capital do the providers of social media such as Facebook hold over its users and should this be regulated? There are countless more, of course.

learning plan 05.16 Identity Theft?

Following up the learning plan on 'identity theft', things may have moved on much further in the gap between writing and publication (always the way with Media Studies; we imagine it must be easier teaching French History in this regard). Responding to a wave of pressure over its use of personal data (which our learning plan deals with) the social network introduced new options in May 2010 for users to more carefully safeguard their privacy – a new 'master control' that lets us decide on the degree of public access we want for particular material; more user-friendly control of the open-source links from Facebook to other sites and less mandatory sharing of information. To some degree, though, all this forces us to confront the central issue of whether there is much point in an extensive social network if there are so many options to limit what's there, and whether media providers should restrict connections in response to the actions of a small minority – cyber-bullies, identity thieves, unethical corporate agents. As the CEO of Facebook puts it:

Although many internet companies have to deal with privacy issues, this is particularly challenging for social networking sites, whose very purpose is the sharing of information. … Millions of users today benefit from making public what was once considered private. Finding the right balance between enabling people to share and express themselves and protecting people's privacy will also pose challenging questions. (Sandbery, 2010: 38)

In the spirit of broadening the reach of 'effects' study as far as possible, a comparison of three academic pieces looking at online digital media is productive. Barrett (2006) looks at *Grand Theft Auto: San Andreas* (see the 'Just Gaming' learning plan (04.11) for another perspective on GTA) through the lens of that classic media concept – representation. Exploring the idea of race and violence being connected to 'neo-liberal fantasies', Barrett argues that the 'ideology of the game' relates directly to current US war discourse. We would have major issues with the idea of a game having a fixed ideology, as the meanings of a game are attributed in the unique playing experience, but that said, Barrett suggests some aspects of the game's environment and narrative reinforce neo-conservative ways of thinking about Afro-American culture that we might view as a negative 'effect':

San Andreas either completely decontextualizes or just outright ignores racist cultural practices that lead to African-Americans being unemployed more than whites, imprisoned more than whites, locked in racial ghettos, and so forth. In ignoring questions of historical racism and injustice, San Andreas suggests that the problems that African Americans experience are due to individual failure. (Barrett, 2006: 114)

This is interesting, whether or not we accept the idea that the game can 'suggest' anything in this way, because the 'effects' of GTA are here defined on ideological lines, rather than in relation to the immersive experience of violence and/or vice. Jarvinen (2004) explores further Gonzola Frasca's concept of simulation and argues that the GTA franchise has been instrumental in increasing the complexity of the system of referents that we would find in any game, thus increasing the immersion of the player, but that, crucially, the frame of reference for *GTA* is irony and parody – a postmodern, intertextual space. Thus for Jarvinen the questions to ask about the game's 'effects' would be as follows:

Does parody as a rhetorical technique reinforce what it parodies? Is parody used in VC as a scapegoat for sexism – does VC, by reintroducing a typical masculine character family from 1980s crime fiction, actually reinforce this type of masculinity? Do the manipulation rules and the causalities implemented through them into the game resist or invite this kind of interpretation? (Jarvinen, 2003: 10)

The point here is that the two approaches are completely different in what they assume (or don't) about where the meanings of a game are exercised and attributed. For Barrett, the game is guilty of a range of negative reinforcements and stereotypes, largely through ignoring history, structure and agency. For Jarvinen, there are only questions to ask and these questions can only be answered by players. Which makes it very hard to analyse videogames in Media Studies lessons, of course, but also very easy to simplify them by thinking about them as fixed 'texts' that we can pin down and assess.

A third article is unrelated to GTA but connected in the sense of being interested in media that is 'in flux'. In a collection of research-informed articles on digital literacy and social learning, Dowdall writes about children producing online digital media. Her argument (which you won't be surprised to read that we support) shows that children can – and often do – make use of the very social media spaces that the 'moral panic' wants to protect them from to create highly literate media material:

> This negative framing can be conceived as a reflection of the reportedly perilous context in which children create digital texts. Equally though, these resources can be regarded as an attempt by policy makers to regain control over children's text production in digital landscapes. There is a risk that this attempt to online text production will actually fail to recognise and celebrate the creative transformative and empowering energies that are being harnessed as children produce their own texts. (Dowdall, 2009: 57).

Further work in this area is provided by the prolific and inspiring Jackie Marsh, a researcher who proves more than anyone that Media teachers need to look further afield for relevant material. When she spoke at the Media Education Association event on moral panics, many of the assembled practitioners were amazed at just how relevant the ideas of someone they had never heard of were to Media Studies. This learning plan will bridge the gap.

 learning plan 05.17 The Jackie Marsh Wiki Meme

So, let's return to the 'mantra': work on audiences is complicated and we need to resist any manifestation of the simplistic model of producer–text–audience effect if we are to bear witness to the complexity of our mediated lives and identities. To this end, the journal *Participations* is essential reading for Media teachers and the learning plan we link to here is a route to it.

 learning plan 05.18 Participations

British film and national identity

To prepare for the range of angles that awarding bodies might opt for in exams, or to give students a choice of focus for coursework, our teaching in this area should cover three perspectives: the British Film industry (changes over time, funding, relationship to America and Europe, dilemmas for producers, audience shifts, government agendas and the relationship of culture to commerce); British films as cultural products (the range of commercially successful and critically acclaimed films on release at the time of the work, with regard to directors, styles and audience responses) and the representation of Britain (in particular, how different films do this in different ways, how this has changed as the notion of being British has changed, and the question of whether British cinema has always suffered, and still does, from a 'burden of representation').

Once again, here is a triangulation, and to focus on one at the expense of another is to skew the topic unnecessarily. And at no point should the intention be to teach students that films are simply 'social documents'. Rather, our work is to facilitate their exploration of the complex interplay between ideas about personal and national identity that are in circulation already and the way our reception of films that deal with these things 'maps' against them. Marking student exams in this area, we have found that the conventional approach tends to be about Social Realism and an unnecessary binary opposition between 'cultural' UK films and a homogenised description of Hollywood. This is problematic for all sorts of reasons, but to mention *Slumdog Millionaire* and *Sideways* as opposed to *Vera Drake* versus *Avatar* illustrates the point. With a film like *This is England*, then, the questions to pose are about critical acclaim in relation to commercial imperatives, and the importance of cultural reflection alongside 'feelgood' depictions.

But these questions cannot be answered without reference to the ways in which films get to be made and seen, in terms of co-funding, production scales, distribution and exhibition. For this reason our suggested starting point is a historical case study on the decline of Film Four alongside some audience research on local cinema demographics. We would do this work before embarking on any textual analysis. Once students are au fait with the BFI categories for defining British films (in which Catetgory A is an entirely British film, funded by UK finance, and staffed by a majority of British personnel; Category B is majority UK funded; C is the more common co-funding scenario and D describes US films with some creative input from the UK), they are not expected to decide that it is a 'bad thing' that, for example, people in the Dudley region get 80% of their film culture from the West Coast of America. What they must come to realise is that sharing a language with Hollywood has been simultaneously a gift and a problem for British film, and your take on this will depend on whether you see film as cultural artefact, commercial product or both. For example, whilst Nick Roddick asserts that '*every memorable achievement to come out of UK cinema since the war has come out of someone's desire to say something, not to sell it*' (1999: 13), Roy Stafford reminds us that '*according to the usual flag-waving of the British press at Oscar time, we should all be excited by 'British' successes such as* American Beauty *(US) and* The Talented Mr Ripley *(US), on the grounds that their respective directors are British or by the 'British' contributions of Michael Caine and Phil Collins to other American movies*'. (2000: 2). Actually, these are part of the same argument, that the media and government define success on the Hollywood model, and films funded by the Film Council and the National Lottery are expected to either compete with blockbusters or settle for low budgets and inadequate marketing. The funding for British cinema is likely to be more restricted than ever in the next few years, due to a combination of the recession and the funnelling of public money into the Olympics, so the commercial imperatives are likely to be even more important.

You need at all times to be very careful not to set up simplistic arguments. Whilst it might at first seem to be 'just plain wrong' that wholly British films have the lowest budgets and are in the minority, it must be said that the examples in this category that do well only make it because American distributors invest in them and many never get seen at all. Anyone making a film in the UK needs to be realistic: America shares our language and we are a tiny audience in comparison. So the temptation to go for the international market will always loom large. The problem is that this approach is untenable as occasional success cannot be sustained on smaller capital resources. Alongside these linguistic, geographical and financial elements, we have the cultural reality of audience expectations. Our students' film culture (alongside TV, games and to a lesser extent music) is increasingly American. Simply telling them this is bad isn't good enough. We have to get into (through reflective work on their part) the reasons for this, and there are links here with Citizenship if you compare the elements of their culture which seem to be more or less American or European.

Whilst under New Labour the Film Council, administrating lottery spend on films, and franchises funded also by this 'idiot tax', created some more visible resources for UK production, the dilemmas faced by the likes of Shane Meadows and Andrea Arnold are described here by Stafford:

> The choices for British producers are: make low budget British films targeted at mainstream British audiences, hoping that the 'peculiarly British' subject matter will attract oversees audiences who will see the films as 'unusual'. A low budget film could cover costs by careful sale of rights in the UK and Europe. Anything earned in the US is then a bonus. Or make low budget films for a 'niche' arthouse audience in the UK and abroad. Or look for partners in Europe and / or America and aim more clearly for an 'international audience'. (Stafford, 2002: 6)

So students should start with the facts – what happened at Film Four was to do with a commercial and cultural mistake. In the 1980s, an editorial-driven approach had led to the production of many groundbreaking films reflecting social issues that, according to their directors, would not be made today. Following the success of the first wave of 'mockney' films in the late 1990s, the company attempted the factory-style approach to commissioning genre/format movies at great pace. When these flopped, the capital was not there to remain solvent (Hollywood players gamble, knowing that one major success will pay for nine losers). On the other hand, lottery funding has led to increased production in other areas, and co-funding, particularly with European companies, keeps Mike Leigh going, with great recent success (*Vera Drake*). The obvious comparative approach (which might be in danger of becoming dated) is to compare a film like *Vera Drake* with *Love Actually* (ensuring textual analysis and consideration of representation of social class and gender is kept in dialogue with knowledge of funding and production). Alternatively, a case study on a range of internationally successful British films can work well, if the focus is on how producers' eyes on the international market can lead to particular representations of London that, to quote a legend, *say nothing to me about my life*. Taking students to different kinds of cinema and focusing on them as an audience group is valuable.

We did some reflective work with my students at Runshaw College, by taking them to Cornerhouse in Manchester to see *My Name is Joe* and researching their responses (McDougall,1999). When students from Halesowen joined their counterparts from all over the country in Bradford for a study day on British film, they were shown clips from *The Land Girls, Sexy Beast, The Crying Game, Secrets and Lies, Brassed Off, East is East, Billy Elliot* and *Notting Hill*. Only the last example prompted a mass expression of disappointment when we moved back from the clip to the presentation slides. What do we do with that reality? The interesting work is to ask students what the reasons are, and work from there.

Dealing with the 'burden of representation (the notion that UK film directors are weighed down by the legacy of 1950s Social Realism, Ealing Comedies and the longevity of Ken Loach), a case study on how recent British films have represented multicultural society in a variety of ways can offer an interesting departure from the Leigh versus Curtis, or Meadows versus Boyle approach. We have, in the past, used *Bend it Like Beckham, East is East, Anita and Me, Bhaji on The Beach, Last Resort, Dirty Pretty Things* and *In this World* to this end. The three 'close study' texts within this range were *Bend it Like Beckham, East is East* (mainly because it overlapped with Film Studies, which some students were also taking) and *In this World*. Here we are setting up a comparison of a nostalgic and partly stereotypical depiction of British Asian life in the 1970s with a contemporary equivalent which has much more of an eye on the international audience, alongside a very different film which, despite being entirely about the nature of British citizenship, is largely set in Asia and Europe. Depending on the time and scale of the work, students can relate these films to the history of 'Social Realism', perhaps focusing on *Saturday Night and Sunday Morning* from the 'Kitchen Sink' period and *Raining Stones* from the Thatcher era.

The important focus is always to ask these questions: who is being represented, by whom, for what purpose and with what range of responses? Albert Finney's portrayal of Arthur Seaton was all about putting new people on the screen within a wider discourse about working-class male ideology (as discussed elsewhere in this book, Arthur understands his alienation, there is no false consciousness to sneer at, and this constructs his heroism, however laden with misogyny his world-view might be). Two of the other films under scrutiny present themselves with this same kind of agenda, combining comedy with realism to depict the existence of 'kinds of people' previously absent from the screen (Asian youth in *East is East*, and a young empowered Asian woman in *Bend it Like Beckham*). But *In this World* stands alone in this study, as Winterbottom provides a partly documentary approach (he went to a refugee camp in Afghanistan and asked two of the residents to be filmed making the journey to London) to set up a more complex and troubling version of this 'representation of the new'.

> We see the characters 'as is' – they are 'ordinary' and 'extraordinary' and we are forced to wonder what we would do in their situation. The drama comes from the situation and the way the characters struggle to respond to it. This is the classic neorealist approach – the opposite of a story 'imposed' on the real world. (Stafford, 2003: 16)

Without due attention to detail, students might well (and they do, on the evidence of exam papers) lump together *In this World* with *Vera Drake* on the one hand, against *Notting Hill* and *Gosford Park* on the other. They shouldn't. Mike Leigh certainly **does** impose a fictional narrative, however authentic his approach might be. Equally, whilst looking like the kind of costume drama Americans love, at the same time *Gosford Park* is as sharp a deconstruction of social class relations as *High Hopes*. Our job here is to give students an understanding of how films relate to cultural identity and nationhood, within an analysis of media texts as sites of conflict between different discourses or world views. Once that is achieved, students can do good work free from lazy categorisation. As always, tasking students with the creation of their own British film, to be shot through with representational devices, is the best way to make this come alive.

There are countless other films that spring to mind if you want to explore the tension between challenging representation and stereotyping – for example, *Billy Elliot*, *Trainspotting* and *The Full Monty* (and there are a plethora of good resources out there for teachers). But once again the more complex and ambiguous texts provide richer analysis. *A Room for Romeo Brass*, *Ratcatcher* and *Wonderland* are essential if only to remind us that British film is incredibly varied in its scope.

The more astute students will take the same approach to the notion of Social Realism as they will to genre – a sceptical scrutiny of the assumptions at work in the circulation of ideas about this kind of film. Comparing a film like *Looking for Eric* to a TV documentary shows us that both texts make claims to realism, and Loach's film certainly establishes a verisimilitude somewhat closer to most of our experiences than, say, *Fantastic Mr Fox*, but the main narrative device employed is melodrama and the kinds of closure and pleasure offered by the later sequences are entirely constructed through neat conventions of plot and story. Real life is far less choreographically staged. Likewise the 'Land of Hope and Glory' resolution and political resonance offered by the ending to *Brassed Off* is tremendously important cinema in our opinion, but one suspects in real life the 'shat upon' residents of Grimley would see their brass band come second or third in the grand final.

Since the first edition of this book, some of the examples above have ceased to be contemporary, so we recommend you keep them in mind for a historical context (and hence we have left them in). However, for a more current exploration of British cinema and identity, we will now discuss some more recent texts – firstly the Richard Curtis collection as a representation of Blair's Britain and then onto Andrea Arnold's *Red Road* and *Fish Tank*, *This is England* as a 'breakthrough' film and *My Name is Eric* as a magic realist, even postmodern fable.

Representation and identity

The way we build up students' grasp of the concept of representation is important. It is far easier to help them with more sophisticated responses to British films and how they represent aspects of identity if we have dealt first with the concept of representation in accessible ways. Here is a suggestion: start with our learning plans that use music to explore representation – Learning Plans 03.06 *Geezers and Birds* and 04.06 *Our House* – with the accompanying discussion of birthday cards and other semiotic artefacts of your/their choice. Then move on to something from outside of their culture; we have used a National Trust magazine and asked students to firstly provide a basic content analysis of ethnicity representation – in this particular edition (Spring 2009) there are no black or Asian people represented at all. Then we discuss the idea that this doesn't mean that the National Trust are racist, but that the 'politics of absence' are very important for us because who is not in the frame will be as revealing as who is. This can be followed up by a classical semiotic 'commutation test' where students think of the most outlandish ways to replace the images of National Trust members (happy families, people on bikes, elderly couples in the countryside, guided tour groups of middle-aged white people in stately homes) with alternative images that would disrupt the representation – obvious examples include a gang of hoodies or a large family of travellers. To be clear the reasons why these would disrupt the representation are very different; we are not suggesting any equivalence! But students, through this activity, get to grips with the idea of a discourse – a coherent belief system that cannot be disrupted with alternatives. The National Trust 'lifestyle' is carefully and consistently coded.

Next we move on to Roland Barthes and his 'Steak and Chips' essay from *Mythologies*:

> Steak is in France a basic element, nationalized even more than socialized. It figures in all the surroundings of elementary life – flat, edged with yellow, like the sole of a shoe, in cheap restaurants; thick and juicy in the bistros which specialize in it, cubic: with the core all moist throughout beneath a light charred crust, in haute cuisine. It is a part of all the rhythms, that of the comfortable bourgeois meal and that of the bachelor's bohemian snack. It is food at once expeditious and dense, it effects the best possible ratio between economy and efficacy, between mythology and its multifarious ways of being consumed. (Barthes, 1994: 70)

At this point students will divide into those that 'get' the idea of mythology and those that say 'it's just food'. So there is some strategic differentiation work to do here. But we are forcing home the idea, repetitively (with different examples), that things represent symbolically – beyond what they 'are in themselves' – but only if we let them, only if we agree on their connotations in a coherent system of discourse and myth. We like to follow this up with questions about the wearing of a tie for a teacher, and what would happen if one day we just agreed to swap the English words for chair and zoo. The answer is precisely nothing so we can discuss the idea that most words are arbitrary, symbolic codes – the exceptions, of course, being onomatopoeia. Next a clip from *Spooks* and a chat about whether if we are being cynical we could say that this is a form of propaganda: the Government, with the BBC, reinforcing through fiction the 'myth' of terrorist threat – not 'myth' because it is a lie, of course (and very importantly), but 'myth' because it is abstracted symbolic consensus, or, as Chomsky would call it, manufactured consent.

Next to Helsby and her 'Representation and Theories' chapter from *Understanding Representation*:

> Media theorists would see the network of messages or discourses emerging from different sources of which the media are one of the most powerful, creating a 'mental set'. Repetition of these messages reinforces the beliefs and makes them appear natural, 'just there' and so confirm the dominant world view, or the 'status quo' for their readers. (Helsby, 2005: 7)

To the extent that we call ourselves 'media theorists' we find this rather an outdated description but following on from 'Steak and Chips' and *Spooks*, it serves to introduce nicely the notion of the 'mental set' which you can return to over and over in your teaching about British film (as we shall see in relation to the Hugh Grant mythology, brilliantly parodied recently in *Outnumbered*).

From Helsby to Leggott's very useful 2008 publication *Contemporary British Cinema* and the chapter on 'Representing Contemporary Britain':

> British Cinema has responded to (and in some cases intervened in) wider debates around sexuality, class, gender and ethnicity, with contemporary representations merely the latest manifestation of a long-running dialogue between a cinema, its people and the world at large. (Leggott, 2008: 83)

This chapter is an excellent example of micro to macro analysis, dealing with a broad range of contemporary films – *This is England, Red Road, Bend it Like Beckham, Kidulthood, Baby Mother* – in relation to class, gender, sexuality and ethnicity. This is important as students need a tight focus on particular elements of 'Britishness' rather than the idea that we are all represented by the films they select.

And now to a direct application and a comparison – firstly a screening of *Red Road* with accompanying attention to Rona Murray's article from *Splice* on 'The New Social Realism':

> *Red Road* represents one experience of our society, which seems to match Foucault's model – that of a society where the ultimate holders of that power are not visible, or even clearly defined, and where the exercisers of regulation are able to direct, unseen, the course of the events. (Murray, 2008: 40)

Murray is applying Foucault's metaphor of the Panopticon to Arnold's film in relation to the omnipresence of CCTV cameras and how the viewer is situated within a set of representations of representations. This is interesting because it is depicting an aspect of contemporary Britain with both social realist and postmodern stylistics.

We can contrast this with a screening of *Love Actually* and the context provided by Tim Adams's article on what he calls 'Curtisland':

> You could find some of New Labour's shiny, happy geography in what we have come to know as Curtisland. *Four Weddings [and a Funeral]* located in a different kind of Britain to any that has been filmed before. It was neither kitchen-sink gritty nor carry-on smutty. It was an apolitical place, full of can-do possibility, obsessed with the educated middle-class, perfectly relaxed about the filthy rich, much more in love with sentiment than ideas, and insatiable in its optimism: it was also in thrall to the idea of happy endings … As the Blair years unfolded, so did Curtisland become more populous. Looked at one way, Britain became the broken-home and teenage pregnancy capital of Europe, looked at another, it was the subject of ever more feel-good, confetti-strewn, loved-up films … Much like Blair's Labour party, the films told audiences across the Atlantic exactly what they wanted to hear about the old country. (Adams, 2009:14)

And then to a more sustained textual analysis – of *Fish Tank*, Andrea Arnold's follow up to *Red Road* which shares the interplay of watching–watcher which draws Murray's Foucaultian interest. The learning plan we link to offers guidance on structure and scaffolding, but suffice to say here that the film will offer a stark contrast to *Curtisland*:

> The thing about the film industry is that it's terribly middle-class, isn't it? All the people who look at it and study it and write about it – are middle-class, so they always see films about the working class as being grim, because the people in the film don't have what they have. I

very much get the feeling that I am seeing a different place. (Arnold, interviewed in Mullen, 2009:17)

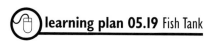

learning plan 05.19 Fish Tank

It is really important, as already said, to minimise the binary opposition students might want to make between social realist and 'fantasy'. *Looking for Eric* works really well for this, as the learning plan shows.

learning plan 05.20 Cantona Socialism

Equally, attention to films which manage to achieve critical acclaim and commercial success despite being skewed more towards social realism than the conventions of 'Curtisland' are valuable. *This is England* is essential for this. Meadows is interesting because his films are as much to do with masculinity and fatherhood (or the absence of) as they are concerned with class politics. And his 'neo-realist' style is, like Andrea Arnold's, a mixture of social realism and more avant-garde and artistic approaches. *This is England* also uses the past to explore the current (like *Life on Mars* and *Ashes to Ashes*) and this might need some careful explaining for students – a contemporary film set in the past but dealing with issues that are relevant in the present is a valid text to study, as opposed to, say, *Saturday Night and Sunday Morning*, which we would only use for historical context.

Film is not isolated so, perhaps for more able students, it is important to make connections across media and indeed across the broader tapestry of life. So when considering the material in the learning plan on the representation of migrants to the UK, we might usefully develop some teaching on the notion of hybrid identity and how the media partly shape this – or help cope with it. Ruddock's (2007) work on diaspora is essential for this discussion, as he brings together existing ethnographic research into the use of media to map hybrid identities on the part of American teenage, Hindu females who engaged with *Friends* and Hindu musicals:

> Both of these media experiences were meaningless on an explicitly textual level; *Friends* was just 'stupid' where Hindu musicals probably means something, but the girls did not know what. But on a cultural level, both resources helped the girls mediate the different worlds they inhabited; *Friends* accessed a high school lingua franca, where musicals contained a sense of Indianness shared with parents. (Ruddock, 2007: 70)

We have written about this in more detail in relation to diaspora and global media elsewhere and the purpose of this book is more about pedagogy than academic 'content'. But our point in this context is important: if students are going to look in detail at how people such as migrants and their children are represented in contemporary media, they need to also consider how those people use a range of media to manage their own cultural hybridity – once again, it's complicated.

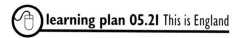

learning plan 05.21 This is England

To summarise, the final learning plan link for this section offers a template for an updated scheme of work on contemporary British film.

🖱 learning plan 05.22 Brit Film Scheme of Work

The learning plan scheme of work supports students looking at the representation of migrants to the UK and so here there are some relevant overlaps with News and Media/Politics (the 2010 election campaign was dominated by 'concern' about immigration). In this context, your students may hold views that are not your own. Your job is to get them reflecting on these views and where they come from in response to films, not to change their minds. Asking these five questions as a context for screening *In this World, Last Resort, Dirty Pretty Things, Somers Town, Ghosts* and *It's a Free World* establishes this reflective approach:

- What is your view of asylum seekers, and where do these ideas come from?
- How are these films British?
- How are asylum seekers represented in different ways?
- How are the films constructed in terms of style and narrative?
- Have these films made you think differently about this issue?

Analysing *East is East* and *Bend it Like Beckham*, the interesting questions are around the blend of realism/authenticity and stereotyping. Some Muslim critics of *East is East* have been concerned about the representation of 'traditional' Muslim values through the patriarch, George. *Bend it Like Beckham*, equally, represents Punjabi identity through the well-worn depiction of a wedding, and Jess is marked out as 'other' to this culture through her desire to play football (the most Western of activities, and traditionally male to boot, if you pardon the pun) on this day. The feelgood narrative alongside the intertextual timing of the release (the World Cup and Beckham's super-celebrity) resulted in this film grossing ten times its production costs. The critical question for students is around the extent to which the film balances its shorthand representations of Punjabi life with a sensitive discourse about gender and identity. Depending on the demographics of your cohort, they may be well placed to answer this question from experience. Could it be argued that the film avoids some of the more important issues about racism in the UK? But perhaps the most interesting angle to explore is the way in which this film seems to stand alone as one which bridges the 'culture or commerce' issue. On the one hand, the film is absolutely a reflection on contemporary British culture and is happy to carry the burden of representation (compared to, say, *Four Weddings and a Funeral*). But on the other, it was produced with America in mind, in the knowledge that soccer in the USA is a game played mostly by young women, the obvious audience for the product. Finally, with an Asian female director, Gurinder Chadha, *Bend It Like Beckham* offers an alternative to the tradition of Social Realist films about British housing estates made by white middle-class men.

This leads us to a final point about British cinema that illustrates the tensions we have felt as Media teachers (McDougall, 2004) between wanting to teach Media from a 'student-first' approach to pedagogy, and the temptation to use the opportunity to show films we believe to be politically important. We have found this difficult in so much as we personally believe that British citizens should encounter films like *Vera Drake, Sweet Sixteen, My Name is Joe* and *London to Brighton* as these films are politically and culturally important within our view of the world. But we can't have it both ways. If we don't think an English teacher should see it as her right to enforce a cultural position on students through suggesting they ought to 'appreciate' Shakespeare (or Toni Morrison for that matter), then we can't abuse our position either.

News and politics

 learning plan 05.23 Seemingly Irrelevant Planned Spontaneity

When Len Masterman wrote *Teaching the Media*, the most compelling case study through which to explore the divergent interests of media and state was the Falklands conflict. Masterman's words in response to that analysis resonate in our climate too:

> The media may not have emerged with much credit as champions of free speech during the Falklands, but it is too cheap and simple a shot to see the media as mere lackeys of the state machine. For one thing, we do need to recognise that the credibility of the media within democratic societies rests upon their ability to demonstrate some independence from government, big business and powerful interest groups. (Masterman, 1985: 191)

Asking students to assess this statement in 2010 would in itself be a tremendously productive activity. After all, the Hutton enquiry and *The X Factor* nature of the 2010 UK general election campaign would seem to suggest a greater degree of media independence than was the case when Thatcher was in power, despite our paranoia about spin. But on the other hand this independence was greatly threatened by the Labour Government, which students might see as having been more concerned with control of news agendas than a democracy ought to allow.

What we must not do is assume our students understand democracy (or its alternatives) fully, or criticise them if they don't. Surely if they are so comfortable in their freedoms that they sometimes lack an awareness of the struggles that have made them so, this is a good thing (presumably the young people with the keenest understanding of freedom are those fighting for it). Either way, they need to gain a working understanding of the notion of a free press before any serious work on testing it out can begin.

 learning plan 05.25 Democracy, Spin, Power

Case studies on the reporting on 9/11, the wars in Afghanistan and Iraq, the Hutton enquiry and the 2010 election campaign can be used within a range of broader areas of study to do with news values, selection, construction and presentation, ideology and news agendas, news audiences, journalism, popular culture and cultural imperialism/ globalisation.

 learning plan 05.25 Matching Tasks

Clearly to cover 9/11, two wars, a major enquiry and an election is a lot to ask of students, but sensible selection of the 'highlights' of each within a scheme of work on media and politics is possible. In this context, it is not so much the reporting of war itself (for example, the role of 'embedded' journalists) that we are concerned with, so much as the reporting of the political decision-making and discourse (in this example the key figures will be Bush and Blair, with Clare Short and Robin Cook in supporting roles). One really 'useful' thing about the coverage of the Iraq war in relation to how papers aligned themselves with politicians was the way in which the *Sun* and the *Mail* took the opposite stance from the *Mirror* whilst the *Express* was more independent. This gets students away from overstating the notion of the tabloid press as a collective, and makes them aware of how very different their news agendas can be, particularly when competing discourses are at work. Patriotism in war time overrides uncertainty about the political justification for the *Sun* (which was pro-Labour after Tony Blair's famous strategic compromise with Murdoch but then switched to Cameron when it sensed he was likely to win, perhaps), whilst the *Daily Mail*'s demonisation of Saddam took it closer to the *Sun* than the *Express* at this time. The *Mirror*'s stance was clear in its unrelenting portrayal of Bush and Blair's departure from the UN as illegal.

Students should start from these obvious differences in tabloid response and then, through research and teaching, map out both historical and current allegiances and agendas to consider questions about whether news agendas are stable or whether they shift in response to single issues (albeit a pretty big one in this case), and if the latter is true, whether these shifts in agenda are related to ethical stances (the editorial agenda) or second-guessing where public opinion will go (a commercial agenda).

Another area we make no apology for mentioning yet again is blogging – Salam Pax (meaning 'peace') offered the world a weblog account of being bombed in Baghdad, stating '*I am not anybody's propaganda ploy – well, except my own.*' Media teachers (including Lewis, 2003, who offers a detailed analysis) seized on this as an example of the kind of war reporting we never got before the technology facilitated it. The blog in question created an opportunity for people to take a 'reality check' on the reports they were given by mainstream media by comparing these 'official' accounts to the internet diary of an ordinary citizen in the battle zone:

> Whatever the true identity of Salam Pax, his blog gave audiences another important perspective on the war – one which was apparently not controlled by the institutions of the Iraqi authorities nor by the US or British military. (Lewis, 2003: 34)

A very useful angle for Media students is that of journalistic sources. Newspaper law and ethics are not areas we often get it into on general Media courses, but in our view better theory arises on vocational courses where students are required to know about legislative and ethical considerations in news reporting than on apparently academic models where a blander 'news values' approach is often taken. To consider a newspaper to be a neat collection of stories arranged around a set of coherent values is to misunderstand the pace and rhythm of news gathering and construction, as journalists will tell you. Any one set of reports on a major issue like the lead-up to the war in Iraq will be the result of a host of interactions with sources and editorial decisions about risk, law and protection. The Hutton enquiry and the death of David Kelly are best understood as narratives about a source and the ability of the Government to seize upon an error in the management of news. To bring this alive, we suggest extracts from Alistair Campbell's diaries where he chronicles these events. But by far the best way of making a case study like this active is to ask a journalist to speak to students about working with sources.

Now to the 2010 general election. In this example, the usual ways of analysing press coverage need adapting as the wars, global recession and various scandals regarding MPs and their expenses had intervened in such a way that there were more ambiguities and departures from traditional agendas than normal. Students (if they are under 40) will have no experience of election campaigns and press coverage that were not 'presidential'. Their expectation is that newspapers will celebrate or demonise party leaders on the day of voting, and this was no exception. But what WAS different was the introduction of live election debates, with huge viewing figures, and the importance of social media to all the campaigns and to the public's reception and exchange of them. And just when Gordon Brown was already struggling to play this new media-sphere game, competing with younger and more 'tweet-savvy' adversaries, he let slip his on-mic insult to a Labour supporter.

At the same time, the emergence of tactical voting as a serious strategy that the electorate could easily understand made the coverage of the lead-up more complex and less patronising in other ways. So we could analyse this duality of cover images, with their straightforward support for the favoured candidate and mocking of the enemy, contrasting with guides to tactical voting on the inner pages, where most newspapers were encouraging readers to make a range of complicated decisions that were anything but presidential – vote Clegg, get Brown, for example (the opposite happened).

What this tells us, again, is that the enemy of the Media student is simplification. We found this in the 'concepts' chapter when considering 'staple' concepts like genre and narrative; we certainly know it about institutions and technologies in times of convergence. And we need to recognise it when teaching our students about news reporting. To say that news agendas and values are fixed and predictable is no longer satisfactory.

The first edition of this book featured a case study on the 2005 election. Not only is that out of date by virtue of there having been another election, and change of government, since, but also it is staggering (at least to people our age) to reflect on the first 'social media election' (allegedly, but we will return to this claim shortly) by considering that in 2005 there was no YouTube, never mind Facebook or Twitter. Obama's prolific and strategic use of social media in his campaign has had the effect of 'normalising' this. But the 2010 election could not have been more different in terms of how the media coverage engaged the voting public. At the same time, though, it was that 'old media' platform, live TV that had the most profound effect, with Nick Clegg winning the popularity contest in the live debates. If anything, social media was most powerful when 'bolted on' to these classic 'watercooler moments':

> It became common practice for viewers to adopt a 'double gazing' stance, sitting in front of the TV with a laptop watching the debates and commenting through social networks.

Thousands of people engaged in live commentary on Twitter – as it became clear Clegg was the winner of the first debate, this was mirrored on the micro-blogging site. (Alani, 2010 – http://www.computerweekly.com/Articles/ 2010/05/14/241237/Did-social-media-change-the-2010-General-Election.htm)

The convergence of 'centre ground' politics in the UK and the attendant narrowing of the media agenda has made it harder to teach this stuff to Media students. We can look back with misty-eyed nostalgia to the days when 'it was the *Sun* wot won it', newspapers had clear and present power and you could compare the *Mail* and the *Mirror* at the time of the miners' strike with a neat content analysis from the Glasgow Media Group. These days, it's not so simple. It isn't abundantly clear whether the *Sun* dropping Gordon Brown made much of a difference, and the live TV debates were clearly (and very carefully) neutral in their construction of the discussion and the rules, which meant the public could ask vetted questions but not respond – no heckling.

Perhaps a more 'clear cut' focus for study is the infamous appearance of BNP leader Nick Griffin on *Question Time* a few months before. Here, a role play for debate activity (see the learning plan link) will work. At the one end of the scale is the ultra-democratic view that the BBC had no choice in a free democratic society; at the other end is the view that the BNP should be censored and in the middle is the view that the BNP have forfeited their right to appear on such platforms by virtue of their own policies being undemocratic. Here is an example of a statement, from a blogger responding on the BBC website, that is very hard to 'pin down':

> I felt embarrassed and ashamed at how Nick Griffin was treated on *Question Time*. I have never, and will never vote for the BNP however that doesn't mean I want a baying audience and panel to harass him to the point he was barely able to finish a sentence. Like it or not, his party has a following and we as members of a democracy have a duty to listen and debate constructively. Where was the debate? I am none the wiser what he thinks as he was never allowed to finish a point. At home I felt embarrassed at how low a level the programme had plumbed. David Dimbleby ducked the hard job of chairing the debate and just joined in with the crowd – he must take responsibility for allowing things to get out of control. The BBC were both courageous and wise to invite him on the programme – having done that they should have ensured he was treated with the basic courtesy that every panel member is entitled to. Will the BBC do the right thing and apologise for how he was allowed to be treated? (http://www.bbc.co.uk/blogs/theeditors/2009/10/nick_griffin_on_question_time.html)

This topic is all about the relationship between politics and media and the extent to which the latter shape the former. Rolling, on-demand news is another determinant, celebrated by some for its way of engaging the public in events – every news item yields activity in the blogosphere – but lamented by others (including the newspaper industry, of course) for creating a state of play referred to by Rosenberg and Feldman as 'No Time to Think':

> By clicking a mouse or punching a master remote device we filter out what we don't wish to see or hear and can select instead from a menu offering only choices that please us or

are familiar. Yes, the echo chamber again, and if only real-life quandries were that easily fixed. They're not. (Rosenberg and Feldman, 2008: 211)

Rosenberg and Feldman are deeply sceptical about the claims of Dan Gillmor, whose 'we the media' thesis (2006) caused so much excitement among the proponents of 'Media 2.0'. Gillmor saw the web as a catalyst for a challenge to this establishment hegemony as ordinary citizens use blogs and other online communication tools to share their own news, which he called 'citizen journalism'. To some extent this is true, but students need to weigh up the debate from an informed perspective. For example, when an innocent member of the public died after being struck by police during the G20 summit protests in London in 2009, yes we got to know about it because a citizen took a photo on their phone. But the means of dissemination were traditional media channels, not purely citizen websites. This is a 'hybrid state' – convergence culture, but the power of the gatekeeper is preserved, even if in a responsive (to the public) mode. Gillmor calls bloggers 'the former audience' and writes about news blogs as a new form of people's journalism. His book details blogs from Iraq which offered an alternative to the Western media's accounts; a range of collaborative Wikispaces, children's news blogs and Persian networkers using the internet for a collective voice in a country where free speech is curtailed, at least, from Gillmor's Western perspective. Here he forecasts the future:

> The spreading of an item of news, or of something much larger, will occur- much more so than today – without any help from mass media as we know it. The people who'll understand this best are probably just being born. In the meantime, even the beginnings of this 'shift' are forcing all of us to adjust our assumptions and behaviour. (Gillmor, 2006: 42–3)

Taking *We the Media* together with Tapscott and Williams's *Wikinomics* (2007), Chris Anderson's *The Long Tail* (2007) and the online interventions of Clay Shirky and Michael Wesch, we get a rounded celebration of the power of contemporary online discourse and social media to challenge the corporate stronghold. But your job is to help students assess the validity of these claims in relation to the longevity of 'Media 1.0'.

Two very helpful champions of balance in all this are David Buckingham and Anthony Lilley. In an extensive research study of 'everyday creativity' and participation, Buckingham (2009) considers Gillmor's claims and suggests that the misleading aspect of 'we the media' is its turning a blind eye to the possibility that the same people who are engaged in politics and action online are engaged in the same things – or would have been – offline. The same can be said of fandom and 'prosumer' activity, of course; the question of whether the internet is the agent or just the repository of such actions is up for grabs. Buckingham does concur, though, with the more balanced idea of what we have called the 'hybrid zeitgeist' – closer to Jenkins' theory of the old and new in tandem:

> In practice, however, the claims made by such advocates of citizen journalism tend to be qualified by a recognition of the continuing need for professional journalism, and indeed for editorial control. Citizen journalism is more frequently seen as a complement to traditional journalism, rather than a replacement for it; it is part of a changed 'media ecosystem' rather than an alternative system in its own right. (Buckingham, 2009: 95)

So students might productively monitor the range of news coverage of a political event and the accompanying public discourse in social media spaces and use that process to 'apply' Buckingham's suggestion, to test it out. With this, consideration of Jenkins's examples (2006) – Photoshop for Democracy; Turd Blossom v. the Obamatar – which share a similar attention to the mixing of professional and citizen journalism in the public sphere:

> This depiction of media change as a zero-sum battle between old powerbrokers and insurgents distracts us from the real changes occurring in our media ecology. Rather than displacing old media, what I call convergence culture is shaped by increased contact and collaboration between established and emerging media institutions, expansion of the number of players producing and circulating media, and the flow of content across multiple platforms and networks. The collaboration between CNN (an icon of old media power) and Youtube (an icon of new media power) might be understood as one such attempt to work through the still unstable and 'untried' relations between these different media systems. (Jenkins, 2006: 274)

Lilley (2010) is a fascinating commentator on the changing media ecosystem since he is a 'media creative' (CEO of Magic Lantern Productions) and a visiting professor at the Centre for Excellence in Media Practice, Bournemouth. Like Buckingham and Jenkins, he pleads for balance, but he adds into the mix the simple idea of scarcity, arguing that in the past the media were trading information, which was scarce and as such a valuable commodity to own, buy and sell. Now what is scarce is our attention. We won't pay for information; Murdoch's dream of constructing a paywall, followed by other media companies desperately trying to charge us for online content, is doomed. How to hold our attention in a world of 'no time to think' is the challenge, he suggests. We like lots of his quotes but here is a good one (and we paraphrase): 'someone visiting a website is just looking for a reason to leave'. Since Lilley's lecture at CEMP, which informs this summary, the live election debates DID hold our attention, and clearly the way that social media responded TO television would strike a chord with the way Buckingham, Lilley and Jenkins see the world.

🖱 **learning plan 05.26** Convergence Culture

We have been dealing so far with the hybridity of old and new media in relation to the coverage of politics at largely the national scale. But the relationship between new media and globalisation is another common topic for students at level 3. As it isn't one of our stated areas of interest in this chapter we will merely introduce the connection here, through looking at the work of McMillin on the alleged need for media academics to depart from a view of the nation state as the 'unit of analysis' and the more cautious scrutiny to power dynamics that we should encourage in our students:

> The opposed political spheres in the case of media globalization refer to the conflict between the unified, utopian, pristine, traditional past and the complex, technology and speed-defined modern present. A critical postcolonial eye scrutinizes the value and purpose of both spheres as ideological constructions and the strategies of recruitment each awards the consuming subject to transform her or him into a loyal and abiding member.

Such a view requires a reading of viewer and consumer choices against the grain of both traditionalism and modernity so that the rights and status awarded to the consumer citizen as subjects constituted within a national frame or transnational one, are continually interrogated for the agency they truly allow. (McMillin, 2007: 190)

McMillin applies the same 'critical eye' to the notion that the centrality of media within society is declining. What is at stake is the bearing witness to difference – in the rhythm of change. Students MUST be reminded that the majority of the world's population is NOT online. At the start of this book we talk about how we might need to think about Media Studies 'after the media'. This refers to the idea of moving away from media texts as a focus of study towards the study of people. But it doesn't mean generalising about everyone as a 'prosumer' or an empowered, transnational digital activist.

These examples will always need to be worked through in the context of a broader debate – in this case usually around the selection and construction of news, news agendas, the free press and democracy or politics and the media. In order to make good sense of the debate and demonstrate such understanding for assessment, students will need to form a narrative out of these 'micro' examples which is seen to test out (without pre-assuming the answers) the hypothesis in the topic. Higher-level work of this kind will also include audience research. At the more simple quantitative level this is to do with who reads what, and at the more complex end students will be evaluating (through the identification of dominant discourses) attitudes towards news and notions of truth and bias.

Fandom

This area has never been treated as a discrete form of Media Studies below higher education and it really should be. The work of Matt Hills has been made more important (or at least its importance more visible) since the 'virtual revolution' and Henry Jenkins has been a key theorist in this area – talking about fan behaviour as a key element in 'convergence culture'. Jon Wardle, more recently, has discussed the interesting connections between fan experiences and learning specifically in relation to how this impacts upon Media pedagogy and so, naturally, this is where our interest lies for this book.

Hills (2010) analyses fandom – most recently with regard to *Doctor Who* – as a form of cultural expression. Whilst many of his examples have nothing to do with 'web 2.0' – Trekkies and Elvis impersonators, for example – it is clear that broadband internet can accelerate fan interpretations and reimaginings of media products – check out the enormous range of 'mash up' and 'sweded' video material on YouTube. From *Harry Potter* fans sharing fan literature online to the many commentary edits of the *Sopranos* finale you can find online, media producers now have to accept that fans can and will upload their own versions of material within hours of the official broadcast. Here we go again – it's complicated:

Though a text like Doctor Who may seem to have obvious 'frontiers' in space and time, such as the bounded minutes of its broadcast, or its sell-through existence as a DVD, in Foucault's terms the text of Who is inevitably caught up in a system of references to other

... texts ... it is a node within a network ... It indicates itself, constructs itself, only on basis of a complex field of discourse. It is thus as a node within a network of discourses that I will think about Doctor Who. (Hills, 2010: 15)

A whole edition of the *Media Magazine* was dedicated to fandom, with Matt Hills contributing. This is an essential resource. Henry Jenkins, who has already received lots of space in this chapter, is another fan-academic worthy of your students' attention and he also turns to web 2.0 as a focus for how the meanings of a cultural product have been negotiated rather than fixed and, importantly, how the media industry is trying to equip itself to cope:

You say 'User Generated Content'. We say 'Fan Culture'. Let's call the whole thing off. The media industry and its consumers alike now operate as if moving towards a more participatory culture, but they have not yet agreed upon the terms of our participation. Even companies that adopt a collaborationist logic have a lot to learn about creating and maintaining a meaningful and reciprocal relationship with their consumers. (Jenkins, 2006: 177)

Wardle (2010) makes a contribution that is of great interest here in its attempt to compare fan experiences with the experiencing of learning. Starting from a recasting of questions asked by Michael Wesch about young people's engagement with unexpected activity as opposed to formally accredited public sphere participation, Wardle asks why fan engagement and formal learning engagement are so disconnected. For Media teachers, this should be pressing:

Perhaps some of the emerging strategies and practices developed by television drama to elicit fan engagement are equally as pertinent to education institutions seeking to improve the learning experience. Being a fan has traditionally had negative connotations with fans being seen as 'cultural dupes, social misfits and mindless consumers' (Jenkins, 1992: 23), as evidenced by popular conceptions of Trekkers and films like The Fan which depicts a baseball fan who becomes increasingly obsessive and insane. Yet since 1988 when Henry Jenkins published Textual Poachers, being a fan has been reconceptualised into something more positive. Drawing on the work of Michel de Certeau, Jenkins describes fans as 'active producers and manipulators of meanings'. This positive conceptualisation of fandom has much in common with notions of deep learning. Since the 1960s learning has moved from traditional behaviourist cognitive approaches to learning theory through to a focus on social practices, whether it be self-directed learning, experiential learning or e-learning.

Wardle goes on to apply the same principles of contemporary theory about 'deep learning' as 'they seem equally true of being a fan as being a learner'. The learning plan we link to here sets this up as a reflective task for your students.

(🖱) learning plan 05.27 Doing a Wardle

Before we move on to the last of our 'topics', another tangent – but an interesting one. Current specifications, to lesser or greater extents, deal with old-fashioned insulations between media formats or sectors. Even the broadest in range, such as the OCR A2 Critical Perspectives in Media unit, which explores themes such as democracy, identity, globalisation and the impact of the internet, still require candidates to write about 'two or more media'. But we know that in the current, hybrid-convergent mediascape, this is only partly appropriate; as we have seen, the relationship between television and the internet was less than clear cut during the 2010 election campaign. Berger (2010) writes about 're-imagined texts', whereby television is 're-imagined' through partial engagement (formal or otherwise) with online fan reception. We have seen how *Doctor Who*, Matt Hills' area of research, is extended to 'hyperdiegisis' across the web and how the fan-critic turned auteur Russell T. Davies can be heralded as an example of 'Media 2.0' par excellence if we think about the way that he embodies the reciprocal relationship of fan and producer, but equally how this is made more visible by the online archive of fan creation. Let's consider the way Berger connects this to *The Wire* through an exploration of 'slash writing':

> The most acclaimed drama of recent years, *The Wire* was set on the mean streets of Baltimore and was concerned with the exploits of a number of street gangs and drug dealers, and their relationship with the police. The series was praised for its epic, novel-like qualities, but what was most significant here is that the most ruthless character, Omar Little, was gay. In *The Wire* Omar's sexuality is not made an issue of – except perhaps when he avenges the murder of his partner, Brandon. Omar is exactly the kind of character a fanfic writer would create (or queer) in the decades previously. Omar was a canonically gay character … Slash became a way of recasting a favorite television program in the slash writer's own terms; a way of expressing their own desires in a fairly safe, but also an increasingly credible arena. For many writers, commenting on and having a conversation with a television character through slash writing is a safer and potentially more fulfilling way of exploring sexual fantasies that with a 'real' person you don't know. For many, slash is a way of bypassing the explicit content in chatrooms and forums, but in a way that still allows for a sexually explicit exploration of desire … Television has appropriated, absorbed and re-purposed many of the properties of the world wide web, but this has been a relationship of mutual exchange, which any appreciation of online fan writing will reveal. Television audiences and 'web users' are the same people, and therefore expect certain things from their media consumption. (Berger, 2010: 180–3)

To repeat the premise, we include fandom and Berger's work on 'slash writing' here in keeping with Gauntlett's condemnation of how Media Studies has annexed the internet to the margins of the subject, when it should be at the centre. We think the same about fandom and this kind of reciprocal producer–fan exchange, so we urge you to support students in considering this activity – plentiful in online evidence – as being at the heart of contemporary media textuality and exchange.

Reality TV

Elsewhere (McDougall, 2009) we summarised the history of this 'genre' and it is helpful to reproduce that here, with some reworking:

In 1965, the BBC broadcast *Man Alive*, a documentary about working-class people and how they live, which at the time seemed groundbreaking but is now derided, especially by Peter Bazalgette (credited with creating the *Big Brother* franchise for Endemol) as patronising in the way it featured middle-class reporters 'investigating' how people live in working-class communities. A decade of similar documentaries about 'ordinary people' followed but things got more interesting in relation to our times when the subjects of *The Family*, broadcast in 1975, became celebrities at the same time as the programme was still being filmed, which was unheard of at the time. So a family wedding happening in the 'real world' but being filmed for the documentary, which was by now a huge success, became a media event and the Wilkins family became a 'normal family' and an Osborne-esque TV family simultaneously.

The late 1970s and 1980s saw further integration of the public into television, with a series of candid camera shows and gameshows making temporary stars out of contestants and unsuspecting participants alike. Camcorders created the opportunity for 'video diaries' to dominate screens in the early 1990s and in 1997 a cluster of 'docusoaps' merged the soap opera, documentary and video diary genres with great effect, most famously with *Airport*. For the first time members of the public featured in such shows realised that they could, like Jeremy Spake, develop a character for themselves which would appeal more generally and lead to contracts for other TV/radio shows and magazine features, something the contestants of *Big Brother* are increasingly in tune to with every series. As the narrator of the BBC series, *How TV Changed Britain*, put it, television was by now 'making ordinary people famous by casting them in their own lives'.

The next step was to develop the 'social experiment' model which we are now so familiar with. This started with *Castaway* in 2000, which unlike *Big Brother* allowed contestants to be aware of the public reaction to them whilst still competing. But this BBC pioneer of the reality TV format was of course eclipsed by *Big Brother* in July 2000, just a few months later. The influence of webcams on the internet distinguished *Big Brother*, which dispensed with a film crew in favour of the 360 degree camera set-up. Whilst the success of *Big Brother* might have been predicted, what was less expected was the convergence of reality TV with the music and performance industries that followed. After the success of the Spice Girls, a conventionally 'manufactured' pop group, *Popstars* was the first programme to make this construction of a band the subject of a television series, with Hearsay emerging as the successful 'product'. Rather than deride this blatant exposure of how music is marketed and created to order, the viewing public demonstrated such an appetite for more that *Popstars* (which next created Girls Aloud) was followed by *Pop Idol, The X Factor* and *Britain's Got Talent*, thus creating a 'lottery culture' in which the idea of dreams coming true is the subject of more and more entertainment, especially on Saturday evenings. The 'postmodern' angle on this becomes more significant when we consider the way that celebrities themselves have 'joined the party'. The contestants on *I'm a Celebrity*… clearly have the intent of resurrecting their profiles by winning the show and we can read this almost as a revenge on celebrity culture. As they eat bugs and expose their flesh for our entertainment, we get to decide whose career is salvaged by this circus act! Ricky Gervais' treatment of this issue in a Boxing Day special edition of *Extras* was a fascinating comedic articulation of the arguments discussed by academic Graeme Turner, which we shall come to.

This relatively new area for Media education tends to be looked at from the perspective of this kind of television's popularity, cultural value and contribution to forms of realism. In each case, the debate will involve taking a stance on whether reality television 'does what it says on the tin'. Is it more 'real' than, say, a soap opera? Is it democratic and interactive, as the likes of Peter Bazalgette will claim, when he compares young people's willingness to interact with the programme by voting and their disinterest in formal politics?

> As the world's academics piled into analysing *Big Brother*'s growing success, one of them had an unusual idea. Stephen Coleman is Professor of e-democracy at Oxford University, studying how new technologies can reinvigorate the democratic process. He isolated and polled two groups – political junkies (PJs) who were mostly older, more conservative and disliked or knew nothing of *Big Brother*, and *Big Brother* fans (BBs) who were younger and broadly not involved in organised politics. 'The most persistent and overwhelming message from the BBs', concluded Coleman, 'concerned authenticity. They regarded politics and politicians as somehow "unreal" and believed that opaque and devious construction of political imagery could be exposed through the lens of transparent media …The discourse of authenticity (who is a "real" person) and transparency (being "seen" to be who one says one is) may well offer significant clues to BBs' reasons for distrusting and disengaging from politics'. Elsewhere this has been called the 'death of deference' – that we no longer automatically believe and respect those in authority over us such as politicians, policemen, teachers and doctors. Whether politicians really have something to learn from the clash between idealism and cynicism is a nice debate. (Bazalgette, 2005: 281–2)

Or is reality TV a crass, dumbed-down betrayal of the public service mission, as Germaine Greer used to say, and judging by her experience on *Celebrity Big Brother*, is unlikely to depart from? And what are the reasons for its popularity? Is this a sign of our lapse into Americanised cultural decline, or is there something more culturally interesting and even empowering about ordinary people dominating the screens? And did the multi-platform, multi-schedule approach generated by *Big Brother* on E4 and the internet signal a paradigm shift?

Since the first edition of this book, 'talent TV' has taken over from 'reality TV' and we are now more interested in the rise and rise of *The X Factor* and all things connected to Simon Cowell. When the 2010 general election campaign was dominated by live TV debates connected to social media, the comparison to a 'talent contest' was much discussed and Simon Cowell was given serious credence for his revelation that he was looking at producing a kind of *X Factor* for politicians. Along with talent TV – a wide range of programmes where contestants compete over several weeks in particular contexts, from *The Apprentice* to *The Choir* – there has been a proliferation of 'reality documentaries' where elite people or celebrities are placed in unfamiliar and threatening situations. *Tower Block of Commons* and *Rich, Famous and Homeless* both put celebrities 'in the mix' with 'real people' for the vicarious pleasure of the viewing public. Michael Portillo even made a programme in which he took on the role of a single parent. Even in these contexts, where the juxtaposition of 'pampered individual' and 'Joe Public' is at the heart of the drama, the same dynamic is at play as in *The X Factor* – the idea that we all want celebrity and emancipation, and that the 'ordinary' public are most interesting when they sense the chance to escape from being so.

Turner (2010) describes this shift as a 'demotic turn' and his view is different to Bazalgette's and Wesch's – and by extension Gauntlett and Jenkins also – in that this is not the same as democratic. The reason for this is that the cult of celebrity creates a new set of expectations of everyday life, so the ordinary person is not featured in the media on 'ordinary' terms:

> No amount of public participation in game shows, reality TV or DIY celebrity websites will alter the fact that, overall, the media industries still remain in control of the symbolic economy, and that they still strive to operate this economy in the service of their own interests. (Turner, 2010: 16)

So for students, the important focus is on this site of 'dissensus'. They might be asked, in an exam, a question about 'we media and democracy' or they might work in a more general frame to look at, or work with, reality TV as a 'genre'. Either way, there is a question to be answered: does this attention to the 'ordinary person' by the media, combined with the idea of 'prosumer' Media 2.0 actually constitute a revolution in the eroding of boundaries between elite and everyday? Or is Turner right when he argues for attention to the more orthodox power dynamics 'behind the scenes':

> I am not interested in arguing that the demotic turn as it is instantiated in reality TV is a categorically 'good' or 'bad' thing. I would argue that it is powerful. Worryingly, though, that power doesn't seem to need to have a principled base. The demotic in reality TV is unruly, unpredictable, or just 'feral' as Annette Hill calls it. As a result, and particularly for the non-western markets I have referred to, the fact that reality TV also operates so effectively as a translator of cultural identities is potentially disturbing. Among the purposes of translation is to enable consumption and thus to enhance the accessibility of the identities such programmes carry. While it may suit the entertainment industry to argue that their projects are harmless enough, programming which sets out to produce cultural identities as a means of marketing a particular product does carry the capacity to generate significant, if unintended, cultural effects. (Turner, 2010: 68)

Helsby, mentioned previously in relation to theories of representation, is the author of a resource pack (2010) on reality TV that we highly recommend. In a section on 'regulation, taste and decency', she discusses the infamous racist attack by the late Jade Goody on Shilpa Shetty during *Celebrity Big Brother* and the subsequent decisions by the programme makers to let the dispute continue live. Taking the same approach as Turner, Helsby asks students to consider the relationship between Susan Boyle's success as 'democratisation', set against a political economy model in which our obsession with celebrity for its own sake (as opposed to as a reward for labour or success) is a symbol of a decline in productivity and culture itself. She sums up this debate thus:

> Celebrity culture is said to be the zeitgeist (spirit) of the times. It is seen as significant because it appears to have established new cultural values not present in previous periods. Depending on your view it can either be a form of democratisation or a symptom of cultural decline. (Helsby, 2010: 64)

Discuss. But with what terms? One piece of advice we consistently give to students is to check their work against the 'every media test'. This just means that if they are working on reality TV, which everybody is familiar with, they should read back their work and calculate the percentage which (assuming their mother is not a Media academic; we know some will be) their mum could have said or written. The learning plan here helps with this.

 learning plan 05.28 The Cowell/Clifford Culture Industry

Having established the debate about the 'effects' of reality TV, next we should 'step up' the theory a little in relation to the idea that any media can be more or less connected to a stable idea of 'reality' in the first place. If we are to judge a text by its proximity to 'the real,' we need to do a little philosophy. Clearly, any text with a claim to be realistic is making a false call. All it can do is attempt to reproduce an audience's dominant sense of reality, to match up as much as possible with phenomenology (point of view). So realistic texts transmit a socially convincing sense of reality. There is a continuum of realism available for us to work with. A piece of German Expressionism is much more overtly 'playing' with the real than, say, *Celebrity Love Island*, but Media students will need to take a challenging position on this. If our notion of the 'most real' is that the presence of the camera is concealed to the subjects, then presumably *Wife Swap* is an anti-realist, even Brechtian intervention, and thus it deserves to be canonised as high culture?

A perennial question on Media teachers' e-forums is the connection between textual analysis and the more sociological work – or 'micro' and 'macro', or even the relationship of the more 'Englishey' work and Cultural Studies. In the case of 'reality documentary', there is a clear need to do both, because the representation of the ordinary person is constructed through the use of a narrative arc, and so an understanding of the effect of such representations in society is dependent on an understanding of the textual design, in this case the narrative structure. This comment from Libby Brooks – in the context of a condemnation of the way that Scottish documentary *The Scheme* exploited (in her view) its protagonists in the name of entertainment – nicely illustrates this micro–macro connection:

> Of course, decent television requires a strong narrative arc – be that the barnpot behaviour of protagonists on *The Scheme*, a local campaign for youth club funding on *Secret Millionaire*, or an MP's queasy stint in a rotting council flat in *Tower Block of Commons*. But what's missing from these primetime parables is the context for social dysfunction, the structural reasons why poverty persists, and any understanding that long-embedded life chances cannot be changed by the momentary intervention of a minor celebrity. The genuine reality is that surviving on benefits is a dull and demeaning affair that makes for rubbish telly. Thus, while documentaries like *The Scheme* may stake their claim for unmediated truth-telling, the demands of the medium mean the visible poor are only ever the antisocial minority, or those randomly selected targets for not entirely benevolent philanthropy. (Brooks, 2010: 38)

A productive approach towards the 'primetime parable', then, will be to ask students to make connections between the narrative arc of a documentary – one group could do this, strategically chosen – and the 'demotic turn' as described by Turner (this is the more complex work). The two groups together can then think about how the documentary might have been different without the arc – in Brooks terms whether this would be 'rubbish telly' – and then theorise the claims, by the likes of Bazalgette, for the democratisation of television. In the end, the contrast will be between ordinary people on screen on the terms of media producers and broadcasters – as objects for our entertainment and scrutiny – and 'we media' created and exchanged on the creators (and users) own terms – an important distinction for students to think about. Of course, when we get into reciprocity between game designers and modders, where the former expect and invite a response from the latter, the hyperdiegetic fan-feedback loop around *Doctor Who* (Hills, 2010) or 'slash writing' (Berger, 2010), it becomes – as ever – more complicated. But, as we said at the end of the big concepts chapter, complicated is good.

Baudrillard's suggestion that reality lives at Disneyland, the postmodern condition described in terms of the knowledge economy and the suggestion in texts like *The Truman Show* and *The Matrix* that one could be perfectly happy in Plato's cave (as long as citizens never get to see the 'truth') all lead us to a pretty complex idea of reality, against which it is increasingly daft to judge how close a TV show can get to it. The 'Lacanian real' is perfect for Media students:

> The signifier has an active function in determining certain effects in which the signifiable appears as submitting to its mark, by becoming through that passion the signified. (Lacan, 1977: 284)

Language (by which we mean the symbolic order, all forms of representation) makes itself present through the lack of its reality. In other words, when we say the word chair, language stands in for the lack of the object itself and after learning the word we are unable to conceive of the 'thing in itself' without reverting to the representation of it in language. It is lost forever, absent in the wake of the presence of its signifier (the word for it). Can Media students usefully consider reality TV within this Lacanian sense of the real? We think they can, if we can find accessible ways in to this kind of stuff, like this application from Belsey:

> Because we have no access to the real, visual realism is not truth, but a way of ordering the visible … [R]ealism positions objects in accordance with a point of view that makes them readily recognisable and, by this means, affirms the identity and confirms the knowledge of the viewing subject. (Belsey, 2005: 131)

So might we adapt Descartes – *I watch, therefore I am*? Either way, we pretty quickly realise that audience reading of texts is where claims to reality stand or fall, as opposed to it depending on production techniques or aesthetic intent. That said, makers of documentary operate with a range of approaches which Sohn-Rethel (2001) describes as expository, observational and interactive modes. The first describes documentary that, usually through voice-over, guides us to a particular point of view or opinion (in the same way as the classic realist text in fiction presents the world view of the hero as a privileged discourse). The observational mode is founded on non-intervention, an unobtrusive approach, often called the 'fly on the wall.' And the interactive mode emphasises the relationship between producer and subject. So students might start by relating a reality TV show to these modes, and they will normally find elements of all three at once. Whilst *Big Brother* was clearly interactive to the extent that the observer speaks to the participants, it claims to be observational (the live webstream was a classic example of a compromised version, as the sound cuts out so frequently for usually corporate reasons). Setting students the simplest of questions will yield the most complex responses: *How real is reality TV?*

To go further into the conventions of realism and documentary (a topic in its own right on some specifications), students can research (and, in balance, be taught about) Bazin and ontology – a big question, but fascinating for students – Soviet documentary and particulary Vertov and 'film truth', Grierson, the British 'Mass Observation Movement' and Free Cinema (which Peter Balzalgette argues, persuasively, was patronising in the extreme compared to today's offerings). In each case, the relationship between the director's voice, the subject/object positions of participants and the degree to which each is interactive are to be assessed. To what extent does reality TV in the twenty-first century draw on these legacies?

To explore debates around the cultural value of reality TV is, in our opinion, mandatory. Once again, critical discourse analysis is the most productive approach. Set up Bazalgette's views (2005), which are clearly framed by his own commercial agenda as a hypothesis to be tested. Students, their peers, families and their teachers can all be interviewed and thrown into the 'statement bank' to be coded and analysed using the knowledge/belief formula previously described. The key questions are these:

- What are the dominant discourses through which reality TV is described?
- How often are people really making statements about their own cultural identity when talking about reality TV?
- What discourses of 'the real' are articulated?
- What descriptions of 'the other' are evident?

This activity is not just intended to discredit the views of those who don't like the genre. Instead, discourse analysis helps students understand how a debate such as this is constructed in relation to wider arguments about popular culture, television and citizenship and people's own sense of cultural distinction. Bourdieu's perspective on the politics of taste is useful:

> Taste classifies, and it classifies the classifier. Social subjects, classified by their classifications, distinguish themselves by the distinctions they make, between the beautiful and the ugly, the distinguished and the vulgar, in which their position in the objective classifications is expressed or betrayed. That is why art and cultural consumption are predisposed, consciously and deliberately or not, to fulfil a social function of legitimating social difference. (Bourdieu, 2002: 7)

This is a fitting way to close a chapter on the big debates about media in society simply because all media learning in this area is as much about the sense people make of media texts (or cultural products), within broader identity politics, as it is about how media products are made in the first place. Interesting Media learning of any kind – at any level – will not only deconstruct texts but start to deconstruct culture itself.

 learning plan 05.29 Pete's Media Blog

Further reading

Adams, T., 2009. 'Welcome to Curtisland', *Observer Film Quarterly*, March.

Alani, F., 2010. 'Did social media change the 2010 election' – blog at http://www.com-puterweekly.com/Articles/2010/05/14/241237/Did-social-media-change-the-2010-General-Election.htm)

Althusser, L., 1971. *Lenin and Philosophy and Other Essays*. London: New Left Books.

Anderson, C., 2006. *The Long Tail*. London: Random House.

Ash, A., 2010, in press. Moving Image, Shifting Positions, Moving Teachers: Adjusting the Focus.

Avery, A., 2010. The Great Media Compromise. Poster presentation, University of Leicester Postgraduate Conference.

Barker, M. and Petley, J., 1997. *Ill Effects: The Media/Violence Debate*. London: Routledge.

Barker, M. and Petley, J. (eds), 2001. *Ill Effects: The Media/Violence Debate*. London: Routledge.

Barrett, P., 2006. 'White thumbs, black bodies: race, violence and neoliberal fantasies in Grand Theft Auto: San Andreas', *Review of Education, Pedagogy and Cultural Studies*, 28: 95-119.

Barthes, R., 1977. *Mythologies*. London: Paladin.

Baudrillard, J., 1998 (ed. Poster, M). *Selected Writings*. Cambridge: Polity.

Bauman, Z., 1998. *Globalisation: The Human Consequences*. London: Polity.

Bazalgette, P., 2005. *Billion Dollar Game: How Three Men Risked It All and Changed the Face of Television*. London: Time Warner.

Belsey, C., 2005. *Culture and the Real*. London: Routledge.

Benyahia, S., 2001. *Teaching Contemporary British Cinema*. London: BFI.

Berger, R., 2010. 'Out and about: slash fic, re-imagined texts, and queer commentaries', in Pullen, C. and Cooper, M. (eds), *LGBT Identity and Online New Media*. London: Routledge: 173–184.

Berger, R. and McDougall, J., 2010. 'Media education research in the twenty first century: touching the void', *Media Education Research Journal*, 1.1.

Bourdieu, P., 2002. *Distinction: A Social Critique of the Judgment of Taste*. London: Routledge.

Branston, G., 1991. 'Audience' in Lusted, D. (ed.), *The Media Studies Book*. London: Routledge.

Brook, S., 2008. 'The heat is on: interview with Julian Linley', *Guardian*, 30.06.08.

Brooks, L., 2010. 'Exotic, extreme, engrossing – tune in to Channel Poverty', *Guardian*, 28.05.10.

Buckingham, D., 2000. *After the Death of Childhood: Growing Up in the Age of Electronic Media*. London: Polity.

Buckingham, D., 2003. *The Making of Citizens: Young People, News & Politics*. London: Routledge.

Buckingham, D. (ed.), 2008. *Youth, Identity and Digital Media*. Cambridge, MA: MIT Press.

Buckingham *et al.*, 2008. *Literature Review for the Bryon Report*. London: DCMS.

Buckingham, D. and Willet, R. (eds), 2009. *Video Cultures: Media Technology and Everyday Creativity*. Basingstoke: Palgrave Macmillan.

Burn, A. and Parker, D., 2003. *Analysing Media Texts*. London: Continuum.

Byron, T., 2008. *Safer Children in a Digital World*. London: DCMS.

Connell, B. (ed.), 2008. *Exploring the Media: Text, Industry, Audience*. Leighton Buzzard: Auteur.

Davey, O., 2005. 'Pleasure and pain: why we need violence in the movies', *Media Magazine*, 12. London: English and Media Centre.

Davies, J. and Merchant, G., 2009. *Web 2.0 for Schools: Learning and Social Participation*. London: Peter Lang.

Dowdall, C., 2009. 'Masters and critics: children as producers of online digital texts', in Carrington, V. and Robinson, M. (eds), *Digital Literacies: Social Learning and Classroom Practices*. London: Sage/UKLA.

Dutton, B., 1997.*The Media*. London: Longman.

Dyer, R., 1994. 'Action!', *Sight and Sound,* October.

Easthope, A. and McGowan, K., 2004. *A Critical and Cultural Theory Reader*. Milton Keynes: Open University Press.

Dyja, E., 2010. *Studying British Cinema: The 1990s*. Leighton-Buzzard: Auteur.

English and Media Centre, 2008. *Doing Ads Study Pack*. London: English and Media Centre.

Fikiciak, M., 2004. 'Hyperidentities: postmodern identity patterns in massive multi-player online role playing games' in Wolf and Perron (eds), *The Videogame Theory Reader*. London: Routledge.

Foucault, M., 1975. *Discipline and Punish: The Birth of the Prison*. London: Penguin.

Freire, P., 1972. *Pedagogy of the Oppressed*. London: Penguin.

Gauntlett, D., 1995. *Moving Experiences: Understanding Televisions Influence's & Effects*. London: John Libbey Media.

Gauntlett, D., 1998. 'Ten things wrong with the "effects model"', in Dickinson, R., Harindranath, R. and Linne, O. (eds), *Approaches to Audiences*. London: Arnold.

Gauntlett, D., 2002. *Media, Gender and Identity: An Introduction*. London: Routledge.

Gauntlett, D., 2007a. *Media Studies 2.0* – at www.theory.org.uk

Gauntlett, D., 2007b. *Creative Explorations: New Approaches to Identities and Audiences*. London: Routledge.

Gauntlett, D., 2009. 'Media Studies 2.0: a response', *Interactions: Studies in Communication and Culture* 1.1: 147–157.

Gee, J. P., 2003. *What Video Games Have to Teach About Language and Literacy*. New York: Palgrave Macmillan.

Geraghty, C., 1991.*Women in Soap Opera*. London: Polity.

Gillmor, D., 2004. *We, The Media*. Cambridge, MA: O'Reilly.

Hall, S., 1981. *Culture, Media, Language*. Centre for Contemporary Cultural Studies Birmingham: Hutchison.

Hartley, J., 2007. *Television Truths*. Oxford: Blackwell.

Helsby, W., 2005. *Understanding Representation*. London: Routledge.

Helsby, W., 2010. *Teaching Reality TV*. Leighton-Buzzard: Auteur.

Higson, A., 1995. *Waving the Flag: Constructing a National Cinema in Britain*. Oxford: Clarendon Press.

Hills, M., 2010. *Triumph of a Time Lord: Regenerating Doctor Who for the Twenty-First Century*. London: I.B. Tauris.

Hodge, R. and Tripp, D., 1996. *Children and Television*. London: Polity.

Hoggart, R., 1967. *The Uses of Literacy*. London: Chatto and Windus.

Jarvinen, A., 2003. 'The elements of simulation in digital games: system, representation and interface in Grand Theft Auto: Vice City' – at www.dichtung-digital.com

Jarvis, P., 2010. *Learning to Be a Person in Society*. London: Routledge.

Jenkins, H., 2006. *Convergence Culture: Where Old and New Media Collide*. New York: New York University Press.

Kendall, A., 2008. 'Playing and resisting: re-thinking young people's reading Cultures', *Literacy*.

Kendall, A., 2008. 'Giving up reading: re-imagining reading with young adult readers', *Journal of Research and Practice in Adult Literacy*, 65 spring/summer: 14–22.

Kermode, M., 2001, *Introduction to C4 Screening of Bad Leiutenant*. London: C4.

Lacan, J., 1977. *The Four Fundamental Concepts of Pyschoanalysis*. London: Hogarth Press.

Lacey, N., 2009. *Image and Representation: Key Concepts in Media Studies*. Basingstoke: Palgrave Macmillan.

Lankshear, C. and Knobel, M., 2006. *New Literacies: Everyday Practices and Classroom Learning*. Maidenhead: Open University Press.

Leggott, J., 2008. *Contemporary British Cinema: From Heritage to Horror*. London: Wallflower.

Lemish, D., 2006. *Children and Television: A Global Perspective*. Oxford: Blackwell.

Lewis, E., 2003.*Teaching TV News*. London: BFI.

Lilley, A., 2010. Inaugural Professorial Lecture at CEMP, Bournemouth University – available at www.cemp.ac.uk

Lister, J., et al., 2009. *New Media: A Critical Introduction*, 2nd edn. London: Routledge.

Livingstone, S., 1999. *Young People, New Media*. London: LSE.

Livingstone, S., 2009. *Children and the Internet*. London: Polity.

Lyotard, J., 1984. *The Postmodern Condition*. Manchester: MUP.

Marsh, J., in press. 'Young children's play in online virtual worlds', *Journal of Early Childhood Research,* 7.3: 1–17.

Martin, R., 2004. *Audiences: A Teacher's Guide.* London: Auteur.

Masterman, L., 1985. *Teaching the Media.* London: Routledge.

McDougall, J., 2004. 'Lads, mags, nuts and *Zoo*', *Media Magazine,* 8. London: English and Media Centre.

McDougall, J., 2004. *Subject Media: The Socio-Cultural Framing of Discourse.* University of Birmingham: http://etheses.bham.ac.uk/556/

McDougall, J., 2008. *AS Media Studies for OCR.* London: Hodder Education.

McDougall, J. and O'Brien, W., 2008. *Studying Videogames.* Leighton-Buzzard: Auteur.

McDougall, J. and Trotman, D., 2010. 'Real audience pedagogy: creative learning and digital space' in Sefton-Green, J. (ed.), *The International Handbook of Creative Learning.* London: Routledge.

McLuhan, M., 1994. *Understanding Media: The Extensions of Man.* London: MIT.

McMillin, D., 2007. *International Media Studies.* Oxford: Blackwell.

Merrin, W., 2005. *Baudrillard and the Media.* Cambridge: Polity.

Merrin, W., 2008. *Media Studies 2.0* – available at http://twopointzeroforum.blogspot.com/

Mullen, L., 2009. 'Estate of mind', *Sight and Sound,* October.

Murray, R., 2008. 'The new Social Realism', *Splice: Studying Contemporary Cinema,* 2.2.

Naughton, J., *Blogging and the Emerging Media Ecosystem,* at http://reutersinstitute.politics.ox.ac.uk/fileadmin/documents/discussion/blogging.pdf

Newman, J., 2004. *Videogames.* London: Routledge.

Newman, J. and Oram, B., 2006. *Teaching Videogames.* London: BFI.

Readman, M., 2009. 'Don't mention the C-word: the rhetorics of creativity in the Roberts report', *Networks 07*: 10-11.

Reid, M., 2002. Teaching Genre. Workshop at BFI Media conference, London.

Rosenberg, H. and Feldman, C., 2008. *No Time to Think: The Menace of Media Speed and the 24 Hour News Cycle.* London: Continuum.

Ruddock, A., 2007. *Investigating Audiences.* London: Sage.

Sandbery, S., 2010. 'Our hiccups on privacy', *Guardian,* 28.5.10.

Sanders, R. and McDougall, J., 2010. *Virtual World Education: Is Experience the New Reality?* Paper presented to the IVERG conference, 2010.

Sardar, Z. and Van Loon, B., 2000. *Introducing Media Studies.* London: Icon.

Stafford, R. (ed), 2000. *Film Reader 2: British Cinema.* Keighley: In the Picture Publications.

Stafford, R., 2001. *Representation: An Introduction.* London: BFI, Keighley: In the Picture Publications.

Stafford, R., 2002. *British Cinema 1990-2002: Teacher's Notes.* Keighley: In the Picture Publications.

Stafford, R., 2003. *Audiences: An Introduction*. London: BFI, Keighley: In the Picture Publications.

Stafford, R., 2003. 'Nowhere to run to? Nowhere to hide for asylum?', *In the Picture 46*. Keighley: In the Picture Publications.

Stafford, R., 2007. 'Global cinema' , *Media Magazine*. London: English and Media Centre.

Stafford, R. and Branston, G., 2006. *The Media Student's Book*, 4th edn. London: Routledge.

Strinati, D., 1995. *An Introduction to Theories of Popular Culture*. London: Routledge.

Tagg, J., 1988. *The Burden of Representation*. Basingstoke: Palgrave Macmillan.

Tapscott, D. and Williams, A., 2006. *Wikinomics: How Mass Collaboration Changes Everything*. London: Atlantic Books.

Thompson, K., 1998. *Moral Panics*. London: Routledge.

Turner, G., 2010. *Ordinary People and the Media: The Demotic Turn*. London: Sage.

Wardle, J., 2010. 'A comparative analysis of learner and fan experience: do contemporary drama structures have the potential to model improvements in the learning experience?' Unpub. PhD thesis, Bristol University.

Waters, M., 1995. *Globalisation*. London: Routledge.

Watson, J. and Hill, A., 2003: *Dictionary of Media and Communication Studies*. London: Arnold.

Willis, P., 1990. *Common Culture*. Buckingham: Open University Press.

Willis, P., Jones, S., Canaan, J. and Hurd, G., 1990. *Common Culture: Symbolic Work at Play in the Everyday Cultures of the Young*. Buckingham: Open University Press.

Winship, J., 1997. *Inside Women's Magazines*. London: Pandora.

Wolf, J. and Perron, B., 2003. *The Video Game Theory Reader*. London: Routledge.

Zizek, S., 2002. 'Welcome to the desert of the real', in Easthope, A. and McGowan, K. (eds) *A Critical and Cultural Theory Reader*. Maidenhead: Open University Press.

6 Supporting Media Coursework

Student-as-expert

This chapter will focus on supporting and extending students with independent audience research and industry case studies, either for critical investigation-style coursework, contextual studies that support practical production, or to develop examples for exam answers on media audiences and institutions. The focus here, as elsewhere in the book, is on moving away from teacher-led transmission of 'facts and figures' and ideological positions – a contentious issue we shall return to later on in this chapter – toward a more bottom-up approach empowering students to 'take charge' of their own independent research.

The best way to help students develop the critically informed and culturally inquisitive attitude to research they need to be successful at this kind of media investigation work, as we have emphasised throughout the book, is to start from what they already understand and to build up from there. It is to reverse pedagogical roles and to position the student, however briefly, as the 'subject-supposed-to-know'. One of the most interesting examples from the culture at large of this 'pedagogy of the inexpert' (Kendall, 2008) comes not from action research in the classroom or from the findings of an academic study, but from a corporate report from the financial heart of the City.

In the summer of 2009, fifteen year-old London student Matthew Robson wrote a short 'research note' discussing briefly the media habits of his friends. What is unusual, however, is that Robson wrote the report not for his teachers, but for the Media & Internet research team at Morgan Stanley where he was on work experience. What is more unusual still, is that his findings made the front page of the *Financial Times*. For a few days in July, the teenager's analysis of the social media habits of his peers, summarised most frequently online and in the press as 'teens don't use Twitter', managed to generate five or six times more feedback than Morgan Stanley's normal reports. Justifying their reasons for publishing the thoughts of an unqualified student, Morgan Stanley Research introduced the report by saying:

> At the vanguard of this digital revolution are teenagers. While their habits will obviously change (especially when they start employment), understanding their mindset seems an excellent way of assessing how the media landscape will evolve. To this end, we asked a 15 year-old summer work intern, Matthew Robson, to describe how he and his friends consume media. Without claiming representation or statistical accuracy, his piece provides one of the clearest and most thought-provoking insights we have seen. So we published it.]
> (Morgan Stanley Research, July 10, 2009)

Leaving aside for a moment the question of why a young person's 'inexpert' attempt at research would get the media traction it did – after all it is hardly a surprise to read that teenagers don't want to pay for online content or prefer Facebook to newspapers – the Morgan Stanley report would seem to offer an example of a young person 'giving voice' to their observations on an unprecedented platform. Of course, many media pundits were critical of Robson's methodology; blogger and social media consultant Suw Charman-Anderson is typical of a number of online commentators who took Morgan Stanley to task for mistaking anecdotal observation for representative data:

> A teenager in a rural setting, or in an inner city estate, or one who feels socially excluded from web culture will have a very different experience than a teen who's well-connected enough to get himself an internship at Morgan Stanley.(Charman-Anderson, 2009)

This neatly draws together the important 'political' issues of cultural capital and the digital divide, complicating what we might otherwise think of as a positive step away from adults surmising the opinions and attitudes of young people. In fact, as David Buckingham and Henry Jenkins and others have argued, as media educators we ought all of us be wary of making assumptions about our students' access to, uses of, and attitudes towards technology and how this affects their relationships with the media in general (see Buckingham, 2010; Jenkins *et al.*, 2006).

As we can all attest from our own classroom experience, it is notoriously difficult to second-guess the scope of our students' background knowledge of the media, the range of their media consumption or their levels of engagement and emotional invest- ment in media forms. For many students, participation in Web 2.0 might consist only of tagging photos of their friends on social networking sites while some of our most socially 'connected' students might not even be on Facebook. Similarly, despite press coverage on how fast games like *GTA IV* and *Call of Duty* 3 sold out on release, many of our students just never play videogames of *any* kind and choose not to do so for a variety of very different reasons. We may also be surprised to learn that some students with iPhones actively choose to 'follow' both N-Dubz *and* Nick Clegg on Twitter, while others might never have been to a live gig despite studying the music industry for their exams. On the other hand, while smart-phones are still fairly uncommon amongst most young people, large CD and DVD collections continue to be a source of pride for many.

We suggest that encouraging all students at the beginning of the course to produce an audit of their media habits in the style of Mathew Robson is an excellent way to problematise many of the commonplace assumptions made about young people's consumption (in the media and by Media teachers!) as well as to introduce students to working with primary research methods early on. Asking your students to keep track of where and when they listen to music or watch television, or how long they spend online and what they are doing while they are there, will help to finesse the claims made both by 'net generation' digital utopians and 'toxic childhood' web denigrators (see Tapscott, 1998; Palmer, 2006).

learning plan 06.01 Media Consumption Audit

The results of such 'classroom ethnography' might surprise and make for interesting discussions, serving also as the basis for more follow-up investigation. For example, fewer students than we might think actually shop online, but discussion of this amongst the class might suggest that this has as much to do with teenagers' limited access to personal cash cards as it does to the easy availability of 'free' downloads. By asking students to consider their own consumption practices we place them, if only momentarily, in the position of the 'expert', as well as 'legitimising' leisure activities as an object for study (the classic, 'So, I can play on my Xbox for home-work?' response).

In addition, by bringing students together to share their findings with each other we are able to compare and contrast the results of their own ad hoc case studies with the trends and tendencies identified by more traditionally 'legitimate' media research. David Buckingham, for example, urges a sceptical attitude of lowered expectations when it comes to thinking about what students are actually doing online, what he calls, 'the *banality* of much new media use':

> Most children's everyday uses of the internet are characterised not by spectacular forms of innovation and creativity, but by relatively mundane forms of information retrieval. What most children are doing on the Internet is visiting fan web sites, downloading music and movies, e-mailing or chatting with friends, and shopping (or at least window shopping). (Buckingham, 2006: 10)

One response to Buckingham's dismissal of much generational internet use would be to address the extent to which Media students conform to or challenge his general picture. Another would be to ask how young people's new media use impacts on the ways they make sense of the bigger media concepts they will encounter on the course; from copyright and ownership, to authorship and creativity. For example, what is the conceptual status of viewer comments posted on YouTube – are these part of the audience reception of the work, an optional extra, or a form of virtual self-realisation ('I woz ere' for the web)?

learning plan 06.02 Generation Game

This learning plan follows on from the Media Consumption Audit and widens the students' fieldwork one step by exploring media history as it has been lived through the changing consumption practices of their parents and grandparents. Again, low-level empirical investigation such as this will help students avoid the tendency to assume things about other people's experiences of domestic media use. As Sonia Livingstone warns, 'audiences are often unpredictable and diverse' (2005: 47), which is why students should be encouraged wherever possible to *do* as much of their own 'real audience ethnography' as they can. Even a cursory exploration of the generational differences between audiences is likely to encourage a varied discussion tapping into media concepts like interactivity, personalisation, globalisation and convergence.

It is a short step from comparing the experience of communal television in the family living room with the 'bedroom culture' of always-on personal media, to being able to discuss more theoretical notions such as the public sphere, social atomisation or Stephen Heppell's idea of 'inbetweenie' time:

If I text someone I don't expect an instant reply, but I do expect a reply soon, or 'nearly now'. Children today spend a lot of time in this new time zone – research suggests it's not as pressured or adversarial as synchronous activity; there is more time for reflection and research before responding. But schools, with their rigid 'time' tables are largely absent from this new learning space. (Heppell, 2008)

That differences in learning styles are more readily accommodated now in lesson planning and institutional frameworks than these generational differences in temporal cognition Heppell identifies is unfortunate, but ultimately unsurprising, considering how difficult it is to get institutions to adopt flexible timetables or cross-curricula delivery. However, there are ways in which we can make more use of these sometimes synchronous, sometimes asynchronous online spaces to enable students to connect more easily with our teaching, and with each other as learners. Virtual Learning Environments (VLEs) allow for students to 'drop in and out' of a course, picking up reading material when desired and uploading assignments when required. The main issue with many excellent VLEs is that learners tend to lack any real sense of ownership of the space. Our own experience has been that it is difficult to get students to reap the benefits of course materials on Moodle as they are reluctant to spend their online time there. Most are 'always' already on their own social networks and have no interest in migrating to our VLEs, or even visiting regularly. Better results, in terms of improved student–teacher communication, advice with work and feedback and sharing of materials and links, has come through co-opting the networks they already inhabit, adopting dedicated course Facebook pages and Twitter feeds that students can 'friend' and 'follow' as part of their existing social media.

learning plan 06.03 Twitter Treasure Hunt

Yet, there are other, self-evident 'generational divides' between students and teachers that continue to impact on the teaching of Subject Media specifically. From technical proficiencies and attitudes towards online privacy to the privileging of textual analysis and ideological critique there is a growing distance between the learning styles of the young people taking media qualifications and the teaching strategies adopted by the teachers delivering them. 'There is an irony about teaching some of the bigger media concepts in a behaviourist model,' argues Jon Wardle, Director of the Centre for Excellence in Media Practice at Bournemouth University, 'trying to teach issues of power and control in a very teacher-directed chalk-and-talk model is invariably self-defeating' (2009: 26).

One example of a more student-centred approach to teaching industry case studies would be to look at streaming versus filesharing. A survey for the UK digital music industry published in 2009 has shown that many 14 to 18 year olds are now streaming music regularly online using services such as YouTube and Spotify(http://www.musically.com/theleadingquestion/downloads/tlq_midem_09_show.pdf). While the number of teenagers who admit to filesharing at least once a month has fallen from 42% in December 2007 to 26% in January 2009, two-thirds of teenagers now describe themselves as regular users of music streaming sites. What is interesting from a comparative study of consumption patterns amongst different audience groups is that 31%

of 14 to 18 year olds listen to streamed music on their computer every day compared with only 18% of music fans overall. Of course the overall picture is more complicated with students exchanging music via Bluetooth and on blogs, as well as through licensed services linked to specific hardware such as Nokia Comes With Music. The likelihood is that you will have regular users of all these facilities in the classroom, so it is really over to them at this point.

 learning plan 06.04 Live Downloading

 learning plan 06.05 Streaming Performance Test

Knowledge prosumers

We live in a world where knowledge is abundant and access is near-ubiquitous. What's scarce is the ability to sift through the information, to extract, synthesise and circulate key ideas to a public that's starving for someone to serve as an intelligent filter … Young people, more adaptive in general and more capable of living with ease in a high-stimulus media environment, make social media seem so easy that people who should really know better will sit still and soak up every word. (Jenna McWilliams, 2009)

Writing on the *Guardian* blog in response to the Morgan Stanley report, McWilliams offers a neat summary of what we consider to be the two horns of the Media 2.0 dilemma. On the one hand, with the super-abundance of information now available through new digital technologies and expanding social media, it is the ability to 'extract, synthesise and circulate' knowledge that becomes scarce, and therefore valuable (see Weinberger, 2007). This has traditionally been the role of the teacher in the 'transmission model' of learning. On the other hand, if it is teenagers who are demonstrably most at ease and seemingly most engaged in these changing technologies and their social transformations, then this leaves teachers seemingly sidelined in a media ecosystem they are increasingly alienated from, both in terms of expertise and experience.

 learning plan 06.06 Students Teach the Lesson

We've begun to see an emerging 'generational divide' in terms of the slow institutional shift from Media as a long-standing adjunct to English delivered by film-buff Literature specialists, to a stand-alone discipline taught by a younger cohort of Media, Film and Communication graduates and ex-industry professionals. However, this would be little more than a change in recruitment practices if it was not matched in a change in teaching and learning, and ultimately a change in the teacher–student relationship. From the 'teacher-as-expert' and a 'chalk-and-talk' model of transmission to the notion of the 'teacher-as-facilitator', we are all familiar with this progressive shift towards a more student-centred pedagogy. This is a move that has only been made more urgent by fast-changing digital media technology and the social and cultural changes that have resulted from it, with all their associated implications for the theoretical underpinnings and conceptual frameworks of our subject. That Media Studies is in a moment of exciting potential transformation is clear; whether we call it Media 2.0, Media 3.0 or Media 1.5 and demand complete rebooting or a less radical upgrade is open for debate. As Jon Wardle observes, 'sometimes student learners are learning from teacher learners who are only just a step ahead' (2009: 26), and this softening of the previously rigid demarcation of pedagogical roles is very exciting.

🖱 learning plan 06.07 Shared Discovery

Keeping in mind Wardle's view, following on from the work of his colleague at CEMP Stephen Heppell, that this 'inbetweenie' pedagogical space is a productive one – if a little anxious making at first – we would suggest that it never hurts to drop the façade of assumed total knowledge and make a feature of the gaps in your own understanding with some shared 'on-the-job' peer learning. On numerous occasions we have had to make impromptu use of free online tutorials or web searches to find out the answer to a student's technical question or institutional query about a media industry. Instead of playing down these instances they can form the basis of mutually beneficial peer-to-peer learning encounters and are just as instructive, in a more ad hoc and improvised way, than having to admit 'I dunno' and waiting for INSET or CPD opportunities to arise.

Such activities as these help to focus our attention on what is a daily reality for many young people: that the internet is now primarily their first port of call when seeking answers (as it is for many older people too, we should add). Our students have grown up in a time when the internet has made it incomparably easy for them to find a 'walkthrough' to 'complete' the latest videogame, take part in discussion threads full of esoteric information on the most convoluted TV dramas, or to view and feedback on hours of instructional 'how-to' video footage describing everything from the best way to apply eyeliner, to how to re-string a ukulele or replace a hard drive. What characterises these learning experiences is not so much that they take place online (in this sense the internet is simply the most expedient medium through which these interactions can now occur) but rather that they exemplify what we might call peer-to-peer knowledge exchanges – models of learning that take place outside traditional pedagogical hierarchies:

> Unlike the classroom, few informal digital activities are organised around a central authority or pedagogue. When asked where their knowledge was from, almost all children refer to the central role played by their friends or siblings. This 'horizontal' knowledge transfer maps well onto informal learning, dependent as it is on casual exchanges and loosely organised activities. … In arenas such as gaming, music or web design children find that knowledge is more likely gained from conversations with someone of their own age than a parent or a teacher. They feel comfortable blurring the line between teacher/student or professional/amateur – exchanging knowledge every day. (Green and Hannon, 2007: 48)

That the kinds of convergent shifts taking place in media production and consumption (see Jenkins, 2006) can be seen as illustrative of potential shifts in media education is an idea that fundamentally underpins the learning strategies in this book and this chapter in particular. Discussing the participatory potential of the web in enabling Japanese youth to form their own amateur media networks, Mizuko Ito ends her article by asking, 'is it possible to legitimate amateur cultural production and exchange as a domain of learning and identity production for young people?' (2006: 64). In line with Ito, and with Green and Hannon and others, we would argue that it is only really by engaging with new learning practices that are 'driven by the motivations of young people's participation in media and peer networks' (Ito, 2006: 65) that media education can hope to be relevant to the new media ecologies that are being shaped by the participation of young people and that are shaping the ways in which these same young people learn.

Though we have used the term 'real audience pedagogy' (McDougall and Trotman, in press) to describe the opportunities for audience interaction and response to media production work offered by digital technologies and the social web, there is a sense in which it also neatly describes this new convergent shift in media education and the reformulating of power relations in the classroom being advocated in the more transgressive moments of this book. In a sense, 'real audience pedagogy' is ultimately a pedagogy based on what *real* audiences are doing – or potentially doing – with *real* media. It is a pedagogy informed by what Gauntlett (2008) identifies as the shift from a 'sit back and be told culture' to a more participatory 'making and doing' culture, from students passively and uncritically soaking up 'Big Media' to actively and critically creating their own 'little media' learning communities.

Take the following interventions by media educators and educationalists that illustrate three ways in which 'Subject Media' is complicating what Mizuko Ito calls 'long-standing distinctions between who are the producers and who are the consumers of knowledge and culture' (Ito, 2006: 65):

> As in open source software, where the underlying code is made available for public knowledge and improvement, the discipline needs to open itself up, allowing our students to see upon what basis it is built and to rewrite and improve it. (Merrin, 2009: 32)

> The best learning almost always occurs in the absence of a teacher, for it is then that learners are free to pursue with great passion the questions that are meaningful and relevant to their own lives. (Wesch, 2008: 5)

> I think that the digital opportunity offers the opportunity for every single student to effectively become a co-creator of the materials that inform the next generation of students. And that's a fantastically attractive proposition.(Lord Puttnam, on New Media Opportunities, OU Podcast)

Just as the way in which cultural practices are circulated and disseminated is fundamentally changing through Web 2.0, each of the authors above is making a call for an equally radical shift in the way knowledge is nurtured and exchanged. It is a call for an opening up of the previously demarcated (and strongly policed) distinctions between pedagogical subject positions of lecturer and student, teacher and pupil, or master and apprentice. As we argue in Chapter 1, it is this challenging of the power relations, ownership and construction of learning itself that is really radical, and yet as Wesch, Merrin, Puttnam and others put forward, it is really nothing more than the idea of giving students authentic opportunities to be co-creators of their own learning. If digital technologies and a participatory culture have enabled young people to create and collaborate together as part of informal learning communities online – making their own web TV channels and videogame mods, for example – why should we not expect them then to 're-mix' or 'mash-up' their formal education? Let us end this section by exploring what this idea of media learners as 'knowledge prosumers' might look like in practice, and consider the example of students 'making and sharing their own pedagogic material' (Gauntlett, 2009a), something we consider constitutes a real shift in dynamics, especially in terms of media research.

MediaMe is a twelve-page, full colour, tabloid-size newspaper written, designed and produced by a class of Level 3 Creative and Media Advanced Diploma students. The paper consists of study materials, articles and activities to help A-Level Media students prepare for their OCR A2 Critical Perspectives exam. The newspaper was produced over a period of four weeks during which the Diploma class researched and planned their materials as well as investigating the preferred learning styles of 16 to 19 year olds by conducting their own 'action research'. They divided themselves into production teams with particular responsibilities and specific roles, including a student-appointed 'quality control' team to oversee the others, and they tested, tweaked and revised their materials by trying them out on students in other classes. The finished paper was visually interesting, engaging, exam specific and up-to-date, consisting of games, investigations and opinion pieces, a comic strip, exam advice and a centre-spread infographic plotting Web 2.0 sites onto a map of the London Underground. The students had workshops on the structure of print publishing and magazine production from an ex-journalist turned Media teacher, they received advice and guidance from a mentor at the excellent English and Media Centre, and their progress was monitored in the class by the subject teacher through regular meetings with the quality control team, who then cascaded information and instructions to the student writers and designers via the various team leaders.

The paper was printed with ink on newsprint – just like a real tabloid newspaper – using an online service provided by Newspaper Club (www.newspaperclub.co.uk) a tool to help people make their own newspapers using online content. The cost of printing was covered by advertising revenue sourced by the students and from sponsorship provided by a local arts venue in Cambridge. The paper was publicised on the OCR Media Studies mailing list and the five-hundred-copy print run sold out in less than a week, going mainly to schools and colleges across the country. A digital version was also made available as a free PDF download on the English and Media Centre website. Feedback from teachers and pupils was generally very positive and their criticisms constructive and fair, while the Diploma students, who were used primarily to working in digital film and animation, enjoyed a new and different challenge, evaluating the project and their efforts positively.

The innovation, in terms of pedagogy, is that technological convergence – in this case of new online communications with conventional, 'old media' print processes – has provided the possibility for 'pedagogical convergence', for students to make and share educational material based on their own learning experiences. Five hundred A-Level

Media students from North London to the North of England are reading the ideas and opinions of Creative and Media Diploma students from East Anglia, and using it as material to help them revise. In addition, A-Level teachers have used *MediaMe* in its digital form as part of their own teaching for the final synoptic exam paper. Some are using the articles as case studies; some are using them as prompts for discussion; some are encouraging students to take issue with the ideas and opinions expressed and to develop their own alternative research and counter arguments. The lines between teacher and student, between peer-to-peer and conventional learning, and between educational resources and amateur production have become truly blurred in an exciting and innovative way.

However, we should not see this single edition revision paper as signalling a complete shift from student-centred to student-*managed* learning, nor should our championing of it be seen as advocating a total 'withering away' of professional pedagogues in favour of education prosumers; just as Henry Jenkins does not see the rise of participatory fandom as spelling the end of professional media production. The success of *MediaMe* was, after all, still heavily dependent on the work of teachers as much as on the active participation, engagement and sense of ownership over the project demonstrated by the students. It was the teachers who first heard about Newspaper Club, who had already established relationships with potential project partners such as the English and Media Centre, who provided technical support and professional insight into industry practices thanks to their own previous career experiences, and who even proofread the final copy for spelling mistakes before it went to print! Ultimately, however, it does demonstrate the productive potential for a more participatory pedagogy, 'as part of the exciting "inbetweenie" space' (Wardle, 2009: 26) being explored together by teachers and students.

On not teaching media politics

There are a number of different starting points for how we enable Media learning about audiences and institutions using this more participatory dynamic. We have seen, for example, how Newspaper Club provides an innovative and experiential opportunity to teach about the press and print publishing as well as for exploring the challenges and affordances of the web for business models and production processes. What better way to study the topic of 'local newspapers' than for students to research, write, publish and promote their own.

In contrast, the 'classic' model of learning about media industries is concerned, in essence, with raising political awareness and addressing questions of power, control, values and beliefs. Despite this book's spirit being to do with learners reflecting on their own pleasures, creative potential and situatedness as consumers more than on transmitting knowledge and ideas for regurgitation, here is an area where it would be very difficult to argue against some 'telling and finding out'. However, as always, the devil is in the detail of the process. So whilst we **do** want students to discover some important truths about who owns what, we need to avoid telling them how to feel about it. A deficit model of Media learning (which is fairly common) is one in which students write heartfelt essays about the evils of Murdoch whilst enjoying Sky and the *Sun*. We might wish students would read the *Guardian*, but that has nothing to do with what we do for a living. So we want to argue that students 'waking up' to the problems of cultural imperialism may well be a very happy outcome of our work with them, but it should never be the objective.

learning plan 06.08 Eye Opener Quiz

If this position seems to be a 'dumbed down' or depoliticised model, let us counter by suggesting that it is never patronising or insulting. We have never thought of Media Studies teaching as a political pursuit or any kind of emancipatory project. Rather, we are fortunate to have had the opportunity to be paid to discuss popular texts and their contexts with young people. One such context is institutional and so it has been part of our vocation to facilitate discussion about, say, the major Hollywood studios and their control of the film industry through vertical integration. But if a student arrives at the conclusion (as they often have) that the reason why people in the Black Country see *Marley and Me* in their droves but either reject or don't know about *Anita and Me* is simply that the consumer experience is more enjoyable within the Hollywood block-buster paradigm, then it doesn't mean we haven't done our job. Indeed, we would be more concerned if a student regurgitated our own views about cinema and cultural identity but didn't really mean it. That would surely be embarrassing.

So let us suggest a set of principles for Media learning about institutions:

1. Students need to know the facts about who owns what and how the patterns of ownership have changed, and these must be accurate and contemporary (which is why it is dangerous to use prepared case study resources).

learning plan 06.09 Collaborative Research

2. Regardless of the kind of course you are teaching, students should find out about employment in media sectors, how it is changing and what it is like to work within legislative frameworks. Again, let us smash open another myth about theory and practice by asking who is better equipped to answer an exam question on broadcasting in the UK in the era of deregulation. Is it the A-Level student being taught this topic for about fifteen hours in total, or the Diploma student producing media products every day for two years within a vocational context that requires them to work within contemporary media law? Even if they have a 'kinaesthetic' learner preference, we would guess they might be more tuned in to the specifics of the regulatory frameworks. So we would always champion an approach that is more vocational, and that ought to include visiting speakers from industry if possible.

learning plan 06.10 Interview a Media Professional

3. Once equipped with the knowledge in a simple 'white hat' sense, students need to know their way around the debates. So the obvious questions are to do with winners and losers. What is at stake in battles for the licence fee? How can the tabloid

press sidestep press complaints and who thinks this matters? Why is there concern over Facebook's privacy settings? How has lobbying by the music industry influenced the Digital Economy Bill? What effect will Rupert Murdoch's 'paywall' have on his revenues and his market share? The broader issues that you can get to from this 'micro' work are to do with globalisation; fragmentation of audience; symbiosis and, again, technology.

learning plan 06.II Self-Supported Study

What we are doing here is trying to give students an informed position so that when they write and talk about these issues they are doing more than we all do when talking in the pub about politics. That, for us, is the acid test – is this the work of a Media student? Is it informed, and accurate? This is far more important than a vague notion of whether it is 'critical' or whether or not we agree with the politics. So, we can establish a triangular relationship between up-to-date facts (who owns what, what has changed, what are the regulations?), the impact of such facts on working practices (the process, ethics and agendas of those making the media) and arguments about the social implications of the changing scene.

We would not necessarily advocate an approach that includes a brief potted history of British politics including New Labour and now, at the time of writing, the Conservative–Lib Dem coalition, so that students understand the terms *left* and *right wing*. Nick Lacey argues that the mainstream political landscape has become so undifferentiated that 'today's 14–19 year olds can be forgiven for not knowing what the difference is between the left and the right' (2008: 21). And yet, if these terms really have so little currency that they need explaining, what is the point of using them? Terms we do need to discuss include 'democracy', 'access', 'impartiality' and 'power', but these are relevant and heartfelt for Media learners. Michael Moore, Mark Thomas, John Harris and others all manage to communicate political ideas without alienating their audiences by deriding their lack of traditional political knowledge and the best Media teaching does the same thing. The worst, on the other hand, sets up the mass media as an object of study along simply demarcated lines of left and right, good and bad, and then condemns its audience for its lack of engagement.

Creative explorations

Borrowing the heading for this section from the title of David Gauntlett's book on new visual methods in the study of media audiences and identities (2007), we would like to advocate, when developing student-focused research units, maintaining a close link between the study of institutions, the analysis of texts and still getting students wherever possible to make things. Students are often most disengaged from research work – whether on audiences, institutions or practitioners – when it is divorced from practical text-work and creative production, and clearly neither deconstruction of meaning or understanding of how ownership impacts on meaning can exist independently of the other, and neither should they be separated off from the possibilities for reflective creativity. Let us take the individual practitioner case study as an example of creative ways to model text-work with contextual study.

In some Diploma specifications this kind of study is presented as an opportunity for students to attend closely to the work of a media practitioner whose example has been an influence in the development of their own creative practice. In others it might be an opportunity to explore how professional practitioners have developed their careers in different industry contexts or for Media Studies, how specific conceptual frameworks and critical methodologies can be applied to the analysis of particular media texts. For example, when studying cinema this kind of investigation is often constructed around the notion of the filmmaker as auteur, and so normally involves the teasing out of key thematic motifs and stylistic traits that can then be traced across the director's oeuvre and interrogating these in the light of institutional pressures, studio influences, synergistic practices and socio-historical factors.

Traditionally such work involves a balance between close textual analysis of particular sequences from individual films and secondary reading from interviews, articles and critical studies in order to contextualise the director's career. This kind of study is often positioned as 'academic' and the teaching of it privileges the developing of study skills, critical research and structured essay writing. While undoubtedly these are crucial factors for producing informative and well-informed investigations, there is still massive scope for introducing greater 'practical' and more creative elements to the exploration of authorial style and institutional influences. To illustrate what we mean, we'd like to offer an example of a more creative and hands-on approach to auteur analysis as pioneered by Barney Oram and his Film Studies team at Long Road Sixth Form College, an example which also serves as a model response to Mizuko Ito's call for the legitimation of amateur cultural production as a fruitful domain of learning. This approach is also at work in Richard Sanders' teaching at Newman University College.

ᐩ **learning plan 06.12** Sweded Remakes

'Sweded' video is an internet 'meme' that mobilises members of the public to reproduce a film sequence or produce a heavily condensed summary of the entire film and share it online, usually via YouTube for playback and comment. The term 'Sweded' has its origins in the Michel Gondry movie, *Be Kind, Rewind* (2008), in which a character who has inadvertently wiped all the VHS tapes in a video rental store first uses the term, insisting his remakes have come from Sweden. A search on YouTube for videos tagged 'sweded' brings up nearly 3,000 hits while many more can be found under 'swede', some of which originated with an online competition on the official *Be Kind, Rewind* website and are archived now on YouTube (http://www.youtube.com/user/bekindrewind). This 'massification' of fan expression has been made possible now that digital cameras and broadband internet have become so widely available that fan video is a ready option for the prosumer enthusiast and media student alike.

How though are we to make sense of the plethora of sweded reworkings of films online? Are they short films? Fan responses? Comedic parodies? Are they actually media texts? From the perspective of the aesthetic criteria and conceptual frameworks we might use when looking at media practical work or analysing 'real' media texts, swedes are another example of 'inbetweenie' cultural phenomena. Swedes are, by definition, at once both playful (they are not supposed to be professional or polished) and a faithful act of respect for a real film. It is therefore impossible to make a qualitative judgement about most sweded content, since the pleasure of this shared material resides in its comedic amateur aesthetics and also its 'for the people' approach to the reproduction and appropriation of expensively made 'real' films. It is, however, by holding in productive tension these two creative attitudes of frivolity and fidelity that swedes provide a very practical and prescient opportunity for students to explore textual deconstruction, generic conventions and their own inventiveness.

Though swedes are parodic versions of films, their producers are, in effect, reproducing the workings of cultural capital. The films chosen for 'sweding' tend to be of a certain 'quality' – they have in many cases been granted the discursive status of 'classics'. The same can be said for the choices of research subject that tend to do well in external assessment, which still seems, unfortunately, to reward practitioner studies of 'dead white males' or genre studies of 'European art cinema', such as the French New Wave or Italian Neorealism. We would argue that behind exam board advice that certain figures or movements repay study thanks to the range of critical material written about them, is a more conventional adherence to the 'canon' and a not-very-hidden-curriculum of received cultural value. While it is obvious that creative and media figures with long-standing and highly praised careers – such as Hockney or Hitchcock – have shelves of books and journal articles written about them and their work, the privileging of print over web-based research that defines most examiners' attitudes is simply an attempt to dissuade students from engaging with more contemporary or provocative figures. Why should it be a surprise that those creative practitioners whose work most excites and inspires our students might tend to be those people, who by virtue of being very much of the moment, of belonging to alternative scenes and movements, or of working in newly emergent cultural forms will by definition not be the subject of academic monographs or special issues of peer-review journals?

learning plan 06.13 Annotated Research List

This is not simply a matter of anti-elitism for it's own sake. While Katie Price/Jordan may well be a perfect case study for discussing post-feminist representations of the female body, 'ladette culture' or the construction of self in reality television, being the author of celebrity autobiographies and ghost-written popular novels still does not make her a particularly relevant choice of creative and media practitioner for extended investigation (as one principal examiner has told us). However, should an institutional preference for academically published critical material preclude, as it would, the study of Shane Meadows as well as Jamie Hewlett or David Shrigley? Despite having made six feature films and seventy-odd short films in his lauded career, Meadows has yet to have a monograph published about him and only in 2010 became, for the first time, the subject of an academic conference. Is this lack of peer-reviewed and academically published criticism really a reason to warn students against exploring his work, especially when a search on findarticles.com finds 414 references to 'Shane Meadows' and Google Books identifies 85 viewable books and magazines that mention the director in some capacity? There is also a vibrant Shane Meadows fan community around www.shanemeadows.co.uk that includes an active forum with a dedicated 'Education and Study' discussion board on which students are invited to post questions. In fact, thanks to Facebook, Myspace and Twitter it is now much easier to get in direct contact with filmmakers, musicians and writers and we have known many students who have even carried out in-depth interviews with the subjects of their case studies via email.

There are two fundamental problems at the heart of much student research work and its relationship with online and offline sources. The first is that most young people are convinced they only need to do online research. As Mark Gellis observed ten years ago, 'students who are already familiar with the Internet often do not want to use anything else':

> It is understandable. The Internet is huge; it is hard for many students to believe that there is information not on the Internet. So why drag yourself down to the Library when you can do all the work in your pyjamas, coffee in hand, and with the newest game playing in another window? (Gellis, 2000: 360)

As of May 2009, the total size of digital content available online has been roughly estimated to be 500 exabytes, or 500 billion gigabytes (and yes, we found this data on Wikipedia). If the internet was huge in 2000, it's got a whole lot bigger since then, and so convincing students of the need to make use of stuff that's not online has got more difficult. Why bother, when there's so much already available in the 'information exaflood'?

And yet, the real problem with the way our students carry out independent research is not just that they use the web to find information rather than traditional offline sources. It's that they use the web *so badly*. 'Google facilitates a quick and simple "method" for completing student assignments', writes Tara Brabazon, but one that encourages students to infer that 'they can answer complex questions about Gramscian hegemony or Stanley Aronowitz's postwork theory as easily as finding their old school friends' (Brabazon, 2008: 18).

Research is now synonymous with search, and for many students this means little more than grazing freely on Google, unquestioningly scanning the highest-ranked items on a results page for easily digestible snippets of answers before ranging off on some other query. Instead Brabazon insists that students must be made to slow down online. 'They must pause, reflect and think', she argues, suggesting a framework of ten questions students should ask of any website:

1. Who authored the information?
2. What expertise does the writer have to comment?
3. What evidence is used?
4. What genre is the document: journalism, academic paper, blog, polemic?
5. Is the site/document/report funded by an institution?
6. What argument is being made?
7. When was the text produced?
8. Why did this information emerge at this point in history?
9. Who is the audience for this information?

10. What is not being discussed and what are the political consequences of that absence? (Brabazon, 2008: 20)

'I know to ask these questions', writes Brabazon, 'I must – overtly and clearly – ensure that students understand why they must probe and frame all information and sources they discover' (20). This is not a call to do away with Google as a viable research tool, or to invalidate Wikipedia as an information source, it is simply a scaffolding framework to improve research skills and the ability to evaluate sources regardless of where they might have been found. As Gellis argues, 'the criteria that distinguish good and bad information are the same whether a source is on-line or traditional. The medium, after all, has nothing to do with the veracity of the information' (Gellis, 2000). As such, Brabazon's questions ought to help students towards the important realisation that 'finding information is not synonymous with understanding information' (Gellis, 2000), and provide a much more constructive response to the problems with internet research than the complaints of colleagues who bemoan the use of Wikipedia by students, or prohibit it entirely (see Jaschik, 2007).

Let us return to our figure of 500 exabytes in the light of Brabazon's ten points. The revision history of the Wikipedia article tells us that the line:

> As of May 2009, the size of the World's total Digital content has been roughly estimated to be 500 billion gigabytes, or 500 exabytes.

was added on 19 May 2009 by a user identified only by their IP address, but who has been regularly editing content on the site since May 2007. What expertise does the author have? Well, according to the articles they have contributed to, this seems mostly to do with popular (and not so popular) music. The source of the data is provided, however, and a citation plus hyperlink refers us to an online version of an article from the *Guardian*, entitled 'Internet data heads for 500bn gigabytes', written by Richard Wray, on 18 May 2009. Wray, the *Guardian's* communications editor, writes that:

> At 487bn gigabytes (GB), if the world's rapidly expanding digital content were printed and bound into books it would form a stack that would stretch from Earth to Pluto 10 times.

While a caption beneath a photo of hi-tech web servers reads:

> A server farm in San Jose, California, holding some of the near-500bn GB of data on the internet.

The anonymous Wikipedia author has clearly paraphrased the key points in Wray's feature, all of which seem to point to the fact that the amount of information stored online is now heading towards the 500 exabyte mark. We also learn from the *Guardian* article that this figure originated in the latest 'Digital Universe' research from technology consultancy IDC and IT firm EMC. A Google search for 'digital universe 2009' locates a press release on the EMC website with more specific statistical data from the IDC report as well as its full title, 'As the Economy Contracts, the Digital Universe Expands'. With that information we were able to find a downloadable PDFof the white paper. At this point, following Brabazon, we could be asking questions about the different audiences for the IDC/EMC report on the one hand and Wray's précis on the other. However, by tracking the research trail in this way, what we actually discover is that the information on Wikipedia is incorrect. By comparing it to the IDC/EMC report we discover that the figure of 487 exabytes actually represents the estimated amount by which total digital content *grew* in 2008. However, before you use that information to berate the anonymous Wikipedia contributor for inaccuracy, it ought to be remembered that they were simply citing a decidedly ambiguous article in a respectable 'old media' print source, the quality of whose information is supposed to be guaranteed by codes of professional practice and robust methodological conventions. It's the reporting that's wrong. As David Gauntlett reminds us, 'Wikipedia is subject to continuous checking and updating – precisely *unlike* anything in print' (2009b: 41). Wikipedia's entry on exabytes can be amended with ease, whereas the 18 May edition of the *Guardian* archived at the British Library Newspaper Collection in Collingwood will always be wrong. Perhaps it's not just Media students, but media professionals that need to learn to be better readers of the web.

 learning plan 06.14 Internet Archaeology

 learning plan 06.15 Word Cloud Essay Plan

 learning plan 06.16 Post-It Presentation

We end this chapter by offering three learning plans that we hope will help make web-based research more about combining critical and creative thinking, and less about ever-increasing access to yet more digital information. The first looks to support web research as a mode of historical enquiry by showing students how to reclaim information about the history of the web before it vanishes 'into the haze of obsolete technology' (Wakefield, 2004: 40). The second uses free online tools to analyse web content visually, while the third offers an alternative to multimedia slideshows and 'infinite canvas' presentations, providing a dynamic, if decidedly 'lo-fi' take on how to best pitch your research findings.

References

Brabazon, T., 2008. 'Transforming learning: building an information scaffold', *Networks,* 3, spring: 16–21.

Buckingham, D., 2006. 'Is there a digital generation?', in Buckingham, D. and Willet, R. (eds), *Digital Generations: Children, Young People and New Media.* New York: Lawrence Erlbaum Associates.

Buckingham, D., 2010. 'Do we really need Media Education 2.0? Teaching Media in the age of participatory culture', in Drotner, K. and Schroder, K. (eds.), *Digital Content Creation: Creativity, Competence, Critique.* New York: Peter Lang.

Charman-Anderson, S., 2009. 'The plural of anecdote is not data'. Retrieved on 31 May 2010 from http://strange.corante.com/2009/07/13/the-plural-of-anecdote-is-not-data

Gauntlett, D., 2007. *Creative Explorations: New Approaches to Identities and Audiences.* London: Routledge.

Gauntlett, D., 2008. 'Participation, creativity and social change' (lecture) – http://www.youtube.com/watch?v=MNqgXbI1_o8 (accessed 31.05.10)

Gauntlett, D., 2009a. 'Media Studies 2.0: a response', *Interactions: Studies in Communication and Culture*, 1.1: 147–157.

Gauntlett, D., 2009b. 'Wikipedia', in Creeber, G. and Martin, R. (eds.), *Digital Culture: Understanding New Media*. Maidenhead: Open University Press.

Gellis, M., 2000. 'Teaching research skills using the internet', in Cole, R. (ed.), *Issues in Web-based Pedagogy: A Critical Primer*. Westport, CT: Greenwood Press.

Green, H. and Hannon, C. (2007) *Their Space: Education for a Digital Generation*. London: Demos.

Heppell, S., 2008. 'Back and forth', *Guardian*, 18 March, http://www.guardian.co.uk/education/2008/mar/18/link.link27 (accessed 31.5.10).

Ito, M., 2006. 'Japanese media mixes and amateur cultural exchange', in Buckingham, D. and Willet, R. (eds), *Digital Generations: Children, Young People and New Media*. New York: Lawrence Erlbaum Associates.

Jaschik, S., 2007, 'A stand against Wikipedia', *Inside Higher Education*, 26 January, http://www.insidehighered.com/news/2007/01/26/wiki

Jenkins, H., 2006. *Convergence Culture: Where Old and New Media Collide*. New York: New York University Press.

Jenkins, H. with Clinton, K., Purushotma, R., Robison, A. J., and Weigel, M., 2006. *Confronting the Challenges of Participatory Culture: Media Education for the 21st Century*. Chicago: MacArthur Foundation.

Lacey, N., 2008, 'Knowing arses from elbows', *In the Picture*, 60. Keighley: In the Picture Publications.

Livingstone, S., 2005. 'Media audiences, interpreters and users', in M. Gillespie (ed.), *Media Audiences*. Maidenhead: Open University Press.

McDougall, J. and Trotman, D., 2010. 'Real audience pedagogy: creative learning and digital space', in Seften-Green, J. (ed.) *The International Handbook of Creative Learning*. London: Routledge.

McWilliams, J., 2009. 'Lost in the new media universe', *Guardian*, 14 July, http://www.guardian.co.uk/commentisfree/cifamerica/2009/jul/14/twitter-teenage-media-habits (accessed 31.5.10).

Merrin, W., 2009. 'Media Studies 2.0: upgrading and open-sourcing the discipline', *Interactions: Studies in Communication and Culture* 1.1: 17–34.

Morgan Stanley Research, 2009. 'How teenagers consume media', http://media.ft.com/cms/c3852b2e-6f9a-11de-bfc5-00144feabdc0.pdf (accessed 31.5.10).

Palmer, S., 2006. *Toxic Childhood: How the Modern World is Damaging our Children and What We Can Do About It*. London: Orion.

Tapscott, D. 1998: *Growing Up Digital: The Rise of the Net Generation*. New York: McGraw Hill.

Wakefield, N., 2004. 'New media, new methodologies: studying the web', in Gauntlett, D. (ed.), *Web Studies: Rewiring Media studies for the Digital Age*. London: Arnold.

Wardle, J., 2009. 'The Creative and Media Diplom – an unfamiliar problem in an unfamiliar context', *PoV*, 1.2, spring: 24–26.

Wardrop-Fruin, N. and N. Montfort, N., 2003. '*The New Media Reader*: a user's manual', in *The New Media Reader*. Cambridge, MA: MIT Press.

Weinberger, D., 2007. *Everything is Miscellaneous: The Power of the New Digital Disorder*. New York: Times Books.

Wesch, M., 2008. 'Anti-teaching: confronting the crisis of significance', *Education Canada*, 48.2: 4–7.

Assessing Media Learning

What is assessment *doing*? How far is it driving pedagogy? As a rule of thumb, the less the better. On the other hand, what is your purpose? To educate, or to drive measurable improvements in 'performance'? Most teachers, sadly, are defined by this question more than any other. One thing is for certain – assessment can never be neutral. It is always subjective, and the more we can involve our students in this subjectivity, the more control we can give them over the judgements made about their work, the more they will achieve. There is no good reason to suspend disbelief in the idea that assessment is some kind of transparent, value free and ideologically pure necessity:

> Assessment is a fundamental element of the curriculum and can take many forms. These different forms of assessment reflect what those designing and delivering the curriculum see as important in terms of student outcomes. They are tied very much to the purposes of the curriculum and beliefs concerning the nature of education. (Bartlett and Burton, 2007: 94)

Given the lack of teacher training specifically in Media, it is hardly a surprise that 'Subject Media' (see McDougall, 2006a) demonstrates a tension between the 'spirit of the subject' – its claims to be an empowering, relevant, even transgressive discipline – and the reality of some of its outdated assessment modes. We see this most explicitly in the confusion expressed by moderators over how they are supposed to be judging practical coursework and in the visible privileging of particular forms of written language within an agreed discourse through which media literacy can be presented and judged. Put bluntly, being able to write a conventional English/Humanities essay is still by far the most important skill a Media student on an 'academic' course can acquire (although this skill is largely already in place, we would argue), whilst vocational learners are still too often harnessed by the need for written evaluations and evidence of planning which distracts from the work itself. Some elements of more recent A-Level specifications have departed from this show me the writing discourse, but generally there is still an anxiety over letting creative work stand alone as evidence of learning, and this is what, in our opinion, still distances Media from Art and Photography and annexes it to English. Ultimately, as Foucault helps us understand, judgement (or subjects' will to be judged) is bound up with claims to legitimate knowledge, and thus power, as Ki's research into GCSE Media students' evaluative work illustrates:

> Although producing a media text is not considered as an end but as a means to understand the ways in which a range of media texts are produced and how they are read and interpreted by different audiences, the institutional requirement for evidence of learning in the form of discursive writing often leaves behind what really happens in the production process. What teachers and examiners alike finally see and eventually look for is nothing but what students (choose to) present or demonstrate for the purpose of assessment in writing. I wondered and I am still wondering to what extent this formalised practice could

tell me about what students have achieved and acquired, or even understood, and how far I could take what they have presented or demonstrated in their evaluative commentaries as evidence of their learning. In this respect, the practice of evaluation is the very place where I can tackle the questions and issues that I have raised but not quite resolved so far. It also serves as a very useful lens through which I can detect the tensions between legitimate knowledge and illegitimate knowledge and the ambiguities in determining power or legitimacy over whose knowledge counts within this subject discipline. (Ki, 2004: 8)

Once again, this book must return to the 'state we're in' and offer suggestions for good practice within these constraints. And since the first edition, we have been pleased to observe a significant move towards making and doing and, crucially, that in some cases the assessment modes are in keeping with this 'spirit'. Take for example recent changes in Media Studies A-Level syllabi encouraging students to detail how they have planned, researched and evaluated their practical coursework by creating podcasts, slideshows or DVD 'extras' such as 'director's commentaries' or video diaries. That such developments are implicated within fraught tensions over 'whose knowledge counts' and what kinds of knowledge are considered legitimate are clear from the *Daily Mail's* snide labelling of the new Media Studies syllabus as 'the iPod A-Level', or by the response of the Queen's English Society to news that media students will earn a fifth of their marks from blogs and podcasts:

> "*This is nonsense. There are very serious issues around literacy – the more pupils are allowed to get away with not writing in proper, well-constructed English, the worse it will be for them.*"
> (*Daily Mail*, 3 January 2008)

Typically, literacy is often cited as the first casualty in the war against traditional assessment methods (see Buckingham, 2003). It is clear that writing an essay with pen and paper in an exam, or on a word processor, or online in a blog all involve different technical practices and perhaps even cognitive processes. The different physical acts of responding to a message by email or by hand-written letter may well encourage the use of different kinds of emotional register, choices of vocabulary, concerns with brevity or length, speed of response and the mindfulness of the act of manipulating a pen. Blogging and podcasting, as encouraged in Media Studies project evaluation, still require appropriateness of language, correct grammar and punctuation and the skills of being able to develop an idea, support an argument with examples and reflect critically on one's own work and the work of others. It is not about lowering standards or reduced expectations in terms of traditional literacy. In fact, for many students with literacy issues (such as dyslexic learners or those for whom English is a second language) podcasting, video diaries or blogs are important strategies for inclusion, enabling learners to express themselves without forever having to struggle to overcome the obstacle of paper and pen.

First a few words about assessing for learning in general. There are a number of reasons for assessment, and being clear about your motives in each case is really helpful for students and teachers. There are differences between assessing with external criteria for moderation, assessing to aid progression, to guide improvement, diagnose problems and offer solutions, test out our teaching, add variety or, crucially, to motivate students (Brown, Race and Smith, 1996: 16). Equally, the power relations in each form of assessment vary, between students assessing themselves for the teacher, students self-assessing on their own, examiners assessing students, students assessing each other, students assessing teachers and, most commonly, teachers assessing students (Meighan and Siraj-Blatchford, 2007: 196). In addition, we should be transparent when telling students what is being assessed, by which we don't mean Bloom's taxonomy (though this might be useful), but we are talking more simply about your intentions, as often students really don't know what it is you are looking for in simple content terms (for example, can you criticise a student for not using examples without checking they know what you mean by an example?). Although this involves educational compromise (reducing everything to assessment), you might do well to accept that today's teenagers have been assessed so intensely since they started school that they have become 'cue-conscious' (Miller and Parlett, 1974). This means they are concerned at all times with what counts and what doesn't, for assessment. The 'cue-deaf', on the other hand, struggle with this crucial aspect of the 'hidden curriculum'.

Meighan and Blatchford (2003) distinguish three ideologies of education within which we can locate assessment modes. The transmission ideology privileges identifiable knowledge that is given and acquired, usually evidenced in written exams. The interpretation ideology assesses the reshaping of knowledge by the learner throughout the course of study, and the autonomous ideology allows assessment to be controlled eventually by the learner. Analysing the kinds of assessment that a) you carry out and b) the awarding body use might well be a sobering experience if you have a sense of your work as liberating.

Trainee teachers are encouraged to use 'Assessment for Learning' (Black et al, 2002) wherever possible, as this form of 'feeding forward' allows greater student autonomy:

> Assessment for learning must involve students, so as to provide them with information about how well they are doing and guide their subsequent efforts. Much of this information will come as feedback from the teacher, but some will be through their direct involvement in assessing their own work. The awareness of learning and ability of learners to direct it for themselves is of increasing importance in the context of encouraging lifelong learning. (Black et al., 2002: 7)

A really good example 'from the patch' is offered on the English and Media Centre's KS3 resource (2004) for Media in English, and it features Stephen Connolly from Haydon School skilfully drawing out a discussion about news manipulation from students' still images. Connolly chooses to let the creative work set up the theoretical discussion, asking questions about how the work seems to reflect news practices.

An example from our own experience of teaching on the first year of the Creative and Media Diploma shows what can happen when students seek to direct the course of their own learning and the implications this can raise for traditional assessment. After being shown Simon Patterson's *The Great Bear* and other variations on the same theme, a class studying TV Drama for the OCR AS Media exam had a go at the TV Genre Tube Map lesson.

learning plan 07.01 TV Genre Tube Map

By the end of the class the learners had managed to create a simplified diagram of two or three of the London Underground lines onto which they had mapped a few conventional TV genres and illustrated in visual terms some typical examples of sub-genres and their hybrids. Despite having achieved the learning objectives set out in the teacher's lesson plan – to demonstrate awareness of genre conventions; to expand intertextual frames of reference – the class were not satisfied with their results and decided instead to 'take over' the next few lessons so as to improve their map. This involved the class arranging themselves into teams with different responsibilities, some doing internet research, some organising and categorising information and others producing drafts of the various tube lines and their interchanges. They worked through ideas collaboratively on large sheets of paper, discussed their progress by drawing on the board collectively adding comments and making changes. They set each other research tasks for homework and even chose to undertake the design of their much expanded map together through the interactive whiteboard, a piece of classroom technology the teacher hadn't even used in the original lesson. Over the course of a week the group showed themselves capable of directing their own learning towards realising a simple goal; to do better than they'd managed initially. Now, it is debatable how much improved the learners' ability to analyse a TV Drama extract for their exam might be after spending a whole week on this activity rather than the single lesson set out in the scheme of work, however there can be no doubting the range and depth of collaborative learning and creative thinking that the learners achieved by – and for – themselves. The 'rub', of course, is that exams still tend to be the 'endgame'. However, Media education, perhaps more than other subjects, allows for this kind of self-directed 'feeding forward'.

Despite some advances (the advent of the Diploma, the increase in coursework in Media A Level), we are surprised that, since the first edition of this book, not much has changed across the board in terms of the obsession we have with production work being explained (generally in words), an incredibly artificial and for most people alienating obligation.

A view that is rarely accepted is that you can't *accidentally* produce a stunning piece of video without theoretical understanding and therefore it is unnecessary and unwieldy to compel a paper trail (or even a blog) to prove it. This position also views with concern the possibility that students can compensate for ropey creative work with good use of language, privileging those with cultural capital over those with genuine creative acumen. A counter argument is that Media Studies is not a form of vocational training and thus practical work can never be 'for its own sake', rather it should be a vehicle for putting theoretical ideas into practice and, as such, there is no substitute for an individual account of how the text is constructed in conceptual terms.

But why? Perhaps Media teachers are much more conservative than we had thought, or are there really some good and sustainable reasons why there should be an element of written work in *all* kinds of media learning? It goes without saying that when we talk about students' learning we are immersed in a set of discourses and framings (Bernstein, 1990), and that pedagogical discourse itself is a form of power. Here are some examples, from a Media Studies web forum, of the 'discourse of restraint' in relation to theory and practice:

> I certainly don't teach media as preparation for entering the media industry – I teach it as a 'consciousness raising' subject that allows students to criticise the effect of the media on society, and develop their understanding of many important issues; something that every young person needs. I believe by making practical coursework 50% it makes A Lever more similar to a 'vocational course' – I believe Media Studies can offer far far more than this very limited expectation.

> If we were simply to accept practical work without any need for academic input or critical thought we would be supporting the production of artifice over content which is the problem with many media products these days.

> I think it should be acceptable for a student to be able to get top marks even if they produce a product which is technically poor, providing that their evaluation is very clear about why they are poor.

Some (doubtless subjective and opinionated) interpretation of these contributions follows.

For a subject which bears such witness to binary opposites in the making of meaning, the 'othering' of vocational learning is surprisingly perennial and, we think, reveals a kind of snobbery that teachers would be reluctant to overtly confess. If education is a form of social ranking, it is never more visible than in the illogical classification of the vocational. The least vocational are the most employable (the media employing Oxbridge historians rather than media production graduates). The truth is that vocational learners become far more 'theoretical' than their 'academic counterparts', simply by spending three or four times as long doing Media. Assumptions made about such courses by teachers with no experience of them amount to a real obstacle to moving the subject forward, a view supported on the e-forum by one teacher:

> Traditional notions of academic and vocational have distinctive class connotations – whether people wish to admit this or not – but new technologies are changing this in respect of what the media artist can do and who has access to what media. It is a process of democratization and it doesn't surprise me that some people would fear this as well.

The concern about contemporary media as art is interesting, and reveals something of the 'evangelical' nature of Media educators, compared to, say, Geography teachers (see McDougall, 2006). This seems to connect with the (old) Masterman thesis – that media products created by students should challenge the orthodoxy, offer something 'better'.

> Practical activity does not, in itself, constitute media education. In particular, the commonly expressed belief that, through practical work, students will automatically require critical abilities and begin to de-mystify the media needs to be challenged. Rather, the link between practical work and analytical activities needs to be consciously forged by the teacher. It must be worked for. It cannot be assumed. (Masterman, 1985: 26)

Do we share this view? Is it part of our mission? Or has digital technology enabled us to move away from either seeing practical work as a vehicle for theoretical reflection and analysis (for example, a news bulletin project to put news values, editorial agendas and manufactured news for target audiences into practice) or vice versa (learning how game designers operate and then having a go yourself). Instead, students are the people charged with 'forging the link' by developing their own theoretical models with which to investigate their own 'technological constructedness'. Working in online domains, downloading and producing music electronically, playing and designing games, experimenting with future gazing for virtual worlds, students are not in the traditional role of theory receipt, but nor are they merely imitating conventions as described to them by teachers. Masterman, writing in the linear age, set up theory as critical and production as uncritical *in itself*, becoming purposeful only when clearly related to analysis. Is this still reasonable? Or is it possible that the notion of equipping students with a critical lens with which they can distinguish mediated representation and discourse from some form of 'reality' is from the past? Aren't videogames (which you read, write and play at the same time) and the proliferation of social media eroding the distinctions between theory and production to the point where the conceptual framework which informs assessment is *"like, so last century"* (or even so *nineteenth* century?!).

On the subject of evaluative writing, and the view that poor work can be good work if the flaws are understood, this view might be more acceptable if it were also the same in exams or written coursework – *'My essay is poor, but here is why'*. This might sound provocative, but it is a serious point. A course which has variety of assessment modes can only stand up to scrutiny if they are taken equally seriously – write a good essay in this part of the course, make a good video here. Again, is that really so off the wall? Do Art teachers reward poor sculpture? This contribution to the e-debate offers an interesting perspective on working in the abstract:

> Don't assume that media production work is 'non-academic'. The understanding of language is abstract, which is why elephants and monkeys don't make shopping lists, because their abstractive powers are limited. If our students want to affect someone with a media artefact, they have to think in abstracts.

So what does all this amount to? Clearly the view that media education is political, that making citizens more media literate and critically powerful is a kind of social goal seems reasonable, and it certainly has great power as an idea. But as access to digital creativity increases more and more, and young people become ever more literate in ways that are 'disconnected' from the parent culture (podcasting and Youtubing for now, but who knows what next?), how does the Media teacher respond? For Steven Goodman, working on a community video programme in New York, this amounts to a 'language gap' – and we can engage with this best through understanding making (video) as 'visual grasping'. Rather than assuming that students must adapt to our (academic) forms of literacy to succeed, isn't it more urgent that we adapt, and transform our ideas about what it means to be critical, or literate? Seeing practice *as* theory allows this. Clearly if you believe that writing down what you know in an academic format is a more robust way of showing that you understand than any other means, or that group work is a lesser form of activity than individual activity, then you will not be persuaded by my argument. But we are asking here for us all to take some time to reflect on such assumptions, to think more seriously about 'the conditions of possibility' (Foucault, 1988) for what students do in the subject. And if we can free our minds to resist the seduction of tradition, who knows?

The remainder of this chapter will suggest a set of strategies for assessing Media work, with each strategy linked to one of the learning plans on the website.

learning plan 07.02 Feed Forward Lesson

The feed forward lesson where you formatively assess students should never be considered a luxury. It is an essential part of the process of preparing students for what, ultimately, it ends up being all about – being marked. Ideally you should have as a matter of department policy, a template for students to identify their own areas for development, which are used by students and staff in negotiation. The key points are a) that this has to be consistently used across a teaching team and always for it to have any purpose, and b) that it is essential, though very difficult, to make students go 'cold turkey' when it comes to marks – i.e., replace marks with comments and key objectives for future work. They will eventually thank you (but it will take a while).

The 'pedagogy of the inexpert' (Kendall, 2008) describes the liberating outcomes of breaking down the boundaries of 'master' and 'apprentice' so we can accept (and even celebrate?) what William Merrin calls the absurdity of being a Media Studies teacher 'when your students know more about media than you do':

> We know the discipline, the texts, ideas and arguments but many of our students surpass us in their knowledge, use and navigation of the contemporary media world: they're at home in it; we're always playing catch-up. (Merrin, 2009: 18)

The fact is, in many cases our students do know more than us and so the contemporary Media teacher simply cannot ever claim to be (and shouldn't want to be) the expert in every learning situation. In keeping with this philosophy, it is really productive to put students in the role of the judge as often as possible – empowering them with the 'law' (as Kafka describes in his parable of the man from the country) in the form of assessment criteria, once translated into their language and then asking them to apply it – to their peers, to themselves, to their teachers. Why not reproduce the conventions of the awarding body standardisation meeting? (If you haven't attended one, you might know someone who has.) This approach will provide novelty (always a good context for learning) and serve to demystify the process by which your students will ultimately pass or fail.

learning plan 07.03 Student Standardisation

Inviting students to peek behind the curtain of rarefied exam meetings and poke around in the mechanics of their own assessment can, by affording an overlap of educational roles, be empowering as well as instructive. Another approach to collapsing traditional master/apprentice rhetorics would be to foster a classroom culture whereby as teachers we encourage our students to assess and feedback to us on *our* practice. This is not a call for popularity contests or a desire to have an idealised image of ourselves as pedagogues reflected back to us by our students, but a drive to learn more about the learners in our classroom, their preferences and particularities. Blurring the distinction between teacher and student roles by drawing on student voice in assessment for learning can, according to a 2004 report by the Specialist Schools Trust and Secondary Heads Association, have a considerable impact on developing a constructive sense of teacher and students as a co-constructed 'community of learners' (SSAT, 2004: 15). Opportunities for students to critically assess their own classroom experiences are rare and, more often than not, course review feedback lessons are cursorily whizzed through in five minutes of end-of-term number circling by students who have already been presented with the same generic questionnaire during identical sessions in their other subjects. Opportunities for students to reflectively engage in the process of giving teachers constructive feedback in ways that are active and creative are rarer still.

While reflective work in an educational context is likely to be in a represented form (e.g. an entry in a learning journal), the potential benefits of using visual methods of representation rather than traditional written approaches are now being explored by researchers. For example, Marilys Guillemin has shown how drawings can be used to explore the ways in which people understand their own experiences of illness. She argues that drawings offer a rich and insightful research method to explore how people make sense of their world, allowing 'participants who are more visual than word oriented the opportunity to express their understanding in a way that best suits them' (Guillemin, 2004).

🖱 learning plan 07.04 Metaphorical Map

One example of drawing as reflective practice we have explored in our classroom practice is asking students to draw metaphorical maps of their experiences on their courses. Students explore the idea of representing the course as a desert island with different aspects of their experiences represented by different locations on the map. Learning activities that students enjoyed or found interesting are represented as positive/inviting locations while less enjoyable elements tend to be represented as geographical features best avoided such as pits, caverns and swamps.

Following on from the work of Richard Sennett, for whom 'making is thinking', David Gauntlett has explored a variety of visual methodologies for critical reflection through creative practice, most noticeably through his work with Lego Serious Play in which respondents use the children's building toy to construct metaphorical models of their own:

> The process of reflection at the start of a task, followed by the physical process of creation (during which further ideas and developments usually emerge), followed by reflection and discussion of what has been made, offers a more complex and multi-layered way of considering a topic. (Gauntlett, 2007: 184)

Creative and Media Diploma teacher Emma Walters has adapted Gauntlett's approach devising her own methodology, *Serious Play Doh*, in which students are encouraged to explore their initial experiences of the new Diplomas by making their own Play-Doh models and then discussing what they have made on video. It is not simply the model or drawing itself that we should be interested in, but the student's interpretation of their own artefact and what this can reveal about aspects of the student experience that might otherwise go unarticulated and ignored.

Reflective drawing is just one way to get students to engage critically (and creatively) with their own learning as part of a summative evaluation of learners' progress by the end of a course. A more formative, ongoing insight into the process by which students develop throughout their Media coursework can be offered by web-blogs such as Blogger, WordPress and e-portfolio solutions such as Moodle. An e-portfolio is an online tool for research, planning and reflection that showcases students' work and forms a record of students' achievements, providing an archive of evidence for assessment and the evaluation of skills. E-portfolios and blogs are an invaluable tool for documenting the process and for reflecting back on the development of understanding, what Media Studies teacher and exam board moderator Gavin Luhrs calls a 'conversation between the students and their progress':

> As a moderator I see lots of blogging going on and it's increasingly well organised and insightful. The value of it for all involved is the way in which it makes transparent the process of coursework – research clearly links to planning which in turn feeds into construction and then the whole thing can be used to evaluate. It's miles better than the research and planning folders of old which were often beautiful and meticulous and completely fabricated. Inevitably blogs result in a fairly descriptive account of the process, but for me that's the beauty of the format – it makes students more conscious of the process with which they are involved. (Luhrs, email)

As well as technological suggestions for the support of research, planning and reflection such as e-portfolios and blogs, we would like to offer three other alternatives to the orthodox timetabled lesson that help prepare students for assessment or that offer a mode for assessment itself: student presentations, tutorials and exam practice workshops. None of these are revelations, we know, but the learning plans we offer might help frame them in more inclusive and engaging ways.

 **learning plan 07.05** Presentations

 **learning plan 07.06** Tutorials

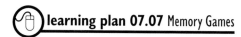 **learning plan 07.07** Memory Games

We hope the advice we give here won't seem too obvious but less experienced teachers in particular often set these things up in ways that are impossible to execute without complaints and inequality. Presentations should never be all on the same topic – if you are bored by the ninth one, imagine how they feel. All they will be thinking about is their own presentation or, once they have presented, who knows? It is only worthwhile if everyone, including you, can take something away from each *different* presentation. Putting them into different roles, organising a 'conference' set up so they can choose which to listen to, asking for peer assessment – these contexts make a difference. Tutorials only work if they are made non-threatening and if students know how they can set the agenda. They simply won't turn up if they are expected to come armed with a mass of work to show you, but they might if you ask them to bring three 'silly questions' about their assignment – everything you wanted to know about the documentary project but were too afraid to ask. And as the learning plan illustrates, you have to rid yourself of the whole 'Educating Rita' delusion! Finally, it is sadly the case that your students, on most courses, need a good memory. This absurd tradition of assessment still prevails and we really ought to be ashamed of it, but we are where we are. Students need to remember stuff and then recall it under great pressure as most courses still feature exams. So exam practice is crucial but probably the most educationally bankrupt, and we would argue morally loathsome practice you will engage in – 'teaching for the test'. But your students deserve the best chance at success and education remains the last legal form of divisive social ranking so we need to help them and we can do this by playing games that support memory training and providing collaborative contexts for so doing – the learning plans we offer include 1 minute, 3 minute and 5 minute essay games, 'consequences', 'Millionaire' and for 80s retro-heads, even *Blankety Blank*.

Finally, a set of 'tips' for preparing students for external assessment which have tended to go down very well at INSET meetings. We must make it clear that these are **not** official recommendations from any exam board, and we are not giving away any big secrets here. That said, here are a dozen suggestions from experience:

1. Accept that assessment objectives are vital. Make them explicit and memorable for students, translate them into their own language and return to them constantly.

2. Translate terms like *limited, minimal, competent, proficient, sophisticated* and *personal engagement* into what they really mean and display them on the wall. The hardest one is *creativity* – as Mark Readman's fascinating work (Readman, 2009) shows us – so good luck with translating that one, but you need to try!

3. Accept that writing skills are paramount (sadly), and teach them.

4. Play safe with theory – train students to use simple ideas, on their own terms, well. Although some examiners are impressed by inaccurate name dropping, they are not supposed to be! Only use 'big name theorists' when you are in control of the material.

5. Integrate as much as you can. Realise that specifications do not often mitigate against overlap. In fact since the first edition of this book there is less evidence of such veneers of ethical constraint, but either way convergence ought to be a theme in your course design.

6. Teach the context of research and provide resources. Make sure students each have a different specific angle, but you can teach the broader topic, even if the 'spirit' of the specification says otherwise or you feel awkward about the 'learned response'.

7. Understand the power of 'spin' in writing up research, if the examiner has not been on the journey. One person's 'chat with friends' is another's focus group. Adopting the discourse of research is half of the battle.

8. Unlike other subjects, finding information the night before the exam is really useful for Media. So don't tell students *'if you don't know it now, you never will'*. An opportunistic bit of time online in the hours immediately before the exam may yield the most topical, contemporary example imaginable (about, say, a new technology, an institutional merger or a piece of breaking news).

9. Moderators are not looking to downgrade students' work. It is more work and bad PR. They work within a 'tolerance', so give the highest marks you possibly can within a mark band.

10. Media awareness is not innate, it can be taught, and it is 50% of the job description of a good Media student.

11. Understand how the awarding process works. Panels, accounting to Ofqual, make horrible assumptions: if more FE colleges are taking the exam, we would expect lower achievement, if more independent schools the opposite. It's not too far away from *Lark Rise to Candleford* in the 'awarding meeting'. Then they try to 'norm reference' the outcomes to avoid too much difference compared to the last year (and too much achievement, with the media in mind). This means a student could take the same exam and perform equally well two years running and get different grades (same goes for coursework). Essentially the correct analogy is a race: where you finish depends on the ability of the other runners, not just your own pace. With this in mind, if you are working with students who are not the beneficiaries of the unequal distribution of cultural capital, you are doing them down if you don't play the system. So make strategic decisions about when to enter particular units.

12. Become an examiner, and you get to attend the standardisation meeting for the exam or coursework unit. This is more useful than this book or a hundred INSET meetings if you want an accurate sense of the board's expectations, and to meet the people who, ultimately, decide your students' fates! You will be comforted and concerned in equal measure. When you return, you can explain to students how the mark scheme only has so much of a function, compared to the importance of presenting to the examiner a sense of their 'ideal student'.

> Assessment, far more than religion, has become the opiate of the people. (Patricia Broadfoot, quoted in Meighan and Harber (eds), 2007: 194)

Anyone with the slightest passion for learning will agree that assessment is a problem and that consecutive policy-makers in the UK have accelerated the Foucaultian nightmare of panoptical assessment to the point where the world of education is exhausted and beginning to fight back (as the teachers' boycott of SATs in 2010 testifies). But this book aims to help you in the classroom and your students will desire your judgement and that of the 'Law' in the guise of the 'absent but present' gaze of the awarding body. The best you can do is maximise the range of contexts for assessment, demystify your criteria, involve learners in the process and ensure fair play.

In the end it's about finding ways of assessing student learning that can do two things. Firstly, we need to produce 'tasks' that allow students to show their theoretical learning in a range of contexts – far beyond the A4 page. For example, in the learning plan that we link to here you will find a Charlie Brooker parody and a song, both of which are responses to a task about web 2.0 that could easily have been an essay. Secondly, we need to make assessment dialogic and formative and in the learning plan we use the work of Dixon (2010) on audio feedback as just one example.

learning plan 07.08 Doing a Dixon

(A section of this chapter has been redrafted from its original publication in the *Media Education Journal*).

References and further reading

Bartlett, S and Burton, D., 2007. Introduction to Education Studies. London: Sage.

Bernstein, B., 1990. *The Structuring of Pedagogic Discourse*. London: Routledge.

Black, P., Harrison, C., Lee, H., Marshall, B. and William, D., 2002. *Working Inside the Black Box: Assessment for Learning in the Classroom*. London: Kings College Publications.

Brown, S., Race, P. and Smith, B., 1996. *500 Tips on Assessment*. London: Kogan Page.

Buckingham, D., 2003. *Media Education*. London: Polity.

Buckingham, D., 2007 *Beyond Technology*. Cambridge: Polity Press.

Foucault, M., 1988. *Technologies of the Self: A Seminar with Michel Foucault*. Amherst: University of Massachusetts Press.

Gauntlett, D., 2007. *Creative Explorations*. London: Routledge.

Guillemin, M., 2004, 'Understanding illness: using drawings as a research method', *Qualitative Health Research* 14: 259–271.

Kendall, A., 2008. 'Giving up reading: re-imagining reading with young adult readers', *Journal of Research and Practice in Adult Literacy*, 65, spring/summer: 14–22.

Ki, S., 2004. *The Evaluation of Practical Production as the Process of Legitimation in GCSE Media Studies*. Unpub. PhD thesis, Institute of Education, London.

McDougall, J., 2004. 'Judging Media learning', *In the Picture* 50. Keighley: In the Picture Publications.

McDougall, J., 2006a. 'Is it really so strange?', *Media Education Journal*.

McDougall, J., 2006b. 'Media education and the limits of assessment', *Media International Australia,* 120: 106–116.

Meighan, R. and Harber, C., 2007. *A Sociology of Educating*. London: Continuum.

Merrin, W., 2009. 'Media Studies 2.0: upgrading and open-sourcing the discipline', *Interactions: Studies in Communication & Culture*, 1.1: 17–34.

Miller, C. M. L. and Parlett, M., 1974. *Up to the Mark*. London: Society for Research into Higher Education.

Readman, M., 2009. 'Don't mention the C-word: the rhetorics of creativity in the Roberts report', *Networks 07*: 10–11.

Sefton-Green, J. and Sinker, R. (eds), 2000. *Evaluating Creativity: Making and Learning by Young People*. London: Routledge.

Further Reading

Althusser, L., 1971. *Lenin and Philosophy and Other Essays*. London: New Left Books.

Altman, R., 1982: *Genre: The Musical*. London: Routledge.

Anderson, C., 2006. *The Long Tail*. London: Random House.

Arroyo, J., 2001. 'Mission sublime', in Arroyo, J. (ed.), *Action/Spectacle*. London: BFI.

Ash, A., 2010, in press. 'Moving image, shifting positions, moving teachers; adjusting the focus', *Media Education Research Journal* 1.1.

Avery, A., 2010. The Great Media Compromise. Poster presentation, University of Leicester Postgraduate Conference.

Baker, J., 2001. *Teaching TV Sitcom*. London: BFI.

Barker, M., 2002. 'Categories of violence', *Media Magazine*, 1. London: English and Media Centre.

Barker, M. and Petley, J., 1997. *Ill Effects: The Media/Violence Debate*. London: Routledge.

Barker, M. and Petley, J. (eds), 2001. *Ill Effects: The Media/Violence Debate*. London: Routledge.

Barrett, P., 2006. 'White thumbs, black bodies: race, violence and neoliberal fantasies in Grand Theft Auto: San Andreas', *Review of Education, Pedagogy and Cultural Studies*, 28: 95–119.

Barthes, R., 1977. *Mythologies*. London: Paladin.

Barthes, R., 1983. *Selected Writings*. London: Fontana.

Bartlett, S. and Burton, D., 2007. *Introduction to Education Studies*. London: Sage.

Bartlett, S., Burton, D. and Peim, N., 2001. *An Introduction to Education Studies*. London: Paul Chapman Publishing.

Baudrillard, J. (ed. Poster, M.), 1988: *Selected Writings*. Cambridge: Polity.

Bauman, Z., 1998. *Globalisation: The Human Consequences*. London: Polity.

Bazalgette, P., 2005. *Billion Dollar Game: How Three Men Risked It All and Changed the Face of Television*. London: Time Warner.

Beetlestone, F., 1998: *Creative Children, Imaginative Teaching*. Buckingham: Open University Press.

Belsey, C., 2005. *Culture and the Real*. London: Routledge.

Benyahia, S., 2001. *Teaching Contemporary British Cinema*. London: BFI.

Berger, R., 2010. 'Out and about: slash fic, re-imagined texts, and queer commentaries', in Pullen, C. and Cooper, M. (eds), *LGBT Identity and Online New Media*. London: Routledge: 173–184.

Berger, R. and McDougall, J., 2010. 'Media education research in the twenty-first century: touching the void', *Media Education Research Journal*, 1.1.

Berners-Lee, T., 1999. *Weaving the Web: The Past, Present and Future of the World Wide Web*. London: Orion.

Bernstein, B. 1990. *The Structuring of Pedagogic Discourse*. London: Routledge.

Bignell, J., 1997. *Media Semiotics: An Introduction*. Manchester: MUP.

Black, P., Harrison, C., Lee, H., Marshall, B. and William, D., 2002. *Working Inside the Black Box: Assessment for Learning in the Classroom*. London: Kings College Publications.

Bolas, T., 2009. *Screen Education: From Film Appreciation to Media Studies*. Bristol: Intellect.

Bourdieu, P., 2002. *Distinction: A Social Critique of the Judgment of Taste*. London: Routledge.

Bourdieu, P. and Passeron, J., 1977. *Reproduction in Education, Society and Culture*. London: Sage.

Bowles, S. and Gintis, H., 1976. *Schooling in Capitalist America*. London: Routledge.

Brabazon, T., 2007. *The University of Google*. Aldershot: Ashgate.

Brabazon, T., 2008. 'Transforming learning: building an information scaffold', *Networks,* 3, spring.

Brey, P., 1998. 'The Ethics of Representation and Action in Virtual Reality', *Ethics and Information Technology*, 1:1.

Brook, S., 2008. 'The heat is on', interview with Julian Linley in *Guardian*, 30.06.08.

Brooks, L., 2010. 'Exotic, extreme, engrossing – tune in to Channel Poverty', *Guardian*, 28.05.10.

Brown, S., Race, P. and Smith, B., 1996. *500 Tips on Assessment*. London: Kogan Page.

Bruce, C., 2002. 'Analyse this!', *Media Magazine*, 2. London: English and Media Centre.

Buckingham, D., 1987. *Public Secrets: EastEnders and its Audience*. London: BFI.

Buckingham, D., 2000. *After the Death of Childhood: Growing Up in the Age of Electronic Media*. London: Polity.

Buckingham, D., 2003. *Media Education: Literacy, Learning and Contemporary Culture*. London: Polity.

Buckingham, D., 2003. *The Making of Citizens: Young People, News & Politics*. London: Routledge.

Buckingham, D., 2006. 'Is there a digital generation?', in Buckingham, D. and Willet, R. (eds), *Digital Generations: Children, Young People and New Media*. New York: Lawrence Erlbaum Associates.

Buckingham, D., 2007. *Beyond Technology: Children's Learning in the Age of Digital Culture*. London: Polity.

Buckingham, D. (ed.), 2008. *Youth, Identity and Digital Media*. Cambridge, MA: MIT Press.

Buckingham, D., 2010. 'Do we really need Media Education 2.0? Teaching media in the age of participatory culture', in Drotner, K. and Schroder, K. (eds.), *Digital Content Creation: Creativity , Competence, Critique*. New York: Peter Lang

Buckingham, D. and Willet, R. (eds). *Video Cultures: Media Technology and Everyday Creativity*. Basingstoke: Palgrave Macmillan.

Buckingham, D., *et al.*, 2008. *Literature Review for the Bryon Report*. London: DCMS.

Burn, A., 2001. 'The rush of images: a research report into digital editing and the moving image', *English in Education*, 35.2.

Burn, A., 2008. 'New media and the future of media education', *Media Education Journal*, 43, summer

Burn, A. and Durran, J., 2007. *Media Literacy in Schools*. London: Paul Chapman.

Burn, A. and Parker, D., 2003. *Analysing Media Texts*. London: Continuum.

Burn, A., Carr, D., Oram, B., Horrell, K. and Schott, G., 2003. 'Why study digital games?', *Media Magazine* 5 and 6. London: English and Media Centre.

Byron, T., 2008. *Safer Children in a Digital World*. London: DCMS.

Caldwell, J. and Everett, A., 2003. *New Media: Practices of Digitextuality*. London: Routledge.

Chomsky, N., 2003. *Doctrines and Visions*. London: Penguin.

Clark, V., 2005. *Media Briefing: The Global Picture & Teaching Notes*. London: BFI.

Cohen, S., 1980. *Folk Devils and Moral Panics*. Oxford: Martin Robertson.

Connell. B. (ed.), 2008. *Exploring the Media: Text, Industry, Audience*. Leighton Buzzard: Auteur.

Creeber, G. (ed.), 2002. *The Television Genre Book*. London: BFI.

Creeber, G. and Martin, R. (eds.), 2009. *Digital Culture: Understanding New Media*. Maidenhead: Open University Press

Csikszentmihalyi, M., 1996. *Creativity, Flow and the Psychology of Discovery and Invention*. New York: Harper Perennial.

Cubitt, S., 2009. 'Digital aesthetics', in Creeber, G. and Martin, R. (eds.), *Digital Culture: Understanding New Media*. Maidenhead: Open University Press

Curran, J., 2002. *Media and Power*. London: Routledge.

Curtis, W. and Pettigrew, A., 2009. *Learning in Contemporary Culture*. Exeter: Learning Matters.

Davey, O., 2005. 'Pleasure and pain: why we need violence in the movies', *Media Magazine*, 12. London: English and Media Centre.

Davies, J. and Merchant, G., 2009. *Web 2.0 for Schools: Learning and Social Participation*. London: Peter Lang.

De Bono, E., 2000. *Six Thinking Hats*. London: Penguin.

Derrida, J., 1977. *Of Grammatology*. London: Johns Hopkins.

Dowdall, C., 2009. 'Masters and critics: children as producers of online digital texts', in Carrington, V. and Robinson, M. (eds) *Digital Literacies: Social Learning and Classroom Practices*. London: Sage/UKLA.

Dutton, B. 1997. *The Media*. London: Longman.

Dyer, R. 1994. 'Action!', *Sight and Sound*, October.

Dyja, E., 2010. *Studying British Cinema: The 1990s*. Leighton-Buzzard: Auteur.

Easthope, A. and McGowan, K., 2004. *A Critical and Cultural Theory Reader*. Milton Keynes: Open University Press.

Egan, K., 2005. *An Imaginative Approach to Teaching*. San Francisco: Jossey-Bass.

English and Media Centre, 2008. *Doing Ads Study Pack*. London: English and Media Centre.

Fearn, H., 2008. 'Grappling with the digital divide', *Times Higher Educational Supplement*, 14.08.08.

Feldman, T., 1997: *Introduction to Digital Media*. London: Routledge.

Fikiciak, M., 2004. 'Hyperidentities: postmodern identity patterns in massive multi-player online role playing games', in Wolf and Perron (eds), *The Videogame Theory Reader*. London: Routledge.

Fiske, J., 1987. *Television Culture*. London: Methuen.

Foucault, M., 1975. *Discipline and Punish: The Birth of the Prison*. London: Penguin.

Foucault, M., 1988. Technologies of the Self: A Seminar with Michel Foucault, eds L. H. Martin, H. Gutman, and P. H. Hutton. Amherst, MA: University of Massachusetts Press.

Fraser, P., 2001. *Teaching Music Video*. London: BFI.

Fraser, P., 2002. 'Production work tips', *Media Magazine*, 1. London: English and Media Centre.

Fraser, P and Oram, B., 2004. *Teaching Digital Video Production*. London: BFI.

Freeman, W., 2010. 'With games this good, who needs film?', *Observer*, 21.02.10.

Freire, P., 1972. *Pedagogy of the Oppressed*. London: Penguin.

Fuchs, C., 2010. Review of *Exit Through The Gift Shop* by Banksy – at http://www.pop matters.com/pm/review/124099-exit-through-the-gift-shop/

Gauntlett, D., 1995. *Moving Experiences: Understanding Televisions Influence's & Effects*. London: John Libbey Media.

Gauntlett, D., 1997. 'Another crisis for Media Studies', *In the Picture* 31. Keighley: In the Picture Publications.

Gauntlett, D., 1998: 'Ten things wrong with the "effects model", in Dickinson, R., Harindranath, R. and Linne, O. (eds), *Approaches to Audiences*. London: Arnold.

Gauntlett, D., 2002. *Media, Gender and Identity: An Introduction*. London: Routledge.

Gauntlett, D. (ed.), 2004. *Web Studies: Rewiring Media studies for the Digital Age*. London: Arnold.

Gauntlett, D., 2007a. *Creative Explorations: New Approaches to Identities and Audiences*. London: Routledge.

Gauntlett, D., 2007b. *Media Studies 2.0* – http://www.theory.org.uk/mediastudies2.htm

Gauntlett, D., 2008. 'Participation, creativity and social change' (lecture) – http://www.youtube.com/watch?v=MNqgXbI1_o8 (accessed 31.05.10).

Gauntlett, D., 2009a. 'Media Studies 2.0: A Response' in *Interactions: Studies in Communication and Culture* 1:1: 147–157.

Gauntlett, D., 2009b. 'Wikipedia', in Creeber, G. and Martin, R. (eds.), *Digital Culture: Understanding New Media*. Maidenhead: Open University Press.

Gee, J. 2003a. *What Videogames Have to Teach us about Learning and Literacy*. Basingstoke: Palgrave Macmillan.

Gee, J., 2003b. 'High score education: games, not school, are teaching kids to think', *Wired*, 11.5.

Gee, J., 2008. Keynote presentation to Future and Reality of Gaming conference, Vienna, 17 October.

Gellis, M., 2000. 'Teaching research skills using the internet', in Cole, R. (ed.), *Issues in Web-based Pedagogy: A Critical Primer*. Westport, CT: Greenwood Press.

Geraghty, C. 1991. 'Representation and popular culture', in Curran, J. and Gurevitch, M. (eds), *Mass Media and Society*. London: Edward Arnold.

Geraghty, C., 1991.*Women in Soap Opera*. London: Polity.

Gillmor, D., 2004: *We, The Media*. Cambridge, MA: O'Reilly.

Goffman, E., 1990. *The Presentation of Self in Everyday Life*. London: Penguin.

Grahame, J., 1994: *Production Practices*. London: English and Media Centre.

Grahame, J., 2001. Being Creative with Minimal Resources. BFI conference workshop.

Green, H. and Hannon, C., 2007. *Their Space: Education for a Digital Generation*. London: Demos.

Guillemin, M., 2004, 'Understanding illness: using drawings as a research method', *Qualitative Health Research* 14: 259–271.

Hall, S., 1981. *Culture, Media, Language*, Centre for Contemporary Cultural Studies Birmingham: Hutchison.

Hanley, P. (ed.), 2002. *Striking a Balance: The Control of Children's Media Consumption*. London: ITC.

Hartley, J., 1999. *The Uses of Television*. London: Routledge.

Hartley, J., 2008. *Television Truths*. Oxford: Blackwell.

Helsby, W., 2005. *Understanding Representation*. London: Routledge.

Helsby, W., 2010. *Teaching Reality TV*. Leighton-Buzzard: Auteur.

Heppell, S., 2006. Keynote speech to the Media Education Summit, Bournemouth – http://www.cemp.ac.uk/summit/podcasts/StephenHeppellKeynote.mp3

Higson, A., 1995: *Dissolving Views*. London: Cassell.

Higson, A., 1995.*Waving the Flag: Constructing a National Cinema in Britain*. Oxford: Clarendon Press.

Hills, M., 2005. *How to Do Things with Cultural Theory*. London: Hodder.

Hills, M., 2010. *Triumph of a Time Lord: Regenerating Doctor Who for the Twenty-First Century*. London: I.B. Tauris.

Hirschorn, A., 2003. 'Sitcoms and absurdism', *In the Picture* 46. Keighley: In the Picture Publications.

Hodge, R. and Tripp, D., 1996. *Children and Television*. London: Polity.

Hoggart, R., 1967. *The Uses of Literacy*. London: Chatto and Windus.

Hopkins, E., 2009. 'The impact of new media technologies', in Sharp, J., Ward, S. and Hankin, L. (eds), *Education Studies: An Issues-Based Approach*. Exeter: Learning Matters.

Horrocks, C. and Jetvic, Z., 1999. *Introducing Foucault*. Cambridge: Icon.

Illich, I., 1973. *Tools for Conviviality*. London: Calder & Boyars.

Ito, M., 2006. 'Japanese media mixes and amateur cultural exchange', in Buckingham, D. and Willet, R. (eds), *Digital Generations: Children, Young People and New Media*. New York: Lawrence Erlbaum Associates.

Jarvinen, A., 2003. 'The elements of simulation in digital games: system, representation and interface in Grand Theft Auto: Vice City' – at www.dichtung-digital.com

Jarvis, J., 2009. *What Would Google Do?* London: Collins.

Jarvis, P., 2010. *Learning to Be a Person in Society*. London: Routledge.

Jencks, C., 2005.*Culture*. London: Routledge.

Jenkins, H. with Clinton, K., Purushotma, R., Robison, A. J., and Weigel, M. (2006). *Confronting the Challenges of Participatory Culture: Media Education for the 21st Century*. Chicago: MacArthur Foundation.

Jenkins, H., 2006. *Convergence Culture: Where Old and New Media Collide*. New York: New York University Press.

JISC, 2009. *Effective Practice in a Digital Age: A Guide to Technology-enhanced Learning and Teaching*. Bristol: JISC.

Johnson, S., 2005. *Everything Bad is Good for You*. London: Penguin.

Joseph, A., 2004. 'Identity crisis: how to create your own digital identity', *Media Magazine*, 8. London: English and Media Centre.

Kabir, N., 2001. *Bollywood: The Indian Cinema Story*. London: C4 Books.

Kendall, A., 2008. 'Playing and resisting: re-thinking young people's reading cultures', *Literacy*, 4. 3: 123–130.

Kendall, A., 2008. 'Giving up reading: re-imagining reading with young adult readers', *Journal of Research and Practice in Adult Literacy*, 65, spring/summer: 14–22.

Kendall, A. and McDougall, J., 2009. 'Just gaming: on being differently literate', *Eludamos: Journal of Computer Game Culture*, 3.2: 246–260.

Kermode, M., 2001. *Introduction to C4 Screening of Bad Lieutenant*. London: C4.

Ki, S., 2004. 'The evaluation of practical production as the process of legitimation in GCSE Media Studies'. Unpub. PhD thesis, Institute of Education, London.

Lacey, N., 2000. *Narrative and Genre*. London: Macmillan.

Lacey, N., 2008. 'Knowing arses from elbows', *In the Picture*, 60. Keighley: In the Picture Publications.

Lacey, N., 2010. *Image and Representation*, 2nd edn. London: Macmillan.

Lacey, N. and Stafford, R., 2002. 'Cut or move the camera? Framing the action', *In the Picture* 45. Keighley: In the Picture Publications.

Lankshear, C. and Knobel, M., 2006. *New Literacies: Everyday Practices and Classroom Learning*. Maidenhead: Open University Press.

Leggott, J., 2008. *Contemporary British Cinema: From Heritage to Horror*. London: Wallflower.

Lemish, D., 2006. *Children and Television: A Global Perspective*. Oxford: Blackwell.

Levan, S., 2000. *York Film Notes: Fargo*. London: York Press.

Lewis, E., 2001. *Teaching TV News*. London: BFI.

Lilley, A., 2009. Professorial Lecture to Centre of Excellence in Media Practice, University of Bournemouth, 11.11.09. http://www.cemp.ac.uk/summit/podcasts/AnthonyLilleyKeynote.mp3

Lister, J., Dovey, J., Giddings, S., Grant, I. and Kelly, K., 2009. *New Media: A Critical Introduction*, 2nd edn. London: Routledge.

Livingstone, S., 1999. *Young People, New Media*. London: LSE.

Livingstone, S., 2005. 'Media audiences, interpreters and users', in Gillespie, M. (ed.), *Media Audiences*. Maidenhead: Open University Press.

Livingstone, S., 2009. *Children and the Internet: Great Expectations, Challenging Realities*. London: Polity.

Luhrs, G., 2002. 'Why convergence matters', *Media Magazine*, 1. London: English and Media Centre.

Luhrs, G., 2005. 'The future will be blogged', *Media Magazine*, 12. London: English and Media Centre.

Lunenfield, P., 2000. *The Digital Dialectic*. Cambridge, MA: MIT.

Lyotard, J., 1984. *The Postmodern Condition*. Manchester: MUP.

Lyotard, J., 1992. *The Postmodern Explained to Children*. London: Turnaround.

Marsh, J. (ed.), 2005. *Popular Culture, Media and New Technologies in Early Childhood*. London: Routledge.

Marsh, J., 2010. 'Young children´s play in online virtual worlds', *Journal of Early Childhood Research*, 7.3: 1–17.

Martin, R., 2004. *Audiences: A Teacher's Guide*. London: Auteur.

Masterman, L., 1984. *Television Mythologies*. London: Comedia.

Masterman, L., 1985. *Teaching the Media*. London: Routledge.

Masterman, L., 2004. 'Visions of media education: the road from dystopia', *In the Picture* 48. Keighley: In the Picture Publications.

McConnell, S., 2003. 'A trip to the seaside', *Media Magazine*, 5. London: English and Media Centre.

Masterman, L., 2006. Review of *The Media Teacher's Book, Media Education Journal*, 40.

McCullough, M., 1998. *Abstracting Craft: The Practiced Digital Hand*. Cambridge, MA: MIT Press.

McDougall, J., 2003. 'Games in the classroom – whatever next?', *Media Magazine*, 6. London: English and Media Centre.

McDougall, J., 2004. 'Judging media learning', *In the Picture* 50. Keighley: In the Picture Publications.

McDougall, J., 2004. 'Lads, mags, Nuts and Zoo', *Media Magazine*, 8. London: English and Media Centre.

McDougall, J., 2004. *Subject Media: The Socio-Cultural Framing of Discourse*. University of Birmingham: http://etheses.bham.ac.uk/556/

McDougall, J., 2006a. 'Is it really so strange?', *Media Education Journal*, 40: 5–8.

McDougall, J., 2006b. 'Media education and the limits of assessment', *Media International Australia,* 120: 106–116.

McDougall, J., 2007. 'What do we learn in Smethwick Village?', *Learning, Media, Technology,* 32.2: 121–133.

McDougall, J., 2008. 'Raggered trousered Wikinomics: "back to the future" for Media Studies', *In the Picture* 60. Keighley: In the Picture Publications.

McDougall, J., 2009. *A2 Media Studies for OCR*. London: Hodder Arnold.

McDougall, J., 2010 'Wiring the Audience', *Participations*, 7.1: 73–101.

McDougall, J., 2010. 'Wiring the Audiencies' in *Participations* Vol 7 Issue 2, at http://www.participations.org/Volume%207/Issue%201/mcdougall.htm

McDougall, J. and O'Brien, W., 2008. *Studying Videogames*. Leighton-Buzzard: Auteur.

McDougall, J. and Trotman, D., 2010. 'Real audience pedagogy: creative learning and digital space', in Sefton-Green, J. (ed.), *The International Handbook of Creative Learning*. London: Routledge.

McLuhan, M., 1994. *Understanding Media: The Extensions of Man*. London: MIT.

McMillin, D., 2007. *International Media Studies*. London: Blackwell.

McNair, B., 2003. *News and Journalism in the UK*. London: Routledge.

McQueen, D., 1998. *Television: A Media Student's Guide*. London: Arnold.

Medhurst, A., 1994. 'The Magnificent Seven rides again', *Observer*.

Medhurst, A., 1996: *Dissolving Views*. London: Cassell.

Meighan, R. and Harber, C., 2007. *A Sociology of Educating*. London: Continuum.

Meigs, T., 2003. *Ultimate Game Design: Building Game Worlds*. Berkeley, CA: Osborne McGraw-Hill.

Merrin, W., 2005. *Baudrillard and the Media*. Cambridge: Polity.

Merrin, W., 2007. http://mediastudies2point0.blogspot.com/

Merrin, W., 2008. *Media Studies 2.0* – available at http://twopointzeroforum.blogspot.com/

Merrin, W., 2009. 'Media Studies 2.0: upgrading and open-sourcing the discipline', *Interactions: Studies in Communication and* Culture, 1.1: 17–34.

Morgan Stanley Research (2009). 'How teenagers consume media', http://media.ft.com/cms/c3852b2e-6f9a-11de-bfc5-00144feabdc0.pdf (accessed 31.05.10).

Mottershead, C., 2001. How to Teach Narrative. BFI Media Studies Conference Workshop, London.

Mullen, L., 2009. 'Estate of ,ind', *Sight and Sound*, October: 16–20.

Mulvey, L., 1975. 'Visual pleasure and narrative cinema', *Screen*, 16.3: 6–18.

Murray, R., 2008. 'The new Social Realism', *Splice: Studying Contemporary Cinema*, 2.2: 30–53.

Musburger, R. and Kindem, G., 2004. *Introduction to Media Production: The Path to Digital Media Production*. Oxford: Focal Press.

Naughton, J., 'Blogging and the emerging media ecosystem', at http://reutersinstitute. politics.ox.ac.uk/fileadmin/documents/discussion/blogging.pdf

Neale, S. and Turner, G., 2002. 'What is genre?', in Creeber, G. (ed.), *The Television Genre Book*. London: BFI.

Nelmes, J. (ed.), 1996. *An Introduction to Film Studies*. London: Routledge.

Newman, J., 2004. *Videogames*. London: Routledge.

Newman, J. and Oram, B., 2006. *Teaching Videogames*. London: BFI.

Newman, M., 2009. 'The Xbox factor: Gaming's Role in Future Assessment' in *Times Higher Education Supplement* via www.timeshighereducation.co.uk/story. asp?storycode=408492

Nock, D., 2004. 'Confessions of a B-movie writer', *Media Magazine*, 8. London: English and Media Centre.

Noddings, N., 1984, *Caring: A Feminine Approach to Ethics & Moral Education*. CA: University of California Press.

Noddings, N., 2005, *Educating Citizens for Global Awareness* (ed.). NY: Teachers College Press.

O'Brien, W., 2003. 'Key media concepts courtesy of Big Brother 4', *Media Magazine*, 6. London: English and Media Centre.

Palmer, S., 2006. *Toxic Childhood: How the Modern World is Damaging our Children and What We Can Do About It*. London: Orion.

Papert, S., 1994. *The Children's Machine: Rethinking School in the Age of the Computer*. New York: Basic Books.

Papert, S. and Harel, I., 1991. 'Situating constructionism'.

Peim, N., 1995. *Critical Theory and the English Teacher*. London: Routledge.

Peim, N, 2000. 'The cultural politics of English teaching', in *Issues in English Teaching*. London: Routledge.

Phillips, N., 'Genre', in Nelmes, J. (ed.), 1996. *An Introduction to Film Studies*. London: Routledge.

QCA, 2005. *Media Matters: A Review of Media Studies in Schools and Colleges*. London: QCA.

QCA, 2008: *Every Child Matters at the Heart of the Curriculum*. London: QCA.

Raynor, P., Wall, P. and Kruger, S., 2001. *Media Studies: The Essential Introduction*. London: Routledge.

Readman, M., 2001.*Teaching Scriptwriting, Screenplays and Storyboards for Film and TV Production*. London: BFI.

Readman, M., 2009. 'Don't mention the C-word: the rhetorics of creativity in the Roberts report', *Networks*, 7: 10–11.

Reid, M., 2002. Teaching Genre. BFI Media Studies Conference Workshop, London.

Riele, K., 2009. *Making Schools Different: Alternative Approaches to Educating Young People*. London: Sage.

Robinson, P., 2002. *The CNN Effect*. London: Routledge.

Rosenberg, H. and Feldman, C., 2008. *No Time to Think: The Menace of Media Speed and the 24 Hour News Cycle*. London: Continuum.

Ruddock, A., 2007. *Investigating Audiences*. London: Sage.

Sampson, A., 2004. *Who Runs this Place?* London: John Murray.

Sandbery, S., 2010. 'Our hiccups on privacy', *Guardian*, 28.05.10.

Sanders, R. and McDougall, J., 2010. 'Virtual world education: is experience the new reality?' Paper presented to the IVERG conference.Sardar, Z. and Van Loon, B., 2000. *Introducing Media Studies*. London: Icon.

Saussure, F. de, 1974. *Course in General Linguistics*. London: Fontana.

Sefton-Green, J., 1999. 'Media education, but not as we know it: digital technology and the end of Media Studies', *English and Media Magazine*, 40. London: English and Media Centre.

Sefton-Green, J. and Sinker, R. (eds), 2000. *Evaluating Creativity: Making and Learning by Young People*. London: Routledge.

Selby, K. and Cowdery, R., 1995. *How to Study Television*. London: Macmillan.

Sennet, R., 2009. *The Craftsman*. London: Penguin.

Shannon, C.E., and Weaver, W., 1949. *A Mathematical Model of Communication*. IL: University of Illinois Press.

Shirky, C., 2009. *Here Comes Everybody: How Change Happens When People Come Together*. London: Penguin.

Shneiderman, B., 2003. *Leonardo's Laptop: Human Needs and the New Computing Technologies*. Cambridge, MA: MIT Press.

Spragon, L., 2004. *Into Animation*. London: BFI Education.

Stafford, R. (ed.), 2000. *Film Reader 2: British Cinema*. Keighley: In the Picture Publications.

Stafford, R., 2001. *Representation: An Introduction*. London: BFI and Keighley: In the Picture Publications.

Stafford, R., 2002. *British Cinema 1990–2002: Teacher's Notes*. Keighley: In the Picture Publications.

Stafford, R., 2002. 'Formats and genres across media', *In the Picture* 44. Keighley: In the Picture Publications.

Stafford, R., 2003. *Audiences: An Introduction*. London: BFI and Keighley: In the Picture Publications.

Stafford, R., 2003. 'Nowhere to run to? Nowhere to hide for asylum?', *In the Picture* 46. Keighley: In the Picture Publications.

Stafford, R., 2003. 'Ofcom is up and running', *In the Picture* 47. Keighley: In the Picture Publications.

Stafford, R., 2007. 'Global cinema', *Media Magazine*, 21. London: English and Media Centre.

Stafford, R. and Branston, G., 2006. *The Media Student's Book*, 4th edn. London: Routledge.

Strinati, D., 1995. *An Introduction to Theories of Popular Culture*. London: Routledge.

Tagg, J., 1988. *The Burden of Representation*. Basingstoke: Palgrave Macmillan.

Tapscott, D., 1998. *Growing Up Digital: The Rise of the Net Generation*. New York: McGraw Hill.

Tapscott, D. and Williams, A., 2006. *Wikinomics: How Mass Collaboration Changes Everything*. London: Atlantic Books.

Tasker, Y. (ed.), 2005. *Action and Adventure Cinema*. London: Routledge.

Taylor, N., 2005. *Search Me: The Surprising Success of Google*. London: Cyan.

Taylor, P., 1999. *Hackers: Crime in the Digital Sublime*. London: Routledge.

Thompson, K., 1998. *Moral Panics*. London: Routledge.

Thusso, D., 2000. *International Communication*. London: Hodder.

Toland, P., 2004. 'What are you playing at? Representations of gender, race and nationality in videogames', *Media Magazine*, 7. London: English and Media Centre.

Turner, G., 2010. *Ordinary People and the Media: The Demotic Turn*. London: Sage.

Tyrell, H., 1988. 'Bollywood in Britain', *Sight and Sound*, August.

Wakefield, N., 2004. 'New media, new methodologies: studying the web', in Gauntlett, D. (ed.), *Web Studies: Rewiring Media Studies for the Digital Age*. London: Arnold.

Walker, C., 2004. 'Are MP3s killing the music business?', unpub. BA dissertation, Coventry University.

Wardle, J., 2009. 'The Creative and Media Diploma: an unfamiliar problem in an unfamiliar context', *PoV*, 1.2, spring.

Wardle, J., 2010. 'A comparative analysis of learner and fan experience: do contemporary drama structures have the potential to model improvements in the learning experience?', unpub. PhD thesis, Bristol University.

Wardrop-Fruin, N. and Montfort, N., 2003. '*The New Media Reader*: a user's manual', in *The New Media Reader*. Cambridge, MA: MIT Press.

Waters, M., 1995. *Globalisation*. London: Routledge.

Watson, J. and Hill, A., 2003. *Dictionary of Media and Communication Studies*. London: Arnold.

Weinberger, D., 2007. *Everything is Miscellaneous: The Power of the New Digital Disorder*. New York: Times Books.

Wesch, M., 2008. 'Anti-teaching: confronting the crisis of significance', *Education Canada*, 48.2.

Willis, P., Jones, S., Canaan, J. and Hurd, G., 1990. *Common Culture: Symbolic Work at Play in the Everyday Cultures of the Young*. Buckingham: Open University Press.

Winship, J., 1997. *Inside Women's Magazines*. London: Pandora.

Withall, K., 2000. 'Exploring documentary truth?', *In the Picture* 40. Keighley: In the Picture Publications.

Wolf, J. and Perron, B., 2003. *The Video Game Theory Reader*. London: Routledge.

Zimmerman, E. and Salen, K. 2003. *Rules of Play: Game Design Fundamentals*. Cambridge, MA: MIT Press.

Zizek, S, 2002. 'Welcome to the desert of the real', in Easthope, A. and McGowan, K. (eds), *A Critical and Cultural Theory Reader*. Maidenhead: Open University Press.

Glossary

AESTHETIC

In Media education usually understood as one type of code amongst several, the aesthetic domain describes *visual* language in cultural contexts. We have used the term in contrast to technical considerations, arguing that digital technology allows the Media teacher to focus less on operational tuition and more on the language of film, for example.

ANCHORAGE

The 'pinning down' of meaning through image being placed in relation to text, or vice versa. The shipping metaphor suggests a wild sea of potential meaning, with the sign (boat) needing to be motivated through grounding.

AUDIENCE

An umbrella term for the person or people reading any media text. Digital technology has led to increasing uncertainty over how we define an audience, with general agreement that the notion of a large group of people, brought together by time, responding to a text, is outdated. Furthermore, advocates of 'Media 2.0' claim that the way people engage with culture is now the 'concept formally known as the audience'. See the journal *Participations* for contemporary research in this domain.

AVATAR

An on-screen icon or representation of the user/player in a computer game. Now in the everyday lexicon as a result of the James Cameron film.

BINARY

Western thought, it is said, is framed by a tendency to think in opposites – e.g. good/evil – rather than embrace ambiguity and difference. In digital coding, binary describes the coding of digits as noughts and ones. See Derrida for the theory.

BRECHTIAN

Referrring to the dramatist Bertolt Brecht, whose key intervention was to make the audience 'ultra-aware' of the artifice of theatre, as opposed to the classic realist tradition of suspending their disbelief.

BRICOLAGE

The construction of meaning through remixing a combination of elements to make a new style. Ranges from surrealist work where things are deliberately put out of context to postmodern media where there is no sense of 'original' material to worry about as everything new is made up of a bricolage of the old – what was already there.

CITIZENSHIP

Our use of the term is not related to the National Curriculum subject. Rather, we are referring to the potential of Media education to foster in students reflective consideration of their place in contemporary democracy and the role of the media in constructing us as modern citizens.

CONVENTIONS

The repeated, normative practices expected within a culture. In the context of Media learning, we are concerned with the normative elements of a particular type of media text.

CONVERGENCE

Hardware and software coming together across media, and companies coming together across similar boundaries, to make the distinction between different types of media and different media industries increasingly dubious. Also, the way that media access is now multi-modal – e.g. watching TV on an iphone – and the means that social media affords us new opportunities to be creative and/or participative is described by Henry Jenkins as '*Convergence Culture*'.

CULTURAL CAPITAL

From Bourdieu and Passeron (1977). Symbolic acquisition that can be exchanged, including qualifications, knowledge, family background, taste, values and other non-material forms of status. Our articulated responses to media texts are sensibly understood within this 'taste-market', we would argue.

CULTURAL IMPERIALISM

Within broader discussions of globalisation, the practice of dominant groups and nations imposing their cultural preferences and claims to legitimate knowledge on other people and nations. Hollywood is the classic example. The assumption tends to be that corporate power is simultaneous with cultural dominance. Made less powerful as an argument by diaspora.

DATA

Original information acquired in learning, usually through research activity. This might be from interviews, surveys, observation or case study work. It is the unique information brought into the classroom by students, self-originated.

DECONSTRUCTION

From Derrida (1977). A philosophy of extended textual analysis, in which it is accepted that we cannot find meaning. Instead we investigate intertextuality and ways in which texts can only be understood in relation to other texts (including ourselves).

DEMOCRACY

Society founded on equality, in which the decision-making powers are elected and are thus representative and accountable. Whether the media is democratic is a very different question, as we do not elect newspaper owners or TV presenters such as Simon Cowell, for example.

DEMOGRAPHIC

Breaking down society or a sample of people by characteristics such as age, gender, ethnicity, occupation, income and socio-economic status (quantitative means).

DIALECTICAL

An exchange of points of view, or **propositions** (theses) and **counter-propositions** (antitheses), resulting in an attempt to reduce the dissensus through the creation of new ideas, which are then new propositions to be countered (a such dialectical thinking is infinite). See Lunenfield (2000) for discussions around the 'digital dialectic.'

DIASPORA

The process by which people who are dispersed around the world take elements of their culture with them so that the cultural imperialism model is disrupted by people using media in relation to hybrid identities. See Ruddock (2007).

DIEGESIS

Describes what is present in the world of a text, as opposed to the extra bits (e.g. soundtrack or voice-over) that exist only for the audience.

DISCOURSE

A coherent system of speaking, thinking and understanding, in language. Systematically organised ways of talking, from Foucault (1988).

ELLIPSIS

What is left out of a narrative, but remains in the story.

ETHICS

Issues of morality (always up for grabs). Often different to legal considerations, an important distinction for students to grapple with.

FALSE CONSCIOUSNESS

Marxist term describing a state of being in which individuals are happily distracted from the truth (by ideology) and are thus convinced, or at least prepared to accept, that things are as they have to be.

FEMINISM

Often misunderstood as an 'extreme', militant politics, for us feminism is nothing more outrageous than the belief that we should oppose any situating of women as unequal to men, or as mere unthinking objects for male scrutiny.

FLOW

A state of mind which happens when someone is involved in activity which is challenging but pleasurable and incrementally more difficult over time, with staggered rewards and feedback.

FRANKFURT SCHOOL

Marxist school of thought, featuring Adorno and Marcuse, concerned mainly with ideology and the role of mass media (the culture industry) in reinforcing hegemony and manufacturing consensus.

GATEKEEPING

The role played by editors, producers, owners and regulators in opening and closing, to greater and lesser extents, the flow of media information through processes of selection and construction.

GLOBALISATION

The proliferation of digital technology, deregulation and convergence combine to allow mutinational and cross-cultural media production and consumption within a global economic system founded on the free market. Arguably digital online media accelerates this process.

HIDDEN CURRICULUM

The set of behavioural codes, practices and additional support needed to be successful in an education system, outside of formal curriculum and institutional policies. From Bowles and Gintis (1976). See Bartlett, Burton and Peim (2001) for an application to contemporary education.

HORIZONTAL DISCOURSE

From Bernstein (1990), a discourse which is 'fed into' by a number of different communities, and is thus spread out, evolving and complex. Media Studies began in this way, we think.

HYBRID

A fusion of more than one media form or a mixing of global and local or a mixing of identities.

HYPERREALITY

A state in which images, and simulations, take on more reality than the state they represent, so that the distinction between reality and representation is no longer sustainable. From Baudrillard (1988).

IDENTITY

Culture and discourse construct subjects (from Foucault, 1988), so for Media Studies the task is not so much to consider the relationship between texts and identities taken on by individuals as to analyse the plurality of identities that subjects play with and the ways in which these are mediated and increasingly virtual.

IDEOLOGY

A dominant set of ideas presenting itself as common sense or truth. Power relations are reinforced through ideology. For Chomsky (2003), the recent military practices of the USA are an example of a super power acting without establishing a traditional ideological consensus.

IMMERSION

Used in analysis of videogames, in two ways: perceptual (the senses are dominated by the experience of the game) and psychological (the player is drawn into the game in the imagination).

INFORMATION ECONOMY

In our post-industrial society, it is suggested (see Lyotard, 1984) that information is the key resource from which wealth can be generated, as opposed to land, raw materials or the means of production.

INTERACTIVE

Media texts which offer audiences the opportunity to shape the text in some way. Choosing from a menu is not interactive if the choices are pre-constructed. Voting for a winner or loser is interactive, but we should distinguish between mass interaction (where you are one of millions making choices) and individual interaction (perhaps a videogame can offer this).

INTERPELLATION

The misrecognition of oneself in a media text (from Althusser, 1971) – for example, women recognising a sense of their gender which was not their construction.

INTERTEXTUAL

The chain of signification, in which texts always make overt or more subtle references to one another. All language is intertextual, and as all experience in culture is languaged, reality becomes intertextual by nature.

KINAESTHETIC

Tactile, physical activity. Some types of learners are assumed to learn more through such practices, but we would advise caution against overstating this, the danger of which is stereotyping and mistaking a preference for an enabling intervention.

LIFEWORLD

The network of experiences of families, hobbies, social gatherings, leading to culturally transmitted ways of understanding the world. In education, there is a tension between the hidden curriculum of schooling and students' lifeworlds, for the majority of people.

LINEAR

In a clear, logical order, moving in one direction.

LITERACY

The ability to read and write. Media education extends such a notion of competence to recognise all forms of writing (e.g. taking photographs) and all forms of reading (e.g. listening to music), and activities which may combine them (e.g. playing a computer game). Media literacy is a much contested area, but at its most basic it describes the practices of (more or less critically) reading contemporary media material.

LOGOCENTRIC

From Derrida (1977), referring to the Greek word 'Logos' (word, speech or reason). Western thought and culture is logocentric as it privileges speech over writing (since Aristotle and his scribe Plato) and sets up as core beliefs the idea that we can strive for a central set of truths and origins as universal principles.

LONG TAIL

Chris Anderson's idea that the large amount of niche markets are now worth as much as the smaller amount of big markets.

LUDOLOGY

The study of play.

MALE GAZE

From Laura Mulvey (1975), an analysis of media images which suggests that the camera represents a male perspective, and as such casts men as subjects and women as objects.

MARKET FORCES

This discourse likens the 'natural' flow of capitalism (competition leading to consumer choice and selection and hence the survival of the fittest) to the laws of nature. Increasingly this discourse is impermeable and all aspects of life, including education, are described in this way. To offer an alternative view is considered 'outdated' within such a hegemonic discourse (less 'sayable').

MARXIST

All theory derived from the works of Marx, founded on a belief that the ruling classes in any time and place maintain their economic and systematic power through controlling not only the means of production but also culture and ideology. Marxist theory, traditionally, seeks to expose the falsity of dominant ideology and reveal the truth previously obscured, and as such it has empowerment of the alienated as its primary objective.

MEDIA ACCESS

Describes the degree of ease with which citizens can be seen and/or heard in the media and respond to the media and be provided with a dialogue with institutions, and the amount of opportunities for people to produce media texts themselves and for them to be distributed – clearly this is greatly increased by social media.

MEDIA LANGUAGE

An umbrella term to describe the ways in which audiences read media texts through understanding formal and conventional structures (for example, the grammar of film editing). Media literacy describes our ability to read and write in this extended sense of language.

MEDIASPHERE

John Hartley describes a 360-degree environment for media consumption, the media-sphere, and says that this fundamentally changes how we need to think about media audiences.

MEDIA STUDIES 2.0

A response to web 2.0, proposed by Will Merrin (2007) and then by David Gauntlett (2007), in which the role of online user-generated content and sharing is seen as fundamental to how we understand media audiences. This makes it mandatory for Media Studies to change how it operates, which impacts greatly on Media teachers like you.

MEME

An idea, or creative item, that is passed on virally from person to person to the point where lots of people know about it and are talking about it.

METALANGUAGE

When we are able to step outside of language to analyse meaning rather than just using language to make meaning, we have a metalanguage. This is an advanced form of literacy.

MICROPOLITICS

The way that small, seemingly insignificant decisions and interactions amount to outcomes that impact on people's lives.

MISE EN SCENE

Everything that is put into the frame (essentially considering the paused moving image as a still image). Includes set design, location, costume, actors and make up, non-verbal communication, colour and contrast, lighting and filter. Primarily an aesthetic practice.

MMORPG

Massively Multiplayer Online Role Playing Games. For example, *World of Warcraft*, *Club Penguin* or *Counterstrike*.

MODE OF ADDRESS

How a text, in any media, speaks to its audience.

MORAL PANIC

Exaggerated media response to the behaviour of a social group. A phrase coined by Stanley Cohen in 1972, this refers to overstated reactions to seemingly deviant aspects of popular culture, usually mobilised by the mass media. Clearly certain videogames have been the subject of widespread moral panics and they are often blamed for declining moral standards in general as well as specific cases of violent behaviour and tragedy.

MULTIMODAL

A form of semiotics, multimodal theory attempts to understand the way that human communication mixes together a variety of forms and how it simultaneously represents, orientates by establishing relations between people and organises (to be clear). For a full account, see Burn and Parker (2003).

MYTH

The key thinker in this area is Roland Barthes, who analysed the way that dominant ideas in a culture take on the status of myth, so they appear natural and neutral. In semiotics, signs and symbols when added together amount to a system of myths.

NARRATOLOGY

For our purposes, the study of videogames as stories – usually seen as in conflict with ludology, but it is possible to combine both theoretical approaches.

NEWS AGENDA

The simple realisation, and subsequent analysis, that a particular news provider will select and construct news within a framework influenced by political, corporate, cultural and commercial objectives.

PARADIGM

A framework of understanding scientific or cultural phenomena. All messages, of any kind, are selected from paradigms. A 'paradigm shift' describes the point at which the usual ways of comprehending culture become outdated.

PARODY

A text which does not simply imitate the style of another (pastiche) but instead is transformative in that it either mocks or shifts in some way the original text's conventions.

PEDAGOGY

Learning and teaching methods, developed from ideas about how learning takes place. Different to curriculum, which describes content, pedagogy is concerned with the how, rather than the what, of teaching, and hence this book is much more pedagogical.

PEER TO PEER

The sharing of media material between two parties in an equal relationship (as opposed to the traditional, hierarchical and commercial seller–buyer interaction).

PHENOMENOLOGY

Theoretical considerations of the relation between consciousness and 'reality', involving analysis of language, culture and being. Embracing phenomenology leads us to depart from assumptions about the nature of reality as existing outside of perception. Much media theory is now, we would argue, a form of phenomenology, especially if the concept of representation is foregrounded and well contextualised in theory and reflection on how complex representation is.

PLEASURE

All forms of engagement with media texts. Crucially, a rejection of judgemental responses to audience choices.

POPULAR CULTURE

See Strinati (1995). Any attempt to define popular culture is situated within a particular theory of it. However, as a way in to more complex questions, we can say that texts which are consumed by a wide range of people, as opposed to a smaller group, configured in some way as an elite, tend to be described as popular and that this implies a derogatory view of tastes. Popular culture has been studied and analysed since the 1960s, and Media Studies is now a 'classic' example of this attention, hence the long-standing discourse of derision around it which is re-circulated every August when the exam results are published.

POSTMODERN

Describes an approach to culture which sees all texts as being intertextual and meaning as mediated rather than representative of a state of original reality. Post-modernists believe that it is no longer sensible to describe media texts in terms of how they represent real life or events, but instead we should see reality as increasingly mediated, so the boundaries between reality and media-reality are blurred. The most famous postmodern philosophers are both French: Jean François Lyotard, who described 'the postmodern condition', and Jean Baudrillard, who said Disneyland was a good example of this blurring of reality and simulation, which he called 'hyperreality'.

POST-PRODUCTION

The editing stage, where material is manipulated using software and transformed into a finished media product.

PRE-PRODUCTION

All forms of idea generation, planning, researching in response to a brief.

PUBLIC SERVICE

Founded on principles of democracy as opposed to profit. Avoid overstating binary oppositions between public service and commercial media, however.

REALISM

A variety of ideas about the degree to which, and the variety of ways in which, media texts represent an idea of reality.

RECEPTION THEORY

Contemporary audience theory is concerned with audience response and reaction and subsequently our understanding of a text's meanings emerge more from attention to audience interpretation than producer intent. Or a variant of the 'death of the author' thesis (from Roland Barthes, 1983).

REFERENCE

Making an explicit mention of a writer or other source in your work and correctly identifying the year of publication, so that someone using your material can follow up this source easily.

REFLECTIVE

Being reflective is very difficult – it is to do with analysing yourself, your ways of understanding the world, your actions and the way you think.

REFLEXIVE

A way of working that demands not only reflecting on one's practices through evaluation, but changing such practice constantly, and ultimately empowering oneself by recognising the 'conditions of possibility' for the work one does.

REGULATION

The surveillance and the threat of action by organisations, sometimes governmental, sometimes from industry, leading to a degree of self-regulation on the part of media institutions, and actual punitive measures in response to self-regulation breaking down. Regulation is sometimes economic, sometimes cultural and always political.

REITHIAN

The rationale for the BBC formulated by Lord Reith (Director General at the time of the BBC's inception) was that it should offer the public information, entertainment and education in equal measure. Opinion is now divided over whether Reith was a bastion of democracy or a patronising elitist.

REPRESENTATION

Students of media are taught that media texts do not present a neutral, transparent view of reality but offer instead a mediated re-presentation of it. Representation entails the processes by which audience members come to understand media texts in terms of how they seem to relate to people, ideas, events, themes and places. This is a very complex idea as the reader of a media text will play an active role in constructing these meanings herself.

RULE ECONOMY

Games are structured so that players need to learn how to operate within a set of boundaries with a range of rules and conditions – from picking up health as you move around a gameworld to remembering how to carry out certain moves at the correct times. This range of rules and criteria to remember is a key feature of a game's structure and it clearly distinguishes videogames from other media forms.

SCHEDULING

The strategic positioning of media texts within broadcasting time. Digital television is increasingly disrupting this approach, since viewers can choose more easily than before when to watch.

SEMIOTICS

The science of signs and symbols. From Saussure's linguistics (1974), and Barthes' structuralism (1977), as I use the term. Essentially, the study of the sign, in terms of its connotations within cultural myth systems (the symbolic order).

SIMULATION

The deliberate artificial imitation of an experience or a process with the intention of making the imitation as close as possible to the 'real thing'. Baudrillard is a key thinker in this area.

SOCIO-CULTURAL

Describes considerations of how our social experiences and cultural choices combine and how meanings are constructed by audiences through experience as much as through any fixed, intended, preferred messages from producers' points of view.

SPECTATORSHIP

How a reader of moving images behaves, which will be culturally specific. Reminds us that, for example, watching a film is not a practice that can be described as though it is a common experience.

SYMBIOSIS

Two forms arranged in an interactive, organic relationship. Used to describe relationships between different media products in commercial terms.

TEXT

All media products are texts, it is argued. But we can extend this term to include people, ourselves and others – anything that is made up of a range of signs that are decoded and interpreted by people. The problem with Media Studies is that it is sometimes too 'Englishey' – when the internal 'properties' of the text are privileged over the ways in which people attribute meaning to media.

TRANSGRESSIVE

A practice which transcends conventional approaches, and either subverts these existing ways of working, or challenges their value.

VERISIMILITUDE

The logical, seemingly authentic world of a text. Not the same as 'realist', because every text has a logical, sensible world constructed through continuity, detail and recognition. So whilst we might not believe that aliens are ready to arrive, *District 9* is believable because it constructs a coherent verisimilitude.

VERTICAL DISCOURSE

From Bernstein (1990). A discourse which is organised hierarchically and coherently, so it can be 'handed down'. Our research (McDougall, 2004) suggests that Subject Media is developing from a horizontal to a vertical discourse, primarily through its modes of assessment.

VIRAL

Describes the spread of ideas from person to person, just like germs spread illness.

VIRTUAL LEARNING

Participating in education without physical access to other students or a tutor, usually through computers and online facilities. There is a great deal of range here, from a lecture presentation put on a VLE to a whole unit learned in Second Life, so try to avoid generalising and always consider the 'conditions of possibility' for virtual learning before you start – not all students are 'digital natives'.

WEB 2.0

The second phase of the internet where the focus shifts from people receiving information and services to people creating and sharing material. It is argued that the second phase of the world wide web starts to take on the appearance of what Tim Berners-Lee originally envisaged. Web 2.0 is defined by collaboration, social networking and the democratic development and distribution of content by ordinary people. Examples are Facebook, YouTube and Wikipedia. The term *Web 2.0* is accredited to Tim O'Reilly.

WE MEDIA

See Gillmor (2004). Ordinary people deciding that they want to create media, through easily accessible technologies such as blogging, digital video, podcasting and v-logging, wikis, YouTube and Second Life.

WIKI

Web-based, shared-authored communication between people to build a set of ideas or a knowledge base.

WIKINOMICS

A term invented by Tapscott and Williams (2006) to describe the impact of Web 2.0 on economics as well as media.

Index